THE BIG BOOK OF
HACKS

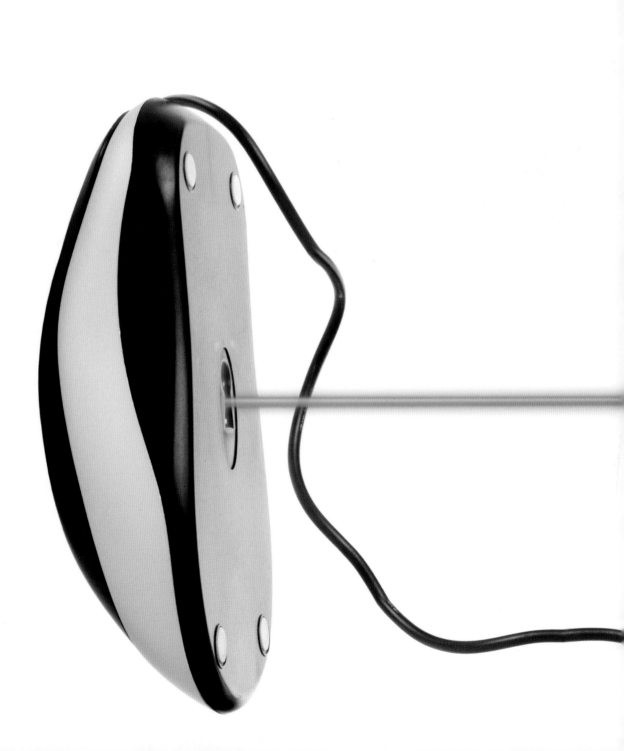

EDITED BY DOUG CANTOR

POPULAR SCIENCE

THE BIG BOOK OF
HACKS

weldon**owen**

contents

GEEK TOYS

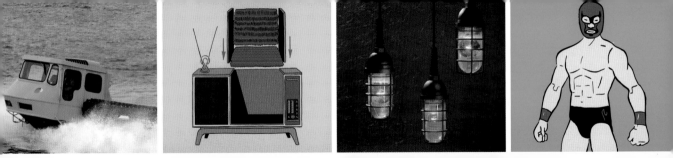

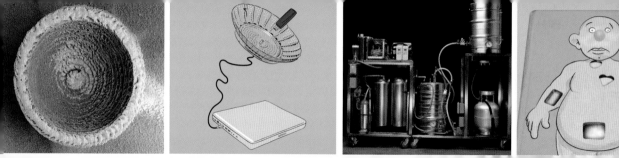

THINGS THAT GO

FOREWORD

Anyone can make anything. That is the lesson of the 140 years that *Popular Science* has been in print. A determined person, working on the weekends, can escape gravity, break the speed of sound, or create a new means of communicating across great distances. And that inventive process begins by tearing things apart and rebuilding them again.

I cannot claim to have been the kind of kid who did that. My instincts around technology were always to keep my belongings clean, dry, and otherwise in perfect working order, not to dismantle or modify them. But my years at *Popular Science* have taught me that that instinct is the wrong one. There is simply too much technology at our disposal not to mess around with it. And when a determined person brings his or her inventive instincts to bear on the gadgets and gizmos that fill our lives, great things can result.

But this book isn't necessarily about building great things. It's about messing around, usually for the simple fun of it. The projects on these pages are based, in part, on the years we've spent pursuing the lone, sometimes crazed hackers who don't just modify technology but blow it apart, just to be able to say they've done it.

I spent an afternoon with our staff photographer, John Carnett, who in his off time had replaced the motor on a four-wheel ATV with a jet engine. The thing required an elaborate start-up procedure and ear protection just to get it rolling, and as he drove me through his Philadelphia neighborhood in it, I cringed to imagine the incredible racket we were making, essentially that of a 747 taxiing past. And yet throughout the process, oblivious to the enemies he was making among the local parents, dogs, and nappers, John wore a look of joy and pride that had nothing to do with serving humanity or inventing something new. He'd just tricked something out— hacked it—in his own way, and in doing so had made his mark on the universe, not to mention on the neighborhood noise ordinances.

It's in that spirit that we, and especially our tireless senior editor Doug Cantor, bring you this entertaining collection of projects. We did it for the hell of it.

Jacob Ward

Jacob Ward
Editor-in-Chief
Popular Science

INTRODUCTION

I was an unlikely candidate to become the editor of How 2.0, *Popular Science*'s do-it-yourself column. I've always been reasonably handy, but when it came to real hands-dirty, open-things-up-and-rearrange-the-parts hacking skills, I was a complete novice.

So I got into the DIY world the same way an experienced DIYer would work on a project: I did some research, talked to seasoned tinkerers, and then dove in. Early on I managed to build a tiny flashlight, hack my cell phone's firmware, and make a pair of bookends from old CDs, all without causing too much damage. Over time I found that with a few hours, a small pile of parts from Radio Shack, and a little patience, I could build some really cool stuff.

Editing How 2.0 has also given me a window into the vast community of smart, dedicated people who have found about a million uses for things like solenoid valves and Arduino microcontrollers. The breadth of their innovations is truly astonishing, and that's what *Popular Science* has tried to show in the pages of How 2.0 each month. We've featured projects ranging from a remote-controlled helicopter only 2 inches (5 cm) high to a remote-controlled bomber with a 20-foot (60-m) wingspan; from a portable solar-powered gadget charger to a 200-pound (90-kg) solar-powered 3-D printer; from a robot built from a toothbrush head and one that can mix and serve cocktails.

Many of these projects have found their way into this book, along with a host of entirely new ones. A few of them are just amazing, audacious things that almost no one could (or probably should) try. Most, though, are easier to replicate. Some take only a few minutes and require little more than gluing parts together.

So if you've never attempted to make anything before in your life, this book provides plenty of ways to start. From there you can take on some of the more challenging projects and develop new skills. Eventually, you might actually find yourself advancing your projects far beyond the versions in the book.

Whatever your skill level and area of interest, I encourage you to roll up your sleeves and (safely) give one of these projects a shot. At times you may get frustrated or even break something. But ultimately you'll be surprised by what you can make, hack, tweak, improve, and transform—and by how much fun you'll have doing it.

Douglas Cantor

Doug Cantor
Senior Editor
Popular Science

HOW TO USE THIS BOOK

So you want to hack stuff—to tear it apart, put it back together with other components, and make it new. We at *Popular Science* salute you, and we've put together these projects to get you started. Many of them come from our popular How 2.0 column, and many come from amazingly inventive individuals out there making cool stuff. (Check out the "Thanks to Our Makers" section for more info.)

Before starting a project, you can look to the following symbols to decode what you're facing.

If you're just breaking in your screwdriver and have never even heard the word *microcontroller*, try out these projects first. Designed to be doable within five minutes—give or take a few seconds, depending on your dexterity—and to make use of basic household items, these tech crafts are the perfect starting ground for the newbie tinkerer.

BUILD IT!

These are the big ones—the ambitious projects that you'll want to sink some real time and cash into, and that will challenge your skills as a builder. How much time and cash, you ask? And just how challenging? The helpful rubric below will give you an idea.

COST

$ = UNDER $50

$$ = $50–$300

$$ = $300–$1,000

$$$$ = $1,000 AND UP

TIME

⊙   UNDER 1 HOUR

⊙⊙   2–5 HOURS

⊙⊙⊙   5–10 HOURS

⊙⊙⊙⊙   10 HOURS AND UP

DIFFICULTY

● ○ ○ ○ ○   One step up from 5 Minute Projects, these tutorials require basic builder smarts, but no electronics or coding wizardry.

● ● ○ ○ ○   Slightly advanced building skills are a must for these projects. Turn on your common sense, and troubleshoot as you go—it's part of the fun.

● ● ● ○ ○   If you see three dots, it means an activity demands low-level electronics and coding skills, or it's pretty rigorous, construction-wise.

● ● ● ● ○   You likely need serious circuitry know-how and code comprehension to do these projects. That, or be prepared to sweat with heavy-duty assembly.

● ● ● ● ●   Hey, if you're reading this book, we figure you like challenges. And projects marked with five dots are sure to deliver just that.

FROM THE ARCHIVES

Popular Science has been doing DIY for a very long time—almost as long as the 140 years the magazine has been in print. Occasionally this book shares a DIY project from our archives so you can try your hand at the hilarious retro projects your grandfather and grandmother built back before, say, television or smartphones.

YOU BUILT WHAT?!

Everyone loves a good success story—tales of everyday individuals who created something so wild that it makes you say . . . well, "You built WHAT?!" You'll find several of these stories throughout the book, and it is our hope that they will inspire you to take your projects to the next level.

WARNING

If you see this symbol, we mean business. Several of the projects in this book involve dangerous tools, electrical current, flammables, potentially harmful chemicals, and recreational devices that could cause injury if misused. So remember: With great DIY comes great responsibility. Use your head, know your tools (and your limitations), always wear safety gear, and never employ your hacking prowess to hurt others. (See our Disclaimer for more information about how *Popular Science* and the publisher are not liable for any mishaps.)

001 PUT TOGETHER A SOLDERING KIT

Soldering is playing with fire, or at least with hot metal. So you need the right tools.

If you're working on electronics projects, chances are you'll want to connect lightweight metal objects like wires, and soldering is the way to get that done. You heat pieces of metal with a soldering iron, then join them together using a molten filler, or solder. Once it cools and hardens, you're left with a strong, electronically conductive bond.

SOLDER This is the good stuff—the material you'll melt to connect metals. Traditionally, solder was a mix of tin and lead, but these days look for lead-free types to avoid nasty health risks. Choose thinner solder for delicate projects, like attaching wires to a circuit board, and thicker solder for projects involving heftier wires or bulkier pieces of metal.

SOLDERING IRON This tool has a metal tip and an insulated handle. When it's powered on, the tip heats up so it can melt solder. There are low- and high-wattage versions: Low wattage is useful for fragile projects, while high wattage is better for projects involving bigger pieces. There are also different types of tips available for the soldering iron.

SOLDERING IRON STAND Buy a stand that fits your iron so you'll have a place to put it down safely when it's hot. (Leaving this thing lying around when it's turned on is a good way to burn down the toolshed before you've even made anything cool with it!)

WIRE-MODIFYING TOOLS You'll likely be soldering a lot of wire, so it's useful to have wire cutters, wire strippers, and needle-nose pliers on hand so you can manipulate the wire. Before connecting wires, you must peel back their insulation to expose the wires, so wire strippers are definitely a must.

CLIPS AND CLAMPS Soldering requires both hands, so you'll need something to hold the materials you're soldering in place. Clips, clamps, and even electrical tape can do the job.

LIQUID FLUX Soldering works best when the items being soldered are squeaky clean, so have liquid flux on hand—it chases away oxides and other goop that can make soldering difficult.

HEAT-SHRINK TUBING You can use plastic heat-shrink tubing to insulate wires before you apply heat and solder them. It's available in several diameters for projects with various wire sizes.

TIP CLEANER Your soldering iron's tip will get a bit nasty as you work, so keep a wet sponge on hand to periodically wipe down the tip.

EXHAUST FAN The fumes from soldering are not healthy to breathe, so you need good ventilation from a fan or an open window to help clear the air.

SAFETY GOGGLES Bits of hot solder can go flying as you work, so don't do it without wearing safety goggles.

LEARN SOLDERING BASICS

Now that you have your soldering gear together, here's how to get it done.

At its most basic, soldering is simply attaching wires to wires. The process is a bit different when you're soldering directly onto a circuit board, but don't worry: We've got you covered with info for each.

SOLDERING WIRES

STEP 1 In a well-ventilated space, with your safety goggles on, plug in your soldering iron to heat it up. Be careful not to touch the tip, which will heat up fast.

STEP 2 Prepare the materials you want to join with solder. If you're connecting two wires, peel back any insulation about 1/2 inch (1.25 cm), and twist the wires together. Place your materials on a surface you don't mind burning a bit, like scrap wood.

STEP 3 Cut a length from the spool of solder and coil it up at one end, leaving a short lead. You can hold on to the coiled end as you apply the solder.

STEP 4 Touch the iron to the point where the wires are twisted together. Leave it there until the wires are hot enough to melt the solder (about 10 seconds), then touch the solder to the wire joint every few seconds until it begins to melt. Allow enough solder to melt onto the wires to cover them, then pull the solder and soldering iron away. Don't touch the solder directly to the soldering iron during this process—that will melt the solder onto the wires, but won't form a firm joint.

STEP 5 When you need to fix a mistake, you can reheat your joint, melt the solder, and reposition the components. If you want to break the connection you made for any reason, you can desolder a joint. For connections like joined wires, you can often simply heat up the joint and pull the wires apart, or cut each wire below the joint and resolder as desired.

SOLDERING A CIRCUIT BOARD

STEP 1 Place the component that you wish to solder in the correct spot on the circuit board and clamp it down, then push the leads for each component through the holes on the board.

STEP 2 Solder the leads to the bottom of the board. (This is easier to do with a fine-tipped, low-wattage soldering iron.) Press the soldering iron to the lead and the metal contact on the board at the point where you want them to connect. Once they heat up enough to melt the solder—just a few seconds—melt a small amount

of solder at the connection point (too much can cause a short, too little won't make a strong connection).

STEP 3 Pull the solder away, then remove the soldering iron a second or two later. Once you've soldered all the leads onto the circuit board, trim off excess wire with a wire cutter.

TRY TINNING

If you're working with components that have to be surface-mounted on a circuit board—ones that don't have leads you can thread through to the back of the board—you'll need to use a technique called *tinning*.

STEP 1 Touch the soldering iron to the point on the board where you want to attach the component. Melt a small drop of solder on this point, then remove the soldering iron.

STEP 2 Pick up the component with tweezers, heat up the drop of solder on the board, and carefully place the component on the solder.

STEP 3 Hold the component in place for a few seconds until the solder cools.

STEP 4 If you need to desolder joints on a circuit board, use a desoldering pump with your soldering iron to melt and remove the solder.

003 STUDY CIRCUIT COMPONENTS

To build a circuit, first you've got to understand its building blocks.

Maps of how current flows through a circuit are called *schematics*. Each component is represented by a labeled symbol, which is connected to other components by lines to represent the current's path.

In this book, we use several circuitry diagrams to show how to attach projects' components, so here we'll introduce you to some of the main circuit components that show up on these diagrams.

TRANSISTORS A transistor amplifies energy flowing to its base pin, allowing a larger electrical current to flow between its collector and emitter pins. The two basic types of transistors, NPN and PNP, have opposite polarities: Current flows from collector to emitter in NPN transistors, and flows from emitter to collector in PNP transistors.

POTENTIOMETERS When you need to vary resistance within a circuit, use a potentiometer instead of a standard resistor. These have a controller that allows you to change the level of resistance: "B" potentiometers have a linear response curve, while "A" potentiometers have a logarithmic response curve.

SWITCHES Switches open or close a circuit. Some are normally open as a default; others are normally closed.

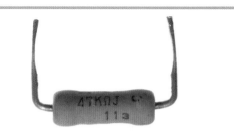

RESISTORS A circuit needs resistance to function. Without it, you'll end up with a short circuit, in which the current flows directly from power to ground without being used, causing your circuit to overheat and otherwise misbehave. To prevent that from happening, resistors reduce the flow of electrical current. The level of resistance is measured in ohms, so check those numbers to make sure a component's resistance matches the level indicated in the circuitry diagram.

CAPACITORS These store electricity, then release it back into the circuit when there's a drop in power. Capacitor values are measured in farads: picofarads (pF), nanofarads (nF), and microfarads (µF) are the most common units of measure. Ceramic capacitors aren't polarized, so they can be inserted into a circuit in any direction, but electrolytic capacitors are polarized and need to be inserted in a specific orientation.

BATTERIES These store power for a circuit, and you can use more than one to increase voltage or current.

WIRE These single strands of metal are often used to connect the components in a circuit. Wire comes in various sizes (or gauges), and it's usually insulated.

DIODES These components are polarized to allow current to flow through them in only one direction—very useful if you need to stop the current in your circuit from flowing the wrong way. The side of a diode that connects to ground is called the *cathode*, and the side that connects to power is called the *anode*. Light-emitting diodes, or LEDs, light up when current flows through them.

INTEGRATED CIRCUITS These are tiny circuits (usually including transistors, diodes, and resistors) prepacked into a chip. Each leg of the chip will connect to a point in your larger circuit. These vary widely in their composition, and will come with a handy data sheet explaining their functions.

TRANSFORMERS These devices range from thumbnail-size to house-size, and consist of coils of wire wound around a core, often a magnet. Made to transfer alternating current from one circuit to another, they can step the power of the current up or down depending on the ratio of wire windings between one coil and another.

004 BUILD A CIRCUIT

Now that you know what goes into a circuit, you can make one.

STEP 1 Assemble all the components that appear on your schematic, along with any tools you'll need to make connections, clamp parts, or trim wires.

STEP 2 To test your circuit before you solder it together, set it up on a breadboard first. Breadboards are boards covered in small holes that allow you to lay out and connect components without soldering them in place.

STEP 3 Once you're ready to construct the circuit, it's best to start by installing the shortest components first. This helps you avoid having to move taller components out of the way, and allows you to flip the board over to hold the component you're working on in place. As you install components, orient their labels in the same direction so they're all legible at once.

STEP 4 Many components have lead wires that you can insert into a circuit board. Bend these leads before you insert the component so that you don't stress the part or the board.

STEP 5 You'll need to hold your parts in place while you solder the circuit together. You can do this by clinching lead wires (bending them slightly on the other side of the board to hold them in place), using tape, or bracing the parts against your work surface.

STEP 6 As you solder, check that each component is aligned correctly after you solder the first pin or lead—it's easier to make adjustments at this point, before you've finished soldering the part in place.

STEP 7 When everything's soldered in place, trim all your circuit's lead wires and test it out.

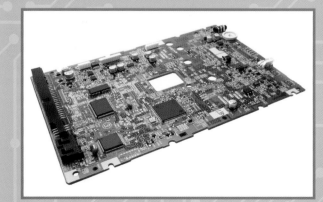

005 CHOOSE A MICROCONTROLLER

Most geeks know a thing or two about microcontrollers. So get these basics under your belt.

A microcontroller is essentially a tiny computer, complete with a central processing unit (CPU), memory, and input and output. It's really useful for controlling switches, LEDs, and other simple electronic devices. Here are a few features you'll want to consider when choosing one for a project.

PROGRAMMABILITY Ideally, you want a microcontroller that you can erase and reprogram a number of times. Some can only be programmed once—these are fine if you're building something more permanent—and some allow you to add external memory for complex projects.

MEMORY Microcontrollers come with a set amount of memory, which is sometimes upgradable, but only to a certain extent. Make sure that the microcontroller you choose has sufficient memory to handle your project.

COMPLEXITY For a more complex project, you'll need to seek out a model with lots of input and output pins and more memory than the lower-end microcontrollers.

PHYSICAL PACKAGING A microcontroller's construction can influence how easy it is to use. For instance, less space between pins can make the device harder to work with. Check out the setup before you put down your cash.

PROGRAMMING LANGUAGE Different microcontrollers use different programming languages. Choose one that uses a language you know or are willing to learn.

SOFTWARE Some microcontrollers have better, easier-to-use software tools than others. If you're a beginner, be wary of using a microcontroller with poorly designed software tools. Ask around among your tech-savvy friends to get a sense of what's right for you.

006 PROGRAM AN ARDUINO

An Arduino is a popular open-source single-board microcontroller. Learn how to program one and let the possibilities take shape.

STEP 1 Arduino microcontrollers come in a variety of types. The most common is the Arduino UNO, but there are specialized variations. Before you begin building, do a little research to figure out which version will be the most appropriate for your project.

STEP 2 To begin, you'll need to install the Arduino Programmer, aka the integrated development environment (IDE).

STEP 3 Connect your Arduino to the USB port of your computer. This may require a specific USB cable. Every Arduino has a different virtual serial-port address, so you'll need to reconfigure the port if you're using different Arduinos.

STEP 4 Set the board type and the serial port in the Arduino Programmer.

STEP 5 Test the microcontroller by using one of the preloaded programs, called *sketches,* in the Arduino Programmer. Open one of the example sketches, and press the upload button to load it. The Arduino should begin responding to the program: If you've set it to blink an LED light, for example, the light should start blinking.

STEP 6 To upload new code to the Arduino, either you'll need to have access to code you can paste into the programmer, or you'll have to write it yourself, using the Arduino programming language to create your own sketch. An Arduino sketch usually has five parts: a header describing the sketch and its author; a section defining variables; a setup routine that sets the initial conditions of variables and runs preliminary code; a loop routine, which is where you add the main code that will execute repeatedly until you stop running the sketch; and a section where you can list other functions that activate during the setup and loop routines. All sketches must include the setup and loop routines.

STEP 7 Once you've uploaded the new sketch to your Arduino, disconnect it from your computer and integrate it into your project as directed.

007 KNOW BASIC WOODWORKING TOOLS

Set up a proper shop with some essential carpentry gear.

You can do most woodworking projects without elaborate table saws and expensive machinery (though they're handy if you have them). But you'll probably want to have these essentials on hand.

MEASURING TOOLS Accurately measuring lengths and angles is essential. A simple tape measure and a combination square (which allows you to measure and check angles) help you mark your cuts accurately.

HAND SAW This is the most basic, inexpensive saw that most of us have stashed somewhere in our garages. You should have one on hand and sharpened for making cuts that don't need to be incredibly precise.

TABLE SAW Now you're cutting with power. This electric saw features a circular saw blade set into a surface, and to make a nice, straight cut in an item, you push it across the blade as it spins. If it sounds dangerous, that's because it is. Be very careful when operating one of these saws.

JIGSAW Use this power tool when you need to make a curved cut in wood or metal. The jigsaw can be difficult to control, and as a result is dangerous—use it only when you require irregular contours or artistic touches.

ROTARY TOOL This simple yet versatile device allows you to cut, drill, sand, and carve into all sorts of materials. It comes with a variety of bits.

BLOCK PLANE This hand tool is useful when you want to soften edges and plane flat surfaces.

DRILL This device is your old faithful—your basic tool for making holes in wood. The size of the hole depends on the bit that you choose.

ROUTER A more advanced cutting alternative, a router is a power tool that accepts a variety of bits and creates hollows in surfaces. It's useful for making different wood moldings and joints.

SANDING BLOCK To smooth wood by hand, outfit a sanding block with sandpaper.

RANDOM-ORBIT SANDER This power sander is useful for faster sanding and large projects.

CLAMPS You'll want to have a variety of clamps on hand to hold your project steady as you glue it together.

WORKBENCH You need a solid surface to work on as you assemble your project.

VISE Some workbenches have a built-in vise, and those designed for woodworking won't damage the wood.

SAFETY GEAR Especially when using power tools, goggles are essential to protect your eyes from flying wood chips, and earplugs or noise-blocking headphones protect your hearing by muffling the noise. A face mask will also keep fine sawdust out of your lungs.

008 MAKE A STRAIGHT CUT IN WOOD

Because sawing straight lines can be trickier than you might think.

STEP 1 Mark your cut with a ruler and pencil, on the sides as well as the top of the wood. When measuring, take the width of your saw blade (called *kerf*) into account, and use an arrow to show which side of the line you'll cut on.

STEP 2 Place your saw on a corner at your mark, and draw it backward with light pressure to create a notch. Repeat this to deepen the notch, then adjust the saw gradually to make a shallow cut along the line on the top surface of the wood. Be careful that you don't press down too hard on the saw; if you do, it could catch.

STEP 3 Using the first groove and your penciled guides, turn the wood and repeat the second step on the other sides. The wood will have shallow cuts on the top and sides.

STEP 4 Turn the wood top up again, and finish sawing through the piece. To avoid splintering, tilt the saw back and support the wood you're cutting as you finish the cut. The grooves on the sides will help keep the saw straight.

009 MASTER WOODWORKING JOINTS

If "butt joint" sounds like a joke to you, grow up and learn these woodworking staples.

TO MAKE A MITERED BUTT JOINT

STEP 1 To join two pieces of wood at a 90-degree angle, you'll first need to mark each piece of wood with a line at a 45-degree angle, drawn from front to back at the corner of each piece. Mark this 45-degree angle on opposite sides of each piece, and join the bottom corners of those lines together with a straight line on the third side. This will mark out the triangular wedge of wood you'll be removing from each piece.

STEP 2 Start your cut at one of the 45-degree lines, cutting a shallow groove. Finish your cut carefully, checking that your cut lines up with both the end corner of the wood and the straight line that you drew. Repeat on the second piece of wood.

STEP 3 Once you've cut each end into a 45-degree angle, line the pieces up with the newly cut surfaces touching. Check to make sure this forms a 90-degree angle, then glue the ends together with wood glue to form a mitered butt joint. Clamp the joint while it dries.

TO MAKE A MORTISE AND TENON JOINT

STEP 1 To create this type of joint, you'll need to cut one piece of wood so that a section protrudes (the tenon) and another piece so that it has a hole (the mortise). First, measure and mark the tenon, making it wide and long enough to create a strong joint.

STEP 2 Use a saw to cut out the tenon. You'll need to cut away a rectangular chunk of wood on each side of a central piece of wood that will form the tenon.

STEP 3 Use the tenon to measure out the mortise on the other piece of wood. Mark a space for the mortise on both sides of the wood.

STEP 4 Choose a drill bit that just fits inside the marks, and drill a hole halfway through the wood. Flip it over, then drill the rest of the way through the wood, using the marks you made in the third step as a guide.

STEP 5 Use a hammer and chisel or a jigsaw to cut the mortise square.

STEP 6 Fit the tenon into the mortise. Depending on your project, you can use a dowel, glue, or a wedge to keep the joint locked together.

010 DRILL A HOLE

Think this is easy? It usually is—especially if you use the right tools and techniques.

STEP 1 Choose a drill bit that's the right size and length for the hole you need to drill.

STEP 2 Mark the spot where you want your hole, then use a center punch to create a dent at the mark. This will help keep the drill bit in place as you work.

STEP 3 Clamp the material you'll be drilling in place.

STEP 4 When you turn on your drill, check to make sure that the drill bit is spinning clockwise.

STEP 5 Drill into the material. As you go, the drill should feel like it's moving smoothly without requiring too much pressure. If that's not happening, stop and check for materials that could be clogging the bit.

STEP 6 When you're drilling, you can put the drill in reverse (spinning counterclockwise) to back out of each hole you make. If the back of a hole isn't smooth, use a deburring tool to remove burrs and splinters.

011 SUIT UP WITH METALWORKING TOOLS

Ready for some metal? You will be— once you have these basics together.

A handful of this book's projects require you to do some metalworking—either shaping it, or fusing one metal piece with another. Now, we wouldn't want you to do that without the right gear, would we?

HOT-CUTTING TOOLS Hot metal is easier to cut than cold, which is why torches and hot-cutting chisels come in handy.

COLD-CUTTING TOOLS Cold chisels are often used to create grooves in metal, and hacksaws are useful for getting through thick, cold metal.

PLIERS These tools help you handle metal that's hot or coated in toxic materials.

VISES AND CLAMPS These secure the metal you're working on, and can also be used to hold multiple pieces of metal together.

FILE A file grates away excess metal, allowing you to reshape a project as needed.

SANDPAPER This is the go-to tool you'll need for smoothing rough patches.

SAFETY GLASSES When you're working with metal, wear welding goggles or a welding hood at all times.

EAR PROTECTION When using tools that make lots of noise, cover your ears to avoid damaging your hearing.

WORK BOOTS Steel-toed or other thick, hard-soled shoes are essential protective gear when you're working with sharp or hot metal.

HEAVY GLOVES Last, but not least, take this important safety precaution: Protect your hands with thick, insulated gloves. Some metal pros wear leather ones, as leather isn't especially flammable—and it looks cool, too.

012 CUT METAL PIPES AND SHEETS

If you're working on plumbing or with metal sheet, you'll probably need to make a cut or two. Here's how.

TO CUT A METAL PIPE

STEP 1 Wearing the appropriate eye protection, clamp the pipe in place on your work table, and mark a line on the pipe where you want to cut.

STEP 2 Place a hacksaw on the marked line, checking to make sure that the blade is perfectly aligned with the mark. Begin cutting, using your non-dominant hand to put gentle pressure on the top of the saw as you move it back and forth across the pipe. Check the alignment periodically as you work to ensure a clean cut.

STEP 3 Carefully remove the cut pipe from the clamp or vise, and smooth the cut edge with a file as needed to avoid sharp edges.

TO CUT SHEET METAL

STEP 1 Place the sheet on your work table, with the section you want to cut protruding over the edge. Hold it in place with clamps, and mark the line where you'll cut.

STEP 2 Use a jigsaw or other cutting tool to cut along the line you marked (the appropriate tool will vary depending on the type and thickness of the metal you're cutting). Hold the sheet with one hand while gently pushing the cutting tool along the line. Slow down if the sheet starts to vibrate excessively.

STEP 3 When you're finished cutting, use a file to smooth the cut edge of the metal sheet, and then unclamp the sheet from your work table.

LEARN TO WELD

It goes without saying that welding is cool. It's also really useful.

Welding allows you to join metals by heating them, then melting or compressing them together. There are several types—such as arc, gas, and resistance. Here's some basic information on arc welding, the most common method.

STEP 1 Safety first. Welding fumes can be really unhealthy, so set up in a well-ventilated area. Arc welding generates UV rays that can easily burn your skin, and molten metal can fly up and hit you, so cover exposed skin and keep a welding hood on the entire time you're working. Wear insulated welding gloves to avoid burns and electric shock, and always use work boots with insulated soles. Finally, use a work table made of nonflammable material.

STEP 2 Before you begin welding, prepare the pieces of metal you want to join. It's useful to bevel the edges you'll be joining, to allow the weld arc to penetrate and create a strong bond. Clean the metal surfaces of all paint, rust, and other contaminants that could interfere with the current created by the welding machine. Once the pieces are prepped, secure them together with clamps.

STEP 3 Attach a ground clamp to the larger piece of metal you'll be welding. The clamp will complete the circuit and allow electricity to pass through the metal once you begin welding.

STEP 4 Choose the right electrode and amperage settings for your welding machine—this will vary depending on your project. Attach the electrode to its holder, called a *stinger*.

STEP 5 Turn on the welder, and hold the stinger by its insulated handle using your dominant hand. You should be wearing all your protective gear at this point.

STEP 6 To begin welding, you need to strike an arc. Choose where you'd like to begin the weld, and tap that point with the end of your electrode. Immediately pull the electrode back slightly: This should create an electric arc between the metal and your electrode. The amount of space you'll need between the metal and the electrode varies depending on your project, and it may take practice to hold a continuous arc.

STEP 7 Move the arc along the path of your weld. This will create a weld bead, formed by the metal from the melting electrode and the base metal. The weld bead forms the bond that will hold your pieces of metal together. Move the electrode in a zig-zag motion to shape the weld bead to the desired width.

STEP 8 Once your weld is done, chip off any slag and use a wire brush to clean up the bond. To avoid rust, paint the metal.

GEEK TOYS

014 THE ULTIMATE ALL-IN-ONE BEER-BREWING MACHINE

Behold this deluxe homemade microbrewery: an elaborate device that boils, ferments, chills, and pours home-crafted ale.

What if there were a machine—a beautiful, shiny machine—and all it did, with almost no work from you, was make you beer? Such was the dream that drove former *PopSci* photographer John Carnett to build what he calls "the Device": a stainless-steel, two-cart brewing system that starts by boiling extract (concentrated wort, or pre-fermented beer) and ends with a chilled pint.

In most home-brewing setups, each step in the process requires moving the beer to a new container by hand, which increases the chance of contamination and requires lifting. Carnett's machine keeps everything in the carts' closed system—he only has to swap a few CO_2-pressurized hoses to move the liquid along.

The delicious brew's journey begins in the boil keg, where concentrated wort extract is heated by a propane burner for 90 minutes. The beer then travels through a heat exchanger—which cools the mix to about 55°F (13°C)—on its way to the fermenting keg. Here, a network of Freon-chilled copper tubes pumps cool water around the keg when the temperature gets too high. After two weeks, the Device pumps the beer into a settling keg, where a CO_2 tank adds carbonation. When you pull the tap, the beer travels through the cold plate, so it's chilled on the way to your glass. That's right: The Device is always ready with a cold pour and consumes no power when it's not actively serving or fermenting.

BUILDING A BETTER BREW
The next step? Adding a third cart to make wort from raw grain instead of extract. But, says Carnett, there's a lot of "testing" of the new design to be done first.

015 DRINK BOOZE FROM A MELON

Turn basic produce into a hilarious drink dispenser.

MATERIALS

Medium seedless
  watermelon

Large spoon

Drill

Knife

Ball valve faucet with
  a handle

Rubber O-ring that fits
  the faucet

PVC-to-faucet adapter

Alcohol of your choosing

STEP 1 Using a knife, cut off just enough of the bottom of your melon so that it sits flat.

STEP 2 Pick the side of the melon that you want to be the front, then cut a hole in the top, toward the rear. Save the piece you've cut out, as you'll use it later.

STEP 3 Scoop out the fruit with a large spoon.

STEP 4 Drill a hole in the melon's front, near the bottom. Using a knife, widen it so it's big enough for the faucet to fit inside.

STEP 5 Gently screw the faucet into the hole. (It helps to stick your free hand inside the melon and guide the faucet into place from the inside.)

STEP 6 Slide the O-ring onto the back of the faucet inside the melon, then install the adapter. Test for leaks.

STEP 7 Load it up with the elixir of your choosing, put the cut-out top back in place, and get your pour on.

016 BREAK INTO YOUR BEER

STEP 1 Use a metal file to wear down a carabiner's hook end so that it fits under a bottle cap's lip. (Be careful not to file it down too much or the carabiner won't close properly.)

STEP 2 Open the carabiner and place the unmodified end against the beer cap, then tuck the hook end under the cap's lip and use it as a lever to pry open your brew.

STEP 3 Carry your carabiner as a keychain so that you're always ready when beer suddenly, magically happens to you.

017 INSTALL A SHOWER BEER CADDY

STEP 1 Buy a cup holder at an automotive parts store. (Some have a hook on the back, which you don't need—remove it by gently breaking it off along the seam or cutting it off with a rotary tool.)

STEP 2 Drill a hole into the back of the cup holder that's just wide enough to accommodate the tip of a suction cup.

STEP 3 Insert the suction cup's tip into the hole, press the suction cup to the shower wall, and load your beer of choice into the caddy.

Carabiner

Filed-down hook end

1

2

Beer bottle

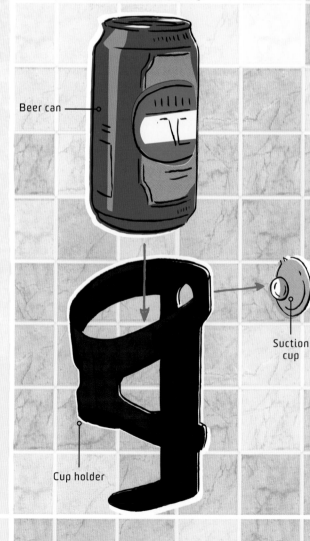

Beer can

Suction cup

Cup holder

018 CHILL YOUR BEER REALLY, REALLY FAST

STEP 1 Drill a hole into the side of a plastic container. The hole should be just wide enough that you can poke the straw of a container of compressed air through it.

STEP 2 Fill the plastic container with as many beers as you can fit. Cover with the lid.

STEP 3 Tape it shut. (Trust us. Otherwise the injected blast of cool air could blow the lid right off.)

STEP 4 Wearing thick, insulated gloves, turn the can of compressed air upside down and insert the can's straw into the hole, being careful not to touch the cans with it.

STEP 5 Squeeze for up to 1 minute.

STEP 6 Open the container and tap on each can's top for a few seconds to relieve the pressure inside. Then open one up and take a big swig—you've earned it.

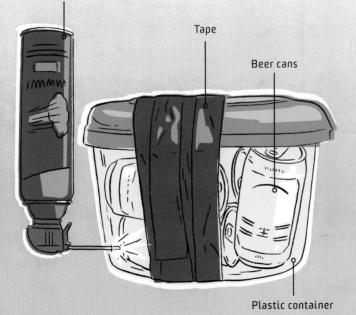

Can of compressed air

Tape

Beer cans

Plastic container

019 DISGUISE YOUR BREW

STEP 1 Using a can opener, remove the top and bottom of an innocent-looking soda can.

STEP 2 Using scissors, cut off the soda can's bottom lip.

STEP 3 Cut along the soda can's seam.

STEP 4 Using a metal file, sand down the can's edges to avoid cuts and scrapes. Get it as smooth as possible.

STEP 5 Wrap the soda can around your beer and enjoy your incognito beverage.

Soda can

Beer can

GEEK TOYS

020 REUSE THOSE RED PARTY CUPS

Keep the infamous cup in play long after the keg's
run dry. (Just rinse out that stale-beer smell first.)

DIY CAMERA LENS HOOD

Fend off glare with an impromptu lens hood. Cut the bottom out of your party cup, and then poke two holes on either side near the bottom. Thread a rubber band through each hole and knot them. Place the cup over your lens, tie the rubber bands around your camera near the viewfinder, and keep rain out of your shots.

MEASURE (MORE) BOOZE

Engineers say that the ridges on party cups are for structural integrity, but people have long used them as measurement lines: the first indentation from the bottom marks 1 ounce (30 mL), the second 5 ounces (147 mL), and the third a full 12 ounces (355 mL).

POOR MAN'S CHANDELIER

Poke holes in the bottoms of about 60 cups. Then glue the cups together along their sides with their open ends facing outward, forming a ball. Insert a bulb from a string of Christmas lights into each hole as you go to make a huge, sparkling plastic orb.

MAKESHIFT BEER INSULATOR

Cut Styrofoam to fit the bottom of your cup and place it inside, then spray a can with nonstick cooking spray. Put the can inside the cup and fill around it with expanding foam. Let the foam dry and trim the excess. Call it a koozie.

021 THE DRINK-SLINGING DROID

This robot tends bar like a pro. And even better, it never needs a tip.

A veteran of the TV show *BattleBots,* Jamie Price has built plenty of destructive machines. But recently he designed a robot with a more mellow calling: offering cold beer and cocktails. The result—a masterpiece of plywood, plastic, aluminum, and electric motors called Bar2D2—serves up everything but the sage advice.

The salesman modeled his machine on the iconic *Star Wars* droid R2-D2, and spent seven months and $2,000 building it. He used a plastic dome from a bird feeder as the head and built the robot's plywood skeleton to match. To make Bar2D2 mobile, Price stripped out the seat, the control system, and a pair of wheels from an electric wheelchair, added a new 12-volt battery, and wired a receiver to the motor so he could control it with an R/C helicopter-type remote.

Price fills each of the robot's six bottles with either liquor or a mixer, and then plugs these ingredients into a software program. The program computes a list of possible drinks, Price picks one, and the software sends pouring instructions to the robot via Bluetooth. A custom circuit board receives the signals and moves actuators that open specific valves just long enough for the robot's air-pressure system to force the right amount of each liquid into a waiting glass.

Bar2D2 has already proven to be a hit among robotics and cocktail fans alike, but Price isn't finished yet. Next he's adding a breathalyzer and an LED-backed projector that displays blood-alcohol content. Give us your keys, Obi-Wan.

BEER ME, BAR2D2
One difficulty was finding a way to move bottles up from the enclosed beer rack to the serving station above. When Price hits a button on his remote, the rod of a motorized caulk gun extends and pushes the beer up from the lower level. He calls it his beer elevator.

022 SERVE SHOTS IN JELL-O CUPS

STEP 1 Mix up your Jell-O and pour it into a muffin tin's compartments, filling each about half full.

STEP 2 Place small pebbles into paper cups to weight them. Put a cup in each tin compartment and cover each with tape.

STEP 3 Wait for the Jell-O to solidify around the paper cups, molding into a cup shape. Remove the cups and pebbles.

STEP 4 Fill up the Jell-O cups with booze. Be popular at a party near you.

023 MAKE DRINKS GLOW IN THE DARK

The magic glowing ingredients? Simple riboflavin and quinine, plus a trippy black light.

FOR BLUE DRINKS:

STEP 1 Mix any drink you want.

STEP 2 Add tonic water.

STEP 3 Drink it near a black light.

FOR YELLOW DRINKS:

STEP 1 Crush up a B2 vitamin and put a pinch of the powder in the bottom of your glass.

STEP 2 Pour in a flavored drink, as the vitamin has a faint bitter taste.

STEP 3 Drink it near a black light.

024 FREEZE LEGO ICE CUBES

Make a mold of LEGO bricks and enjoy the world's geekiest ice.

MATERIALS

A LEGO base plate
and bricks

Petroleum jelly

Mold compound

Craft knife

Food coloring, if desired

STEP 1 Wash and dry the base plate and blocks.

STEP 2 Build a LEGO tray on the base plate: Make four sides three blocks in height, then place single bricks inside the border, spacing them evenly with one or two row of bumps between each.

STEP 3 Coat the tray in petroleum jelly, then slowly fill the tray with the mold compound and set aside for at least 12 hours. Bang on the table to prevent bubbles.

STEP 4 Peel the mold out of the LEGO tray and trim any random bits off with the craft knife.

STEP 5 Wash the mold and turn it over. Fill the depressions with water (add food coloring, if you roll that way), slide it in the freezer, and await your cubes.

025 COOK A HOT DOG WITH ELECTRICAL CURRENT

An LED display lights up the room and nukes your hot dog, too.

MATERIALS

Power cord

Wire strippers

Two alligator clips

Soldering iron and solder

Hot dog

Nonconductive plate

Two metal forks

Assorted LEDs

STEP 1 Using wire strippers, cut off the end of the power cord and peel back the outer insulation. Snip back the green ground cord and strip the ends of the remaining two wires.

STEP 2 Solder one small alligator clip to each of the stripped wires.

STEP 3 Put the hot dog on a nonconductive plate (ceramic works nicely). Secure each alligator clip to a fork, and stick the forks into the hot dog.

STEP 4 Stick some LEDs into the hot dog.

STEP 5 Very carefully plug the cord into the wall. Don't touch the hot dog or any of the rest of the contraption while the cord is plugged in.

STEP 6 The hot dog will cook in a minute or two. Not that you're going to eat it, right?

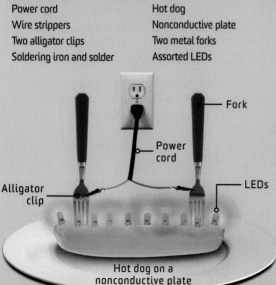

Fork

Power cord

Alligator clip

LEDs

Hot dog on a nonconductive plate

WARNING
Use this activity to impress your friends with your electrical chops, not your culinary skills. Eating the resulting hot dog is a seriously bad idea. Also, keep water very far away from this science experiment!

026 MOD YOUR TOASTER FOR FAR-FROM-AVERAGE TOAST

Because bread tastes a lot better with funny faces on it.

COST	$
TIME	⏱
EASY ● ● ○ ○ ○ HARD	

MATERIALS

Toaster
Paper
Pencil
Craft knife
Glue stick

Aluminum flashing
Utility knife
Metal file
Bread that needs toasting

STEP 1 Unplug your toaster and remove the insert—that's the part that holds bread slices in place. Measure the space between the insert's two prongs.

STEP 2 Cut two pieces of paper to fit between these two prongs. Draw or print a shape that you want to see on your breakfast onto the paper. Include a tab on either side of each shape that you can wrap around the prongs to hold your design in place inside the toaster.

STEP 3 Use a craft knife to cut out the negative spaces around and in your design, creating a stencil.

STEP 4 Glue the paper pieces to aluminum flashing. Use a utility knife to cut the shapes and their tabs out of the flashing, then smooth the edges with a metal file.

STEP 5 Gently and thoroughly wash off the glue and remove all the paper. With the toaster unplugged, use the shapes' tabs to hook them to the toaster insert.

STEP 6 Plug the toaster in, replace the insert, put in some bread, and make some really fun toast.

☠ **WARNING**
Toasters may seem harmless enough, but once they're plugged in they're juiced with powerful voltage. No prongs, aluminum flashing, or paper bits should come into contact with the toaster's electric heaters.

027 WIELD A POTATO LAUNCHER

Potatoes—they're not just for the dinner table. Build this cannon and see spuds fly.

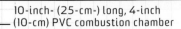

COST	$$
TIME	⏲ ⏲ ⏲ ⏲
EASY ● ● ● ○ ○ HARD	

MATERIALS

- 2 feet (60 cm) of 16-gauge insulated wire
- Wire strippers
- BBQ igniter
- Various PVC parts (see diagram below)
- Soldering iron and solder
- PVC primer
- PVC pipe cement
- Drill
- Two 8-by-2½-inch (20-by-6.35-cm) machine screws
- Leather gloves
- Electrical tape
- Hair spray
- Potatoes

STEP 1 Cut the insulated wire in half and strip back a bit of the ends of each piece.

STEP 2 Find the fine wire near the igniter button's lip. Twist this wire's end with one stripped insulated wire; solder them together. Secure with electrical tape.

STEP 3 Locate the igniter's main wire near the base. Cut it, leaving about 2 inches (5 cm) at the plug end. Strip, twist, and solder the end with the other insulated wire.

STEP 4 Prime the adapter, coupler, combustion chamber, and bushing. (Don't get primer on the threads.)

STEP 5 Immediately apply pipe cement to the parts of the adapter, coupler, combustion chamber, and bushing that will fit together. Cement the coupler and bushing to the combustion chamber, and the adapter to the coupler.

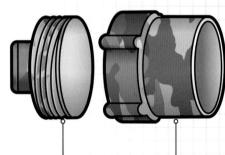

BBQ igniter

Machine screws

10-inch- (25-cm-) long, 4-inch (10-cm) PVC combustion chamber

4-inch (10-cm) threaded plug

4-inch (10-cm) clean-out adapter

4-inch (10-cm) PVC coupler

STEP 6 Right the assembled pieces and twist them while pressing, then check that the combustion chamber fits 1 1/2 inches (3.75 cm) into the coupler and equally far into the bushing.

STEP 7 Wait 10 minutes for the cement to dry, then drill two holes in the combustion chamber at a 90-degree angle to one another, closer to the coupler than the bushing. Drive in two machine screws, leaving 1/4 inch (6.35 mm) between them inside the pipe.

STEP 8 Prime one end of the 36-inch (91-cm) pipe—this is your barrel—and the smaller, exposed end of the bushing. Apply pipe cement and twist to seal.

STEP 9 Wrap the ends of each of the insulated wires around the screws in the combustion chamber. Then tighten the screws and insulate with electrical tape.

STEP 10 Wearing leather gloves, lash the ignitor button to the combustion chamber's side using electrical tape.

STEP 11 Let the contraption dry for 48 hours before using it. (Otherwise, it may blow up—trust us on this stuff.) Test the igniter button to make sure there's a spark. If there is, twist on the threaded plug at the end.

STEP 12 Place the launcher on the ground and securely lodge a potato into the end of the barrel, about 2 inches (5 cm) inside. Rotate the potato to mold it into a cylindrical shape that fits tightly in the barrel.

STEP 13 Remove the end cap and spray a two-second blast of hair spray into the chamber. Close it again.

STEP 14 Pick up the launcher, point it in a safe direction, and press the BBQ igniter. Watch that tater go!

4-by-1 1/2-inch
(10-by-3.75-cm)
reducing bushing

36-inch- (91-cm-) long,
1 1/2-inch (3.75-cm)
PVC barrel

BUILD IT!

028 IMPROVISE A PLANETARIUM

Gaze at a starfield featuring twinkling constellations of your own devising.

COST	$ $
TIME	☺ ☺ ☺
EASY ● ● ● ○ ○ HARD	

MATERIALS

LilyPad Arduino
Breakout board
USB cable
Velcro
Sewing needle and thread
Two same-size pieces of black fabric
Conductive thread
Wire strippers
Single-stranded wire

Six LEDs
Soldering iron and solder
Scissors
Fiber optic filament
Electrical tape
3.7-volt polymer lithium ion battery and a mini USB charger for them
Small clear beads
Hot-glue gun

STEP 1 Connect your LilyPad Arduino to your computer using a breakout board and a USB cable. Then load it up with the code at popsci.com/thebigbookofhacks.

STEP 2 Sew Velcro around the edges of the fabric pieces, and sew the LilyPad Arduino near the edge of one fabric piece using conductive thread.

STEP 3 Strip the wire and make small loops. Solder the loops to the six LEDs' connectors, making "buttons."

STEP 4 Create a pattern and print it out in a size to fill your ceiling. Tape it onto the other piece of fabric—not the one you attached the LilyPad Arduino to.

STEP 5 Look at your pattern and decide where you'll need the most fiber-optic bundles. Space the LEDs so the filaments can extend from them to fill the pattern.

STEP 6 Sew the buttons onto the fabric piece that you sewed the LilyPad Arduino to, connecting each LED to one of the LilyPad Arduino terminals with conductive thread. Use terminals 3, 5, 6, 9, 10, and 11.

STEP 7 Cut fiber-optic filaments into varying lengths and gather them into six bundles of 10 to 20 strands. Tape the ends of the filaments in each bundle together.

STEP 8 Attach the battery to the LilyPad Arduino; each LED will light up. Then use electrical tape to secure the filament bundles over the LEDs and to the fabric.

STEP 9 Thread the filaments through the second piece of fabric, following the pattern. It helps to use a small, sharp tool to poke holes for the filaments. When finished, remove the pattern.

STEP 10 Slide a clear bead onto each filament and hot-glue it on the underside of the fabric. Trim the filament.

STEP 11 Use the Velcro to connect the fabric pieces together with the filaments in between them. Hang it up with small nails or hooks, lean back, and admire your new starry, starry night.

029 PUT ON A LIQUID LIGHT SHOW

Project extreme grooviness with this simple psychedelic setup.

MATERIALS

Cardboard sheet
Scissors
Overhead projector with
 bottom lighting
Two thin, round glass nesting
 bowls
White wall or sheet
Water
Water-based dye
Mineral oil
Oil-based dye
Eyedropper

STEP 1 Measure and cut the cardboard sheet so that it fits over the projector base. Cut a hole in its center that's slightly smaller than the small glass bowl.

STEP 2 Place the cardboard on the projector surface. (It will mask the bowls' edges and keep your hands from blocking the display.)

STEP 3 Position the projector so that the light shining through the cutout completely fills your target screen and the edges aren't visible.

STEP 4 Add just enough water-based dye, such as food coloring, to a glass of water to produce a light tint.

STEP 5 Place the larger glass bowl on the projector surface face up, so it's centered over the cutout. Pour the colored water in it so that its bottom is covered.

STEP 6 Combine mineral oil with oil-based dye in a separate container, and fill an eyedropper with it.

STEP 7 Drop small amounts of colored oil into the water with the eyedropper.

STEP 8 Place the small glass bowl inside the large bowl. The water and oil mixture should just fill the space between the two bowls.

STEP 9 To start the light show, turn on the projector (and some psychedelic tunes) and move the bowls gently. Rotate them to swirl the liquids, or lift and lower them to move the image in and out of focus.

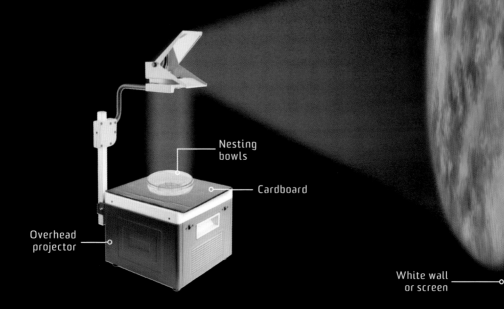

Nesting bowls

Cardboard

Overhead projector

White wall or screen

030 JAM OUT TO A SOUND-REACTIVE LIGHT BOX

Watch beats blink in time with a slick-looking LED display.

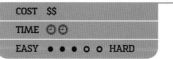

COST	$$
TIME	☺☺
EASY	● ● ● ○ ○ HARD

MATERIALS

Sheet of 3-mm Plexiglas
Ruler
Table saw
Drill with a glass bit
Audio cable
18-volt adapter
Fine sandpaper
Hot-glue gun
Six white 5-mm LEDs
TIP31 transistor
Electrical wire
Soldering iron and solder

STEP 1 To make the box, measure the Plexiglas into four 6-by-2-inch (15-by-4.7-cm) pieces and two 2-by-2-inch (5-by-5-cm) pieces. Cut them with a table saw outfitted with a plastic-cutting blade.

STEP 2 Drill two holes near a corner in one of the long pieces: one for the audio cable that will go to a stereo and one that's large enough to fit the plug on the adapter cord. Go lightly or the Plexiglas may break.

STEP 3 Using a circular motion, sand both sides of the pieces and the surfaces of the LED bulbs to get a cloudy, frosted look.

STEP 4 Hot-glue three of the rectangular panels together along their long edges, then glue the square pieces to the ends. Sand the joints after the glue dries.

STEP 5 Pull the audio cable through one of the box's holes and peel back the plastic to expose its wires on the inside of the box.

STEP 6 Wire the electronics according to the circuitry diagram. If you want more LEDs, buy an adapter that provides each LED with 3 volts.

STEP 7 Put the circuit in the box. Pull the adapter plug through the hole in the box, then glue it in place.

STEP 8 Glue the last Plexiglas piece onto the box. Plug the audio cable into your stereo's speaker output and plug the adapter into a power outlet.

STEP 9 Pick a song, and see it in lights.

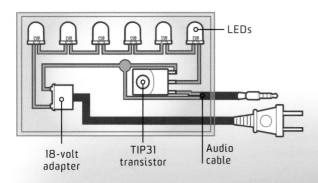

LEDs

18-volt adapter

TIP31 transistor

Audio cable

031 WAVE AN LED LIGHTER AT A CONCERT

Power ballads sound even more epic with this lighter mod.

MATERIALS

Dead lighter with absolutely no fluid inside

Pliers

Hacksaw

3-volt LED

Soldering iron and solder

Electrical wire

Two AAA batteries

Aluminum-foil duct tape

Superglue

STEP 1 Check to make sure your lighter is empty. If not, hold down the lever until the lighter fluid evaporates.

STEP 2 Using the pliers, pry off the metal shield at the top of the dead lighter. Carefully remove the striker wheel, fuel lever, spring, and fuel valve inside; set aside.

STEP 3 Cut ¼ inch (6.35 mm) off the bottom of the lighter with the hacksaw. Pry out the plastic divider.

STEP 4 In the middle of the metal shield's underside, create a dent with your pliers—this will be a contact point for the switch.

STEP 5 Solder the LED's negative lead to the shield near the dent and the positive lead to a piece of electrical wire 1 inch (2.5 cm) in length.

STEP 6 Solder a piece of wire 1 inch (2.5 cm) in length to the underside of the metal part of the fuel lever.

STEP 7 Put the spring and fuel lever inside the lighter. Reinsert the metal shield and thread the long wire attached to the LED through the flint tube.

STEP 8 Line the batteries up with opposite polarities next to each other, then tape a piece of stripped wire across them using aluminum-foil duct tape.

STEP 9 Follow the circuitry diagram, connecting the LED and fuel lever's wires to the batteries with aluminum-foil duct tape.

STEP 10 Slide the batteries inside and glue the bottom back on. It's slow-jam time.

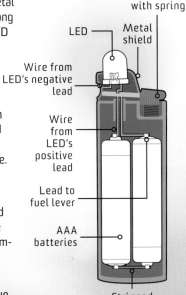

Fuel lever with spring

LED

Metal shield

Wire from LED's negative lead

Wire from LED's positive lead

Lead to fuel lever

AAA batteries

Stripped wire

---

5 MINUTE PROJECT

032 PARTY WITH AN LED GLOW STICK

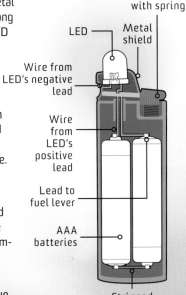

STEP 1 Using tape, attach a 3-volt LED's longer lead to a coin battery's positive side and its shorter lead to the negative side.

STEP 2 Disassemble the ballpoint pen. Discard everything but the pen tube.

STEP 3 Place the LED into the tube and tape the battery in place. Dance.

033 AN LED-LIT DISCO DANCE FLOOR

When dance fever hit MIT, students built a computer-controlled, LED-lit disco floor.

A group of undergrads at the Massachusetts Institute of Technology took on a challenge more daunting than classwork: disco. Before a dorm party, Mike Anderson, Grant Elliott, Schuyler Senft-Grupp, and Scott Torborg worked night and day for a week to build a computer-controlled, pixelated dance floor out of 1-by-4-foot (30-by-120-cm) boards, LEDs, tinfoil, paper towels, and old computer parts. The result would make Travolta weep with joy.

Each of the 512 pixels contains three LEDs pointed down at a square of paper towel that sits in a larger piece of foil. The foil reflects the light up through the plastic floor, while the paper towel mutes its glow. (LEDs stay cool, so the towels won't ignite.) A computer controls each pixel individually, and the open-source software generates 25 disco-tastic patterns, enabling DJs to match the light show to the music they're playing—and code-savvy disco fans to add new light patterns. What's more, by varying the intensity of each bulb, the students can blend light from the red, green, and blue LEDs housed in each pixel to produce any color. And should the party get extra wild (and with a dance floor like this, it will), the platform's wooden frame and thick layer of Lexan plastic make it nearly indestructible.

After earning minor fame at MIT (one of the inventors scored dates because of his uncanny soldering skills), the students began upgrading the floor. Their latest model has a prebuilt circuit board and instructions, so anyone can turn a basement into a discotheque.

HOW GEEKS GET DOWN
Everyone who actually worked on the floor and isn't a professional model, raise your hand.

034 MAKE A SONIC TUNNEL OF FIRE

See your favorite song burst into flame with this classic Rubens' tube.

This may be one of the best bad ideas of all time, and we have physicist Heinrich Rubens to thank for it: He found that if you make a sound at one end of a tube, you get a standing wave equivalent to the sound's wavelength inside the tube—and that the best way to demonstrate this principle is with waves of flame synced with music. Right on, Heinrich.

COST	$$
TIME	⏲ ⏲ ⏲
EASY ● ● ● ○ ○ HARD	

MATERIALS

4-inch (10-cm) ventilation ducting	Epoxy putty
Nail	Hose T-connector
Drill	Propane tank
Duct tape	Teflon tape
Latex sheets	Two 4-inch (10-cm) brackets
Scissors	Screws for your brackets
Two hose splicers	Scrap wood
	Media player and speakers

STEP 1 Leaving 4 inches (10 cm) at either end, mark off every ½ inch (1.25 cm) down the length of your ducting. (Do it on the side without the seam.)

STEP 2 Gently tap a nail at each interval, creating divots that will be easy to drill. Then drill through each resulting depression.

STEP 3 Wrap a strip of duct tape around each end of the tube. Then cut two squares of latex and tape them across both ends of the tube, creating an airtight seal.

STEP 4 Select two spots for fuel entry in the seam, each about one-third of the way across the tube. Tap the locations with a nail to create depressions, then drill two holes large enough to accommodate your hose splicers.

STEP 5 Install the hose splicers, securing the edges around the fuel entry holes with epoxy putty.

STEP 6 Attach the T-connector to the propane nozzle, then the hose splicers to the T-connector. Wrap the ends of the all the components with Teflon tape.

STEP 7 Using screws, attach brackets to scrap wood to make a stand. Then mount the tube onto it.

STEP 8 To use, tape all holes to create a seal. Then pump the tube full of propane for 2 minutes.

STEP 9 Remove the tape and test the tube by lighting one hole. If the flames are 1 inch (2.5 cm) high, it's ready.

STEP 10 Place a speaker as close as possible to one end of the tube (without actually touching the end's latex seal). Hit play, and watch those sound waves ignite.

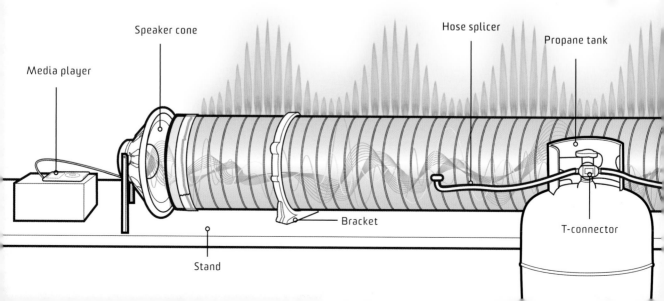

Media player · Speaker cone · Hose splicer · Propane tank · Bracket · Stand · T-connector

YOU BUILT WHAT?!

SHOOT A PROPANE-POWERED FIREGUN

Fire enthusiasts have long used propane "poofers" to shoot huge fireballs for special effects. But for this particular model, *PopSci* contributor Vin Marshall tried a new approach that incorporates striking visual elements as well as a bit of science. It took 40 crazed hours of near-nonstop parts acquisition, construction, and testing in a friend's partially collapsed warehouse to finish the poofer. Why would someone go to all that trouble just to shoot fireballs over the Philadelphia skyline? The better question is, why not?

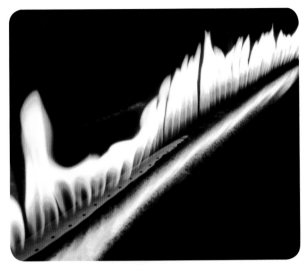

THE RUBENS TUBE IN ACTION
Why just listen to "Light My Fire" when you can listen to it *and* see its sound wave expressed in real flames?

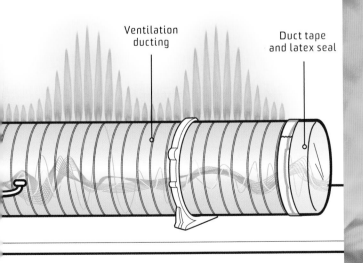

Ventilation
ducting

Duct tape
and latex seal

035 TURN YOUR CAMPFIRE GREEN

STEP 1 Pour ¼ inch (6.35 mm) of copper sulfate into a small paper cup. (You can use common tree-root killers, which contain copper sulfate.)

STEP 2 Melt old candle stubs in a double boiler, and pour the wax into the cup over the copper sulfate.

STEP 3 Stir the copper sulfate and wax together until the chemical is coated.

STEP 4 After it cools, peel off the sides of the paper cup.

STEP 5 When you're done cooking at your campsite, throw the copper-sulfate-infused wax into the hottest part of the fire and watch the green flames start licking.

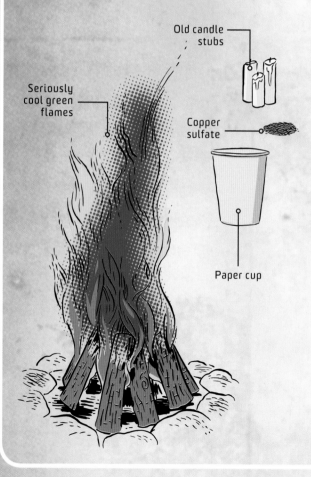

Old candle stubs

Seriously cool green flames

Copper sulfate

Paper cup

036 HOLD A FLAMING BALL IN YOUR BARE HAND

STEP 1 Use scissors to cut away a 2-by-5-inch (5-by-12.5-cm) strip of cloth from an old T-shirt. Roll the cloth into a ball.

STEP 2 Thread a needle with about 2 feet (60 cm) of sewing thread.

STEP 3 Push the needle all the way through the fabric ball, securing the loose end of the fabric strip.

STEP 4 Wind the thread around the ball many, many times. When you're almost out of thread, pull the needle through an existing loop of thread, then tie it off and remove the needle.

STEP 5 Soak the ball in isopropyl alcohol; squeeze out any excess that may drip onto your hands.

STEP 6 Wash any fluid off your hands, light up your fireball, and let it blaze around in your hand. (The less-adventurous can put on heat-resistant gloves.)

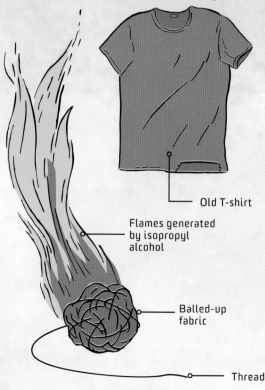

Old T-shirt

Flames generated by isopropyl alcohol

Balled-up fabric

Thread

037 SET OFF A SPINNING FIRE TORNADO

STEP 1 In the center of a lazy Susan, mold clay into a base for a fireproof bowl. Press the bowl into the clay, and place pieces of molding clay along the edges of the lazy Susan.

STEP 2 Measure the lazy Susan's diameter and roll a piece of screen into a 36-inch- (90-cm-) high cylinder of the same diameter. Use straight pins to secure the cylindrical shape.

STEP 3 Pour kerosene onto a rag; place it in the bowl.

STEP 4 With a fire extinguisher nearby, carefully ignite the rag in the small bowl with a long-handled lighter, then place the screen cylinder over the lazy Susan, pressing it into the pieces of molding clay.

STEP 5 Give the lazy Susan a whirl. Stand back and watch devious, fiery nature at work.

STEP 6 To extinguish, don heat-resistant gloves, wait for the lazy Susan to slow, and remove the screen. Then snuff out the small bowl with a larger fireproof bowl.

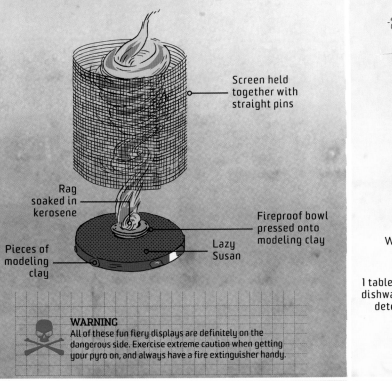

Screen held together with straight pins

Rag soaked in kerosene

Pieces of modeling clay

Lazy Susan

Fireproof bowl pressed onto modeling clay

WARNING
All of these fun fiery displays are definitely on the dangerous side. Exercise extreme caution when getting your pyro on, and always have a fire extinguisher handy.

038 IGNITE A HOMEMADE SPARKLER

STEP 1 Using a rotary tool, make a small hole into the top of a medicine bottle's lid.

STEP 2 Fill the bottle about one-fourth of the way with water and add 1 teaspoon of salt.

STEP 3 Add 1 tablespoon each of powdered dishwashing detergent and baking soda, and then put the lid on.

STEP 4 Carefully hold the flame of a lighter or match over the hole until the gas you've just created ignites, firing your sparkler. Celebrate.

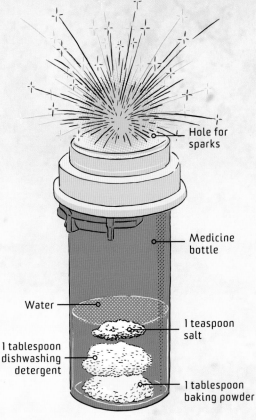

Hole for sparks

Medicine bottle

Water

1 teaspoon salt

1 tablespoon dishwashing detergent

1 tablespoon baking powder

039 WREAK HAVOC WITH THE ULTIMATE SQUIRT GUN

Water guns have never been more fun. No, really, we mean it.

This wet weapon is way more than a squirt gun; it's a powerful water cannon that shoots more than 1 quart (950 mL) of water up to 50 feet (15 m) in less than 10 seconds. But don't be a jerk. Keep your H2O gun's spray away from other people's faces.

COST	$$
TIME	☺ ☺
EASY ● ● ○ ○ ○ HARD	

MATERIALS
Drill

Various PVC parts (see diagram below)

PVC cement

Waterproof grease

Bucket of water

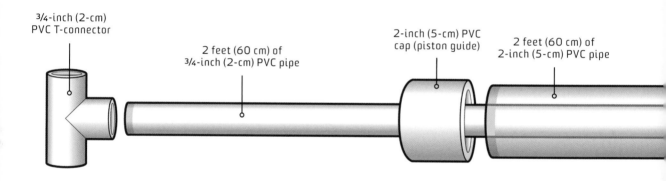

3/4-inch (2-cm) PVC T-connector

2 feet (60 cm) of 3/4-inch (2-cm) PVC pipe

2-inch (5-cm) PVC cap (piston guide)

2 feet (60 cm) of 2-inch (5-cm) PVC pipe

STEP 1 Use a drill to make a ¼-inch (6.35-mm) hole in the center of one 2-inch (5-cm) cap and a 1¼-inch (3-cm) hole in the center of the second cap. The first is your nozzle; the second is the piston guide.

STEP 2 Glue the T-connector to the small pipe with PVC cement. When gluing, immediately insert the pipe into the fitting and turn it to distribute the solvent evenly. Hold the joint for about 30 seconds to make sure it sets; wipe off excess glue with a rag.

STEP 3 Slide the piston guide over the small pipe with the open end facing away from the T-connector.

STEP 4 Glue the reducer bushing to the small pipe's end, the coupler to the reducer, and the 1¼-inch (3-cm) pipe to the coupler with the PVC cement.

STEP 5 Slide the O-ring over the small 1¼-inch (3-cm) pipe and glue the 1¼-inch (3-cm) PVC cap to the pipe.

STEP 6 Glue the nozzle onto the big pipe. Let the apparatus dry.

STEP 7 Apply a small glob of waterproof grease to the inside of the 2-inch (5-cm) PVC pipe. Insert the piston into the body and push and pull a few times to evenly spread the goop. When it seems sufficiently lubricated, firmly push the piston guide onto the body.

STEP 8 To load, use it like a giant syringe: Compress the handle and stick the huge squirt gun's end into a bucket of water, then pull up on the T-connector to draw water into the pipe.

STEP 9 Super-soak somebody near you.

040 MAKE A MINI CATAPULT

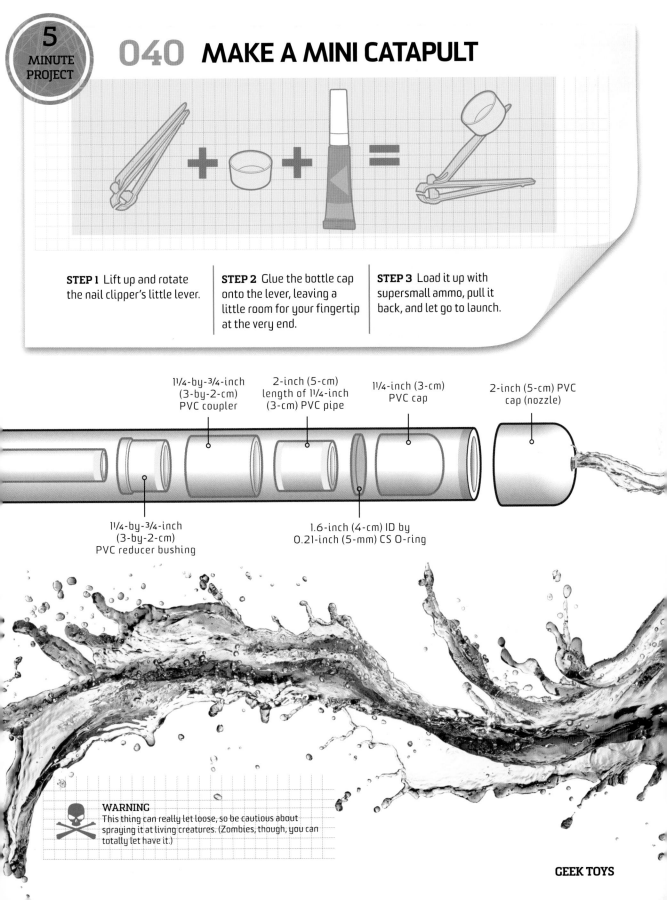

STEP 1 Lift up and rotate the nail clipper's little lever.

STEP 2 Glue the bottle cap onto the lever, leaving a little room for your fingertip at the very end.

STEP 3 Load it up with supersmall ammo, pull it back, and let go to launch.

1¼-by-¾-inch (3-by-2-cm) PVC coupler

2-inch (5-cm) length of 1¼-inch (3-cm) PVC pipe

1¼-inch (3-cm) PVC cap

2-inch (5-cm) PVC cap (nozzle)

1¼-by-¾-inch (3-by-2-cm) PVC reducer bushing

1.6-inch (4-cm) ID by 0.21-inch (5-mm) CS O-ring

WARNING
This thing can really let loose, so be cautious about spraying it at living creatures. (Zombies, though, you can totally let have it.)

GEEK TOYS

041 PLAY WITH A BIKE-PART SPIROGRAPH

Those mathy whirls of color from your childhood can be yours all over again.

MATERIALS

Bike chain	Jigsaw
Thin plywood	Superglue
Tape	Colored pens
Pen	An assortment of chain rings

STEP 1 Arrange a bike chain on the plywood in a perfect circle and tape it down. Faithfully trace around the chain's outer rim, being careful not to move it.

STEP 2 Using a jigsaw, cut out the circle and discard it. Line up the chain so that it fits inside the circular hole.

STEP 3 Use superglue to secure the chain all the way around the inner edge of the hole in the plywood. Let this dry overnight.

STEP 4 Place the plywood frame over paper. Put a chain ring on the paper and insert a colored pen through one of its bolt holes to make contact with the paper.

STEP 5 Keeping your pen in the chain ring's bolt hole, trace around the bike chain to lay down an awesome design. Experiment with chain rings that have different numbers of teeth for patterns of varying complexity.

---

5 MINUTE PROJECT

042 TURN JUNK MAIL INTO PENCILS

STEP 1 Cut a strip of paper—with colors or a pattern that you like—so it's 16½ inches (42 cm) in length and 5 inches (12.5 cm) in width.

STEP 2 Apply glue along a long edge and apply a piece of mechanical pencil lead to it, then roll your paper snugly around the pencil lead.

STEP 3 Continue applying glue every 1 inch (2.5 cm) and rolling up the paper little by little.

STEP 4 Let the pencil dry overnight. Use a craft knife to sharpen it and start scribbling.

043 SET UP A TURNTABLE ZOETROPE

See LEGOs come to life with this classic animation trick.

COST	$$
TIME	◷ ◷
EASY	● ● ○ ○ ○ HARD

The world saw its first modern zoetrope in 1833, and since its invention the device has paved the way to cinema as we know it. This playful update uses a strobe light to interrupt your view of a series of still objects as they go around and around on a record player—causing your eye to perceive them as if they were in motion. It's not 1833 anymore, but the effect is still pretty mind-boggling.

MATERIALS

Protractor	Superglue
A record to sacrifice	Record player
18 LEGO miniature figures	Strobe light

STEP 1 Using the protractor, measure and draw lines every 20 degrees on the sacrificial record. Space out the LEGO figures around the edge of the record according to these marks, and glue them down.

STEP 2 Put the LEGO figures in positions of your choosing—think about creating the look of continuous motion by carefully changing each one's position incrementally from that of the one before it.

STEP 3 Set the record player to 33⅓ RPM.

STEP 4 Adjust your strobe light to flash ten times per second and position it so that it's pointed at the zoetrope at close range.

STEP 5 Turn out the lights, turn on the record player and the strobe, and watch those LEGO figurines start dancing, running, battling, or doing whatever you want them to do.

044 THE REAL IRON MAN SUIT

This homebuilt superhero suit looks as good as the silver-screen version.

Anthony Le has been a fan of Iron Man since he was a kid. When he heard that the comic-book superhero was hitting the big screen in 2008, he was inspired to build his own Iron Man suit. That version was more of a costume, but his next edition—finished just in time for the movie's sequel—edges much closer to the real thing. With its dent-proof exterior, motorized faceplate, and spinning mock Gatling gun, his take on the movie's War Machine suit could easily frighten a supervillain—not to mention kids in the theater.

To make the suit, Le—who is a fitness consultant by day—studied some concept sketches of the suit posted on the Internet. He focused on the War Machine suit, donned by Stark's buddy Jim Rhodes in *Iron Man 2*, in part because "it just looks more hardcore." He used thin, high-impact urethane for the armor, cutting it into plates and joining them with some 1,500 rivets and washers. He sculpted a clay helmet mold and then used a mix of liquid resin to create the final product. He added a replica of the machine gun on the suit's shoulder made of PVC pipes and other materials. But that was just cosmetic work. He also added a small servo motor that opens the faceplate, as in the movie, and built a gun out of pipes and a motor. LEDs in the eyes and chest-plate further add to the illusion.

All the LEDs and the motors that drive the gun and the faceplate have their own batteries hidden within the suit's large frame. Inside the chestplate, Le added a hands-free button that activates the helmet. When the faceplate is open, he just stands up and points his arm forward, causing his chest to press against the button, triggering the servo motors in the helmet to close the mask. This, in turn, switches on the red LEDs set inside the eye openings, which are large enough for him to also see out of. To open the mask up again, he presses another button.

Le wore one of his suits to the Children's Hospital in Aurora, Colorado, to cheer up the kids, and the staff was so pleased they made him his own ID card. The name listed? Iron Man.

HARD TO MISS
The material Le used for the armor is thin but takes stress well. "You can throw it against the wall, and it won't even be damaged," he says. Le has a cult following among fans of the movie featuring Iron Man—he wore the suit to the theater to see *Iron Man 2*.

045 MIX MAGNETIC SILLY PUTTY

STEP 1 Mix 1 tablespoon of basic craft glue and 1 cup (240 ml) of water in a plastic bag, then add 1 tablespoon of borax. Squeeze to make the putty.

STEP 2 Wearing gloves and a face mask, spread out the putty and sprinkle about 2 tablespoons of iron oxide powder onto it. Work it in for about 5 minutes.

STEP 3 Introduce a magnet to your putty and watch it move and change shape.

046 COOK UP FERROFLUID

Believe it or not, this spiky stuff is a fluid. Put it on a magnet and it goes nuts.

MATERIALS

Syringe
Ferric chloride solution
Distilled water
Steel wool
Coffee filter
Household ammonia
Oleic acid
Kerosene

STEP 1 With a syringe, measure 10 ml of ferric chloride solution and 10 ml of distilled water into a container.

STEP 2 Add a small piece of steel wool. Stir or swirl the solution until it turns bright green, then filter it through a coffee filter.

STEP 3 Add 20 ml more ferric chloride solution to your filtered green solution. While stirring, add 150 ml of ammonia.

STEP 4 In a well-ventilated area, heat the solution to near boiling. While stirring, add 5 ml of oleic acid. Keep heating until the ammonia smell is gone (about an hour).

STEP 5 Let cool, and then add 100 ml of kerosene. Stir until the black color attaches to the kerosene.

STEP 6 Pour off and collect the kerosene layer in a bowl.

STEP 7 Place a magnet under your bowl's bottom and watch

047 CATCH A THRILL ON A BACKYARD COASTER

Sure, it may not do loop-de-loops, but our lawyers tell us that's a good thing.

COST	$$$$
TIME	⏱⏱⏱⏱
EASY ● ● ● ● ● HARD	

MATERIALS

5-by-5-inch (12.5-by-12.5-cm) wooden posts

Drill

Screws and bolts

4-by-4-inch (10-by-10-cm) wooden posts

2-by-4-inch (5-by-10-cm) boards

Measuring tape

Circular saw

Gray sun-resistant 1½-inch (3.75-cm) PVC pipe

Heat gun

PVC of a slightly smaller diameter that fits snugly inside the main PVC size

Casters fitted with skateboard wheels

Rectangular piece of wood or particleboard

Car seat with seat belt

Rope

STEP 1 Survey your land and choose a spot for your backyard coaster.

STEP 2 Design your track. Note that you can't have a hill that is higher than the previous peak. If you're creating multiple hills, the car must continuously build enough energy by descending hills to make it up subsequent hills and around corners. Try starting with a downward slope from about 9 feet (2.75 m) followed by a hill that measures about 6 feet (1.8 m) at its crest. End the track with a steep uphill that the car won't be able to climb over, which will stop it.

STEP 3 Lay down 5-by-5-inch (12.5-by-12.5-cm) posts on the ground as a base. Screw the posts together with a drill.

STEP 4 Saw the 4-by-4-inch (10-by-10-cm) posts to varying heights that match your design's elevation changes. Then screw the posts along the top of the 5-by-5-inch (12.5-by-12.5-cm) floor to create your elevation. Leave 1 foot (30 cm) between each post.

STEP 5 Mark and cut 2-by-4-inch (5-by-10-cm) boards into slats as long as the width of your track. Lay these across the tops of the 4-by-4-inch (10-by-10-cm) posts and screw them into place.

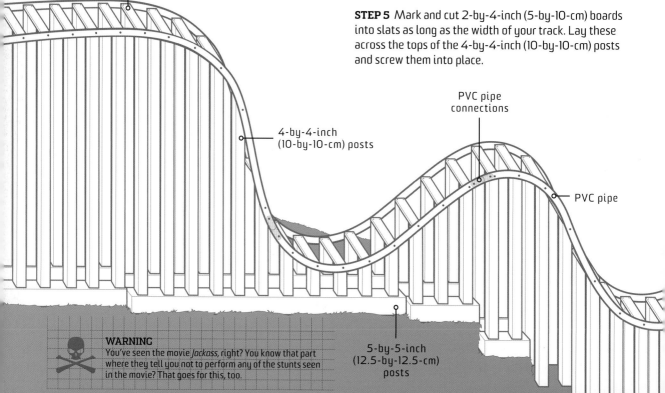

2-by-4-inch (5-by-10-cm) boards

4-by-4-inch (10-by-10-cm) posts

PVC pipe connections

PVC pipe

5-by-5-inch (12.5-by-12.5-cm) posts

WARNING
You've seen the movie *Jackass*, right? You know that part where they tell you not to perform any of the stunts seen in the movie? That goes for this, too.

STEP 6 Drill holes through the gray PVC pipe, and then use the drill to screw through these holes into the sides of the 2-by-4-inch (5-by-10-cm) boards, forming the rails and sides of your track. Use a heat gun to mold the PVC to curves. As you go, connect segments of PVC securely by sliding a 1-foot (30-cm) section of the smaller diameter pipe into the PVC that's already in place. Screw it in, then slide on the new piece and screw that in as well.

STEP 7 To make the coaster car, screw wheels onto the bottom of a flat piece of wood that's 3 feet (90 cm) long and about the width of the track. One set of wheels should roll on top of the PVC and the other should ride along the outside.

STEP 8 Check to see if the car works by rolling it on the track, and make adjustments to wheel placement if necessary.

STEP 9 Bolt the car seat equipped with a seat belt onto the coaster car, leaving room in front for the rider's tucked legs.

STEP 10 Attach a long piece of rope to the car—you can use this to pull the coaster backward up the first slope for a rider to board.

STEP 11 Test the roller coaster. Place the car on the track and put a sack of flour on it to serve as a crash-test dummy. Test more than once. If the tests are successful, consider someday cautiously trying it yourself.

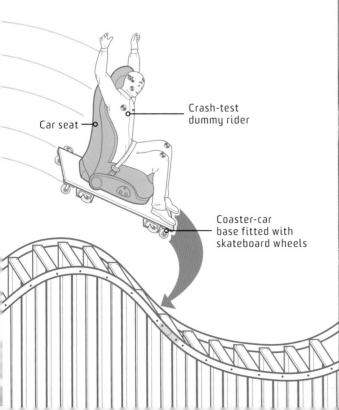

Car seat

Crash-test dummy rider

Coaster-car base fitted with skateboard wheels

WATER-POWERED JET PACK

When Raymond Li decided to build a jet pack propelled by water instead of rocket fuel, most of his friends thought he had gone crazy. Worse, engineers told him it would be impossible to manage the water's mass and thrust to keep it stable in the air. Li, however, figured that if he attached a hose to his pack, and put the engine and water pump in a separate vessel—which ended up being an extensively modified Jet Ski—that dragged behind him, he could seriously reduce his weight, and therefore the amount of thrust needed to stay aloft. In theory, a stiff hose filled with heavy, pressurized water would also add drag, stabilizing the jet pack for better forward flight control. It took four prototypes and more than 200 flight tests to get it right. But now, with a mere 30-pound (13.5-kg) pack, the Jetlev-Flyer generates 430 pounds (195 kg) of thrust and lets Li fly forward at 22 miles per hour (35 km/h) up to three stories high. That's quite an upgrade from your average day at the lake.

048 SET UP A PINBALL GAME AT HOME

Because arcades can't stay open all the time, and you're out of quarters, anyway.

COST	$$
TIME	⊙ ⊙ ⊙
EASY ● ● ● ○ ○ HARD	

MATERIALS

Peg-Board
Saw
2x4s
Wood glue
Nails
Hammer
Drill
3/4-inch (2-cm) drill bit
1/2-inch (1.25-cm) drill bit
1/8-inch (3-mm) drill bit
5/16-inch- (8-cm-) diameter hex bolt with nut

3/8-inch- (9.5-mm-) diameter spring
Wood
Wood pegs
Bicycle bell
Rubber bands
Scrap wood
PVC pipe elbows
Rubber hose
Marbles

STEP 1 Use the saw to cut the Peg-Board to your desired size to form the base of the pinball machine.

STEP 2 Measure and cut 2x4s to make a frame. Glue and nail it into place.

STEP 3 Nail a 2x4 under the top of the frame to prop it up at a slight angle.

STEP 4 Drill a hole about 1/2 inch (1.25 cm) in diameter in the bottom frame piece's right corner. Insert the hex bolt and slide the spring over the bolt.

STEP 5 Attach the nut to secure the spring on the bolt. Pull the bolt down to compress the spring—this is the ball launcher. Place a piece of scrap wood alongside the bolt to create a guide for the ball.

049 Play DIY Skee-Ball

Go analog with a good old-fashioned Skee-Ball toss.

MATERIALS

1-inch (2.5-cm) particleboard
1/2-inch (1.25-cm) particleboard
1/4-inch (6.35-mm) particleboard

Saw
Wood glue
Nails
Rubber ball

STEP 1 Use the saw to cut pieces of particleboard according to the measurements in the diagram.

STEP 2 On the board that serves as a ramp, trace your ball at one end to create a circular shape. Then add 1/4 inch (6.35 mm) all around this shape, and cut it out.

STEP 3 Build the game using nails and wood glue, making sure that the ramp fits against the back wall and that the opening is large enough for the ball to drop in.

STEP 4 Cut a hole into one side of the box so that you can reach in and grab the ball after scoring tosses.

STEP 5 Stand about 8 feet (2.4 m) away and toss the ball so that it rolls up the ramp—if it goes in the hole, that's one point. Any player who scores may continue until he or she misses; the first to score 15 points wins.

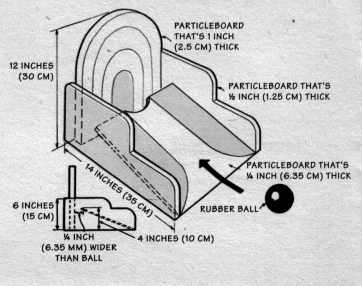

PARTICLEBOARD THAT'S 1 INCH (2.5 CM) THICK

12 INCHES (30 CM)

PARTICLEBOARD THAT'S 1/2 INCH (1.25 CM) THICK

14 INCHES (35 CM)

PARTICLEBOARD THAT'S 1/4 INCH (6.35 CM) THICK

6 INCHES (15 CM)

RUBBER BALL

1/4 INCH (6.35 MM) WIDER THAN BALL

4 INCHES (10 CM)

STEP 6 Toward the bottom of the game, drill through the side boards to create a ¾-inch (1.9-cm) hole in each. Drill another hole next to the first so that the holes meet, making a long oval hole on each side of the board.

STEP 7 Mark the center of the oval hole on the top of the board, then drill into it from above with a ⅛-inch (3-mm) drill bit. Repeat on the other side.

STEP 8 Cut two pieces of wood into paddles of your desired length. Sand the edges.

STEP 9 Drill a ⅛-inch (3-mm) hole from the top near the ends of the paddles. Slip the paddles into the holes in the side boards.

STEP 10 Place a nail through the holes in the frame, through the paddles, and into the holes' bottom. Tap it with a hammer to secure them in place. Place a peg on either side of each paddle to restrict its range.

STEP 11 To create tunnels, nail down rubber hoses sliced in half lengthwise and PVC pipe elbows, and for good bumper action, extend rubber bands between pegs or nail scrap wood to the Peg-Board. If you want spinners, try foam X shapes secured loosely with a nail. Don't forget a ramp and bicycle bell.

STEP 12 Load up the launcher with a marble, pull back the bolt, and release it—let the game begin.

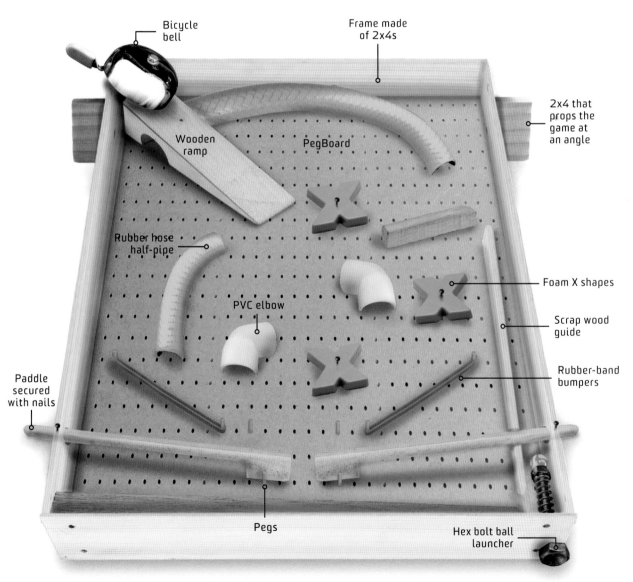

Bicycle bell

Frame made of 2x4s

2x4 that props the game at an angle

Wooden ramp

PegBoard

Rubber hose half-pipe

Foam X shapes

PVC elbow

Scrap wood guide

Paddle secured with nails

Rubber-band bumpers

Pegs

Hex bolt ball launcher

050 BUILD A MINT-TIN RACER

STEP 1 Use a drill to make five holes into your tin: two on both of the tin's long sides and one in the top corner of the lid.

STEP 2 Measure and cut two wooden sticks so they are long enough to traverse the width of the mint tin with about ½ inch (1.25 cm) extra on either side.

STEP 3 Slide the axles through the holes in the side of the tin, and attach bottle-cap "wheels" to the sticks with hot glue.

STEP 4 To deck out your racer with a flag, insert a straw into the hole in the tin's top, and tape a triangular flag to the straw's top.

STEP 5 Detail your racer however you like.

Straw flag

Mint tin

Wooden stick axle

Bottle cap wheel

051 SHAKE UP A MARTINI IN A MINT TIN

STEP 1 Drill a hole into one end of the mint tin and insert a plastic nozzle. (You can buy these in bulk online or at home-improvement stores.)

STEP 2 Buy or fill two travel-size bottles: one with gin or vodka, one with vermouth.

STEP 3 Place the booze bottles, a paper cup, and an olive inside the tin.

STEP 4 When you need an emergency drink, remove all the tin's contents and pour the bottles into the tin.

STEP 5 Close the tin and shake it well.

STEP 6 Loosen the nozzle, pour into the cup, and garnish with the olive.

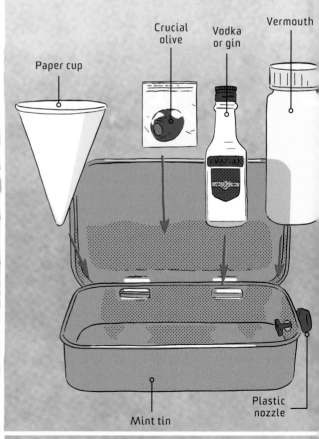

Crucial olive

Vodka or gin

Vermouth

Paper cup

Mint tin

Plastic nozzle

052 STRUM A MINT-TIN GUITAR

STEP 1 Position the tin so that its label is facing you. Then trace the stacked ends of three rulers onto the far right side to make a rectangle.

STEP 2 Using a drill, make a hole in the rectangle on the box's side, then cut out the rectangle outline with tin snips.

STEP 3 On the other side of the box, just below the lid's lip on the side, make three evenly spaced holes for the guitar strings. Thread the strings through and knot them off inside the box.

STEP 4 Remove the insides of a cheap ballpoint pen and cut the clear tube to about the width of your mint tin. Then cut it in half lengthwise. Make three notches in it for your guitar strings.

STEP 5 Use a hot-glue gun to glue the pen tube facedown onto the tin lid on the side where you've made holes for the strings.

STEP 6 Insert one ruler into the rectangular cutout so that it goes about halfway into the mint tin. Secure it with a hot-glue gun.

STEP 7 Cut a credit card to the ruler's width. Bend one edge up and glue it to the ruler about ½ inch (1.25 cm) from the ruler's end.

STEP 8 Cut the other two rulers down to 1 inch (2.5 cm) shorter than the exposed ruler. Glue them on top of the first ruler.

STEP 9 Drill holes for the eyebolts into the end of the bottom ruler. Insert and secure them with nuts on the ruler's bottom.

STEP 10 String the strings over the pen tube and tie them off around the eyebolts, and start strumming the hits.

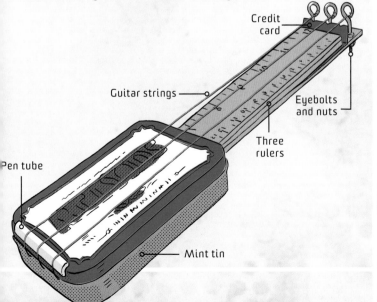

Credit card

Guitar strings

Eyebolts and nuts

Three rulers

Pen tube

Mint tin

053 CARRY A POCKET BILLIARD SET

STEP 1 Use a craft knife to cut a piece of foam to fit inside a mint tin. It should be just about level with the tin's top.

STEP 2 Remove the foam and place it on green felt. Trace around it, then cut out the shape. Test it to make sure that it fits nicely inside the tin.

STEP 3 Take a small bead (aka, one of your pool balls) and place it in a corner of the felt. Cut a hole around it to make a pocket. Then trace the scrap to make pockets in the other three corners.

STEP 4 Glue the felt down onto the foam. Trace and cut the pocket shapes out of the foam, too.

STEP 5 Assemble the seven beads into a triangle. Place a piece of copper wire along one side of the triangle; mark its length.

STEP 6 Use this measurement to fold the wire into a triangle shape with sides of equal length.

STEP 7 Cut a small-diameter copper rod to make a pool cue.

STEP 8 Rack 'em up wherever you go.

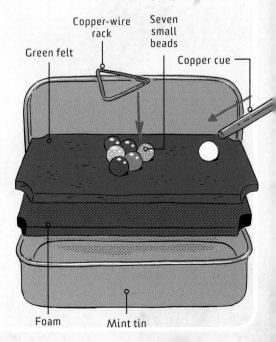

Copper-wire rack

Seven small beads

Green felt

Copper cue

Foam

Mint tin

054 BUILD A MINI ARCADE GAME

No room for a full-on console? Make a mini version for countertop play.

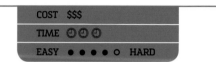

COST	$$$
TIME	⏱ ⏱ ⏱
EASY	● ● ● ○ HARD

MATERIALS

Netbook
½-inch (1.25-cm) medium density fiberboard
Ruler
Screws
Screwdriver
Hinge
Hole saw
Buttons and joystick
Label paper

Paint
Table saw with a plastic-cutting blade
Plexiglas
I-PAC 2
Electrical wire
Soldering iron and solder
Hot-glue gun
USB cable
Legal arcade software

STEP 1 Take apart your netbook and measure its LCD screen, obtaining the dimensions on which you'll base your arcade design.

STEP 2 Measure and cut ten pieces of medium-density fiberboard for the arcade's body (one each for the back, top, bottom, and sides) and five pieces for the front.

STEP 3 Screw it together. Mount a hinge in the back so you'll be able to open it up and access your electronics.

STEP 4 Measure and cut holes in the front of the arcade for the buttons and joystick using the hole saw.

STEP 5 Come up with a design for your arcade and print it on the label paper. Paint the arcade your desired color, then apply your label to the arcade.

STEP 6 Use the table saw with a plastic-cutting blade to cut Plexiglas pieces that fit over the pieces of board, and screw them over the label paper to protect the design.

STEP 7 Place the buttons and joystick and wire them according to the I-PAC 2's instructions.

STEP 8 Cut an additional piece of fiberboard to mount behind the LCD, propping the LCD up inside of the arcade. Make a hole in this board for wires.

STEP 9 Use the table saw to cut a piece of Plexiglas and mount it in front of the LCD.

STEP 10 Mount the I-PAC 2 and the base of the netbook inside the back panel of the arcade with hot glue.

STEP 11 Solder the LCD wire and USB wire directly to the I-PAC 2 board.

STEP 12 Open the arcade's back and turn on the netbook. Download and install legal arcade software, and get your game on.

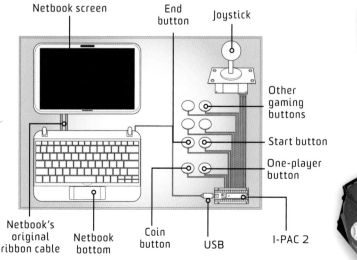

Netbook screen
End button
Joystick
Other gaming buttons
Start button
One-player button
Netbook's original ribbon cable
Netbook bottom
Coin button
USB
I-PAC 2

055 CINCH A NINTENDO-CONTROLLER BELT

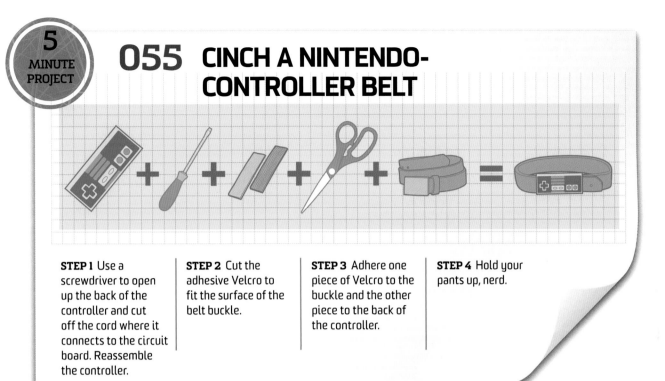

STEP 1 Use a screwdriver to open up the back of the controller and cut off the cord where it connects to the circuit board. Reassemble the controller.

STEP 2 Cut the adhesive Velcro to fit the surface of the belt buckle.

STEP 3 Adhere one piece of Velcro to the buckle and the other piece to the back of the controller.

STEP 4 Hold your pants up, nerd.

YOU BUILT WHAT?!

THE LEGO PINBALL MACHINE

In the hands of Netherlanders Gerrit Bronsveld and Martijn Boogaarts, LEGOs are no kid's toy. The duo's hobby is piecing together thousands of colored bricks—and other LEGO-made components, including programmable computers—into complex creations. Twenty-five LEGO hockey sets and 13 LEGO computers make up this arcade with a rubber band–powered kicker and sensor-activated bumpers, targets, and gates. A round will set you back 50 cents.

056 SET UP A SUPERSIZE GAME OF OPERATION

This classic kids' game may be all grown up, but it'll still leave you in stitches.

COST	$
TIME	🕐🕐🕐
EASY ● ● ● ○ ○ HARD	

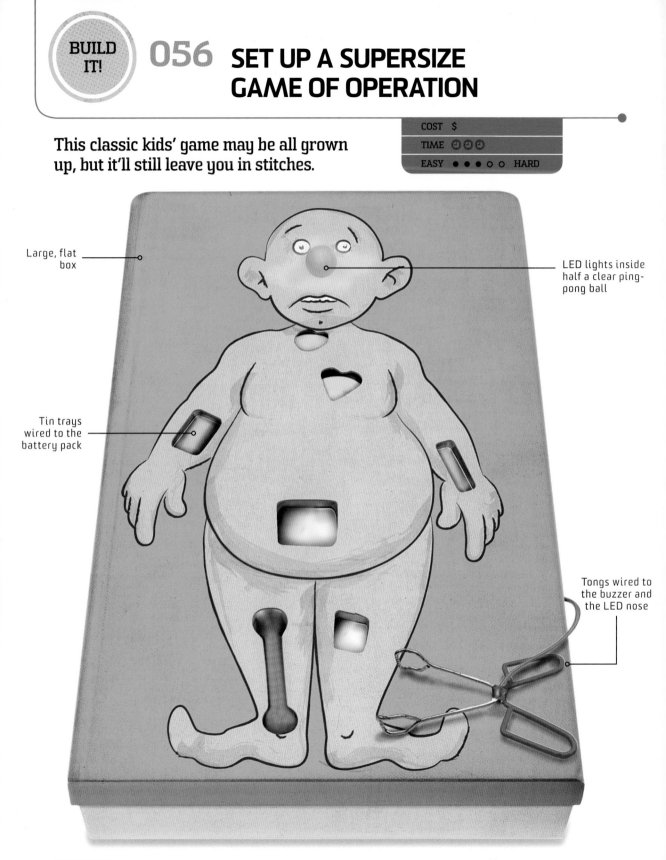

Large, flat box

LED lights inside half a clear ping-pong ball

Tin trays wired to the battery pack

Tongs wired to the buzzer and the LED nose

MATERIALS

Large, flat box

Paint

Seven "body parts"

Box cutter

Disposable tin oven trays

Tape

Gray paper

Wire strippers

Buzzer

Three AA batteries and holder

Threaded electrical wire

Five red LEDs

Five 100-ohm resistors

Soldering iron and solder

Metal tongs

Multimeter

Clear ping-pong ball, cut in half

STEP 1 Paint your box and sketch an outline of the patient's body, adding as much detail as you want.

STEP 2 Outline the body parts you'll be "surgically removing." Add at least ½ inch (1.25 cm) around the outlines, then use a box cutter to cut them out. Cut a hole for the nose that can fit all five LEDs, and a hole in the side of the box so you can easily access its interior.

STEP 3 Cut up and/or combine the oven trays so that they fit closely around each body part, then tape them under the holes. Line the trays' bottoms with gray paper.

STEP 4 Strip plastic off the ends of the buzzer's wires and those of your battery holder, then connect the buzzer's positive end to the battery pack's positive end.

STEP 5 Twist each positive leg of the five LEDs to a resistor, then wire all five resistors to a length of threaded electrical wire. Solder this wire to the battery holder's positive wire.

STEP 6 Twist the buzzer's negative wire to each LED's negative leg. Solder in place.

STEP 7 Cut a piece of electrical wire long enough to extend from underneath the "patient's" head to outside the box, where the players will pull it all over the board. Attach one end of this wire to the buzzer's negative wire.

STEP 8 Strip the protective coating on the tongs, then twist the other end of the wire attached to the buzzer's negative wire around the bare space. Tape it in place.

STEP 9 To wire the oven tins, cut a long electrical wire for each, making sure that it will reach the battery pack's location near the head. Tape each wire to an oven tin, then connect it to the battery pack's negative wire.

STEP 10 Tape the red LEDs in the hole for the nose and glue half of a ping-pong ball on top. Tape the battery pack and buzzer nearby.

STEP 11 Decorate your patient, drop body parts into the tins, and page your friends to come "operate."

057 Play Giant Checkers

Fact: If something is fun, making it larger makes it even more fun.

MATERIALS

Particleboard

Saw

Paint

U-shaped nails

Two pole hooks

STEP 1 Cut nine 4-foot- (1.2-m-) square pieces of particleboard, and arrange them in a 12-foot (3.6-m) square. (Using segments will allow you to store and transport the board.)

STEP 2 Mark a grid of squares that each measure 1 foot (30 cm). Paint the squares in alternating colors of your choice.

STEP 3 Use a saw to cut 24 discs that measure 8 inches (20 cm) in circumference. Paint half the discs one color, half another color.

STEP 4 Hammer a U-shaped nail partway into the center of each disc.

STEP 5 Use the pole hooks to pick up and move playing pieces by the nail loops.

058 MAKE A REFLECTION HOLOGRAM

Holograms aren't just for the holodeck. Make a 3D image of an object near you.

MATERIALS

Class 3A laser diode with an output of 3 to 4 mW

Tweezers

Battery pack

Wooden clothespin

Holography processing and development kit

Distilled water

A small solid object

PFG-03M 2.5-by-2.5-inch (6.35-by-6.35-cm) holographic plates

Cardboard

Matte black spray paint

STEP 1 Open up the laser diode and, using a pair of tweezers, remove the lens and the small tension spring. Hook the diode up to a battery pack.

STEP 2 Secure the clothespin in an upright position, and prop the laser diode between the clothespin's prongs.

STEP 3 Prepare the chemical processing solutions with distilled water and lay out the trays according to the holography processing and developing kit's instructions.

STEP 4 Set up the object that you want a hologram of 15 inches (40 cm) from the laser. Glue or tape it down if you're concerned about movement.

STEP 5 Make the room fairly dark, and adjust the laser in its holder so that the beam spreads out horizontally, with the object centered in its light.

STEP 6 Place cardboard in front of the laser to block light from reaching the object.

STEP 7 In the darkest area, remove a holographic plate from its container and (after immediately closing the container) lean the holographic plate against the object so that the sticky, emulsion-coated side touches it.

STEP 8 Request that everyone in the room hold still, and lift the piece of cardboard to expose the holographic plate to the laser light for about 20 seconds. Replace the cardboard.

STEP 9 Process the exposed holographic plate according to the holography kit's instructions, and then spray-paint the sticky side of the plate black.

STEP 10 When the plate is dry, place it in front of any incandescent (unfrosted) light source—a flashlight or the sun, for instance—to see the hologram take shape.

Now the force can always be with you, too.

MATERIALS

10-inch (25-cm) piece of 1.25 inch (3-cm) PVC pipe	Pliers
Black spray paint	2½-foot (75-cm) length of ¾-inch (2-cm) frosted polycarbonate tube
Drill	Two AA batteries
4 feet (1.2 m) of electrical wire	Soldering iron and solder
Wire strippers	On/off switch
30 LEDs	Duct tape

STEP 1 Spray-paint the PVC pipe black—this is your handle—then drill a hole in it for the on/off switch.

STEP 2 Cut two 2-foot (60-cm) lengths of electrical wire and strip both.

STEP 3 Attach the positive leads of the LEDs down the first wire, evenly spacing them. Then attach the LEDs' negative leads to the other stripped wire. Use pliers to crimp the LEDs' legs, securing them to the wires.

STEP 4 Drill a hole in the polycarbonate tube's top. Pull the string of LEDs into the tube through the other end, thread its wire through the hole, and tie it off.

STEP 5 Place the batteries next to each other with their polarities facing opposite directions. Attach a piece of wire across their ports with aluminum-foil duct tape.

STEP 6 Solder two wires to the on/off switch and thread it through the hole for the switch in the handle, first bringing it up through the hole in the bottom.

STEP 7 Insert the tube into the handle so that the wires from both the LED string and the switch dangle out of the handle's end. Tape the handle and tube together.

STEP 8 Solder the negative wires from the switch and LED string to the battery pack's negative port, and the positive wires from both to the positive port.

STEP 9 Duct-tape the handle's bottom to hold the battery pack inside. Turn it on and go get a Sith.

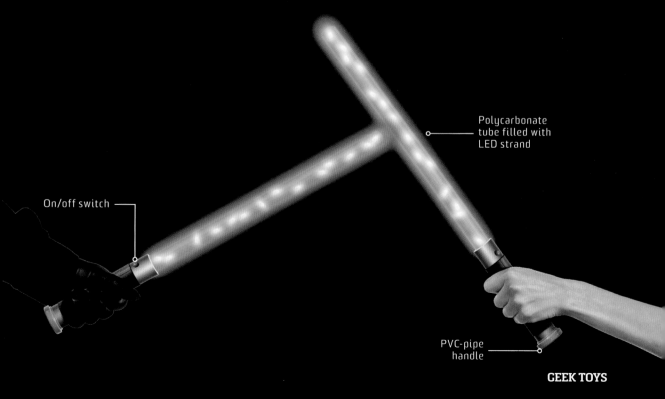

Polycarbonate tube filled with LED strand

On/off switch

PVC-pipe handle

GEEK TOYS

060 HACK YOUR MAGIC 8 BALL

Can you make this fortune-telling gizmo say whatever you want? It is decidedly so.

COST	$
TIME	⏱
EASY ● ○ ○ ○ ○ HARD	

MATERIALS

Magic 8 Ball
Plexiglas cutter
Screwdriver
Razor

Sandpaper
Extra-fine permanent marker
Superglue

STEP 1 Use a Plexiglas cutter to cut through the glue at the ball's equatorial seam, then carefully pry it open.

STEP 2 Inside there's a cylinder of blue dye. Remove the screws that hold it in place, and then pour out and reserve the liquid. Fish the answer ball out.

STEP 3 Pat the answer ball dry. Use a razor and sandpaper to scrape off the existing messages.

STEP 4 Write the messages you desire on the ball using an extra-fine permanent marker. Wait for the ink to dry.

STEP 5 Put the answer ball inside the cylinder, and then transfer the blue liquid back into the cylinder, too.

STEP 6 Glue the cap on the cylinder and reinsert it inside the two halves of the Magic 8 Ball.

STEP 7 Glue the ball back together, let it dry, and enjoy rewriting the future.

061 GO ANYWHERE WITH VIRTUAL-REALITY GLASSES

. . . anywhere that Google Street View goes, that is.

MATERIALS

Safety goggles
Large piece of cardboard
Pencil
Craft knife
Tape
Smartphone

STEP 1 Lay the safety goggles on the cardboard so that they're facing forward. Trace around the shape, adding at least 2 inches (5 cm) in front.

STEP 2 Roll the goggles up so that they're resting on an end. Trace around that side, adding extra space again.

STEP 3 Using the craft knife, cut out your tracing as one piece, then fold it so you have a four-sided rectangular tube that fits perfectly around your goggles. Secure it with tape and slide the goggles just inside.

STEP 4 On a separate piece of cardboard, trace the cardboard box's front, leaving 1-inch (2.5-cm) tabs on either side. Cut it out, then trace your smartphone onto its center. Cut out the shape of your phone, making

a window, and insert this cardboard piece into the rectangular tube opposite the goggles.

STEP 5 Dial up Google Street View and locate a place you've always wanted to go and tape your phone over the window.

STEP 6 Don your virtual-reality glasses, and take a walk someplace far, far away.

062 FILE-SHARE WITH A USB DEAD DROP

Camouflage a USB flash drive so that you can swap files on the sly.

MATERIALS

USB flash drive
Screwdriver
Plumber's tape
Drill with masonry bit
Cement
Paint, if desired

STEP 1 Stick your USB drive into your computer's port and upload any files you want to share, then remove it.

STEP 2 Scout for a good place to put your dead drop. You may need a drill with a masonry bit to make a hole in concrete, like the one you see here.

STEP 3 Slide your USB inside and use cement to secure it in place. Don't get any cement on the USB itself. If you want extra camouflage, paint a bit around it.

STEP 4 Scram—and let your contacts know where the secret docs are. To retrieve files from a dead drop, just line your laptop's USB port up with the USB drive and slide them together.

Coin battery

Alien-esque embellishments

Vibrating pager motor

Double-sided foam tape

Toothbrush head

063 BUILD A BRISTLEBOT

All the fun of a hyperactive pet, minus all the annoying shedding.

MATERIALS

Toothbrush with angled bristles
Rotary tool
Double-sided foam tape
Pager motor
Glue
Coin battery
Electrical tape
Decorations

STEP 1 Use a rotary tool to cut the head off a toothbrush. Apply double-sided foam tape to the back.

STEP 2 Salvage a pager motor with two wires and connect the wires to a coin battery, positive to positive and negative to negative. Tape the wires in place on the battery with electrical tape.

STEP 3 Add decorations, then attach the motor and battery to the foam tape on the toothbrush. Watch the robot merrily frolic.

064 MAKE A MINI WHIRLING MOTOR

Send current up over a magnetic field for some head-spinning results.

MATERIALS

6 feet (2 m) of enameled copper wire
C battery
Wire strippers
Electrical tape
Two safety pins
AA battery
Magnet

STEP 1 Wrap the wire several times around the C battery, leaving a few inches of excess at each end.

STEP 2 Slide the coil you just made off the battery. Pull one end of the excess wire through the coil, and then wrap it multiple times around the coil to hold it together. Leave about 1 inch (2.5 cm) of excess. Repeat with the other end of the wire.

STEP 3 Strip the bits of wire extending from the coil.

STEP 4 Using electrical tape, secure safety pins to both ends of the AA battery with the hinge ends sticking up.

STEP 5 Stick the coil's stripped ends through the holes in the hinge ends so the coil is centered over the battery.

STEP 6 Place the magnet on top of the battery, then give the coil a push and watch it spin.

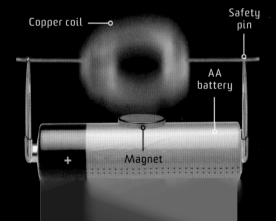

Copper coil

Safety pin

AA battery

Magnet

Plastic coat
hanger "handle"

Plastic tube
fingers

String loops that
control each finger

065 RIG AN ANIMATRONIC HAND

Need an extra hand? Build one—just don't blame us if it gets you in trouble.

MATERIALS

Marker
Paper
Plastic tubing
Craft knife
Nylon string
Black tape

CD case
Hot-glue gun
Plastic clothes hanger
Cell foam
Glove, if desired

STEP 1 Outline your hand with a marker on a piece of paper, and mark where the joints and knuckles are.

STEP 2 Cut five "fingers" from the plastic tubing—they should be as long as the distance from your middle fingertip to your wrist.

STEP 3 Cut a V-shaped notch in the underside of each finger to make joints.

STEP 4 Insert a 3-foot (90-cm) length of nylon string into each finger. To secure the string, pull it all the way out of the fingertip, then loop it through the notch closest to the fingertip and tie a knot. Tape it down at the fingertip and at the wrist.

STEP 5 Snap off a thin plastic strip from the spine of a salvaged CD case. Place the plastic strip over the four fingers about where they would meet the top of the hand. Hot-glue the strip to the fingers.

STEP 6 Place the hand palm up. Apply tape around the base of the fingers, then hot-glue the thumb to them (just don't melt the plastic). Remove the tape when dry.

STEP 7 Cut another length of tubing 1 foot (30 cm) long. Thread each of the strings extending out of the wrist end of the finger tubes through the new tube.

STEP 8 Cut another piece of plastic from the CD case and glue it so it straddles the finger tubes and the arm tube, stabilizing the wrist.

STEP 9 To make a handle, cut open a plastic coat hanger and glue the pieces together into a square shape. Then glue it to the end of the arm.

STEP 10 Give your new hand the gift of human touch by applying thin pieces of foam to the fingertips and the palm of the hand. Put a glove on it if you like.

STEP 11 Make loops in the ends of all the finger strings using tape or knots. Hold one end of the square handle against the palm of your own hand, then insert your fingers into these loops and practice gently tugging on them to make the hand move creepily about.

066 THE ELECTRIC GIRAFFE

It walks, it blinks, it seats six, and it blasts Kraftwerk. Meet one man's enormous pet project.

It started with a 7-inch (18-cm) walking toy giraffe and a desire to see Burning Man—the annual art-and-rave party in the desert in Black Rock, Nevada—from a higher vantage point. A year later, Lindsay Lawlor rode into the desert art festival atop Rave Raffe, a 1,700-pound (771-kg) robotic giraffe sporting 40 strobes, 400 LEDs, and bone-shaking speakers.

Lawlor wanted his Burning Man ride to be a true walking vehicle, so he copied the small toy's locomotion system on a massive scale. The front and back legs opposite each other step ahead at the same time, propelled by an electric motor. When those legs land, hydraulic brakes lock the wheeled feet, and the other two legs take a step. Canting from side to side, Raffe lumbers ahead at about 1 mile per hour (1.6 km/h). A 12-horsepower propane engine runs only to recharge the batteries, so the beast is quiet and efficient, while a pneumatic pump raises and lowers the giraffe's massive neck. When Lawlor let Raffe shuffle off alone in the desert, it walked for 8 hours.

Since the giraffe's debut, Lawlor (a part-time laser-light-show designer) has added new features, including computer-controlled flashing giraffe spots, an electroluminescent circulatory system, and a gas grill.

067 CREATE AUDIO ART OUT OF CASSETTE TAPE

Get your John Cage on with a hack that's half musical instrument, half graffiti.

COST	$$
TIME	☺ ☺ ☺
EASY ● ● ● ● ● HARD	

MATERIALS

Cassette player and recorder
Screwdriver
Wire strippers
Electrical wire
Scissors
Rubber thimble
Superglue
Glove

Project box
Drill
On/off switch
Soldering iron and solder
Battery and battery holder
Velcro
Strips of audio tape

STEP 1 Pop open the cassette player's door. Push the play button to make a metal mechanical component called the *playhead* slide down. Remove the screws securing the playhead.

STEP 2 Turn your attention to the cassette player's back. Remove all the screws and open up the case. Take a good look at the circuit board, noting where the playhead, speaker, and battery leads connect.

STEP 3 Unscrew and extract the circuit board with the speaker and playhead attached. Detach the drive motor and microphone from the circuitry itself.

STEP 4 Find the contacts that move together when you hit the play button. Sever the wires connecting them to the play button, but not the ones to the circuit board.

STEP 5 Cut the wires that connect the playhead and speaker to the circuit board.

STEP 6 Cut holes in the rubber thimble and thread the playhead's wires through them. Glue the playhead's base to the end of the thimble, and then glue the thimble over the finger of a glove.

STEP 7 Fit the circuit board into the project box, and drill holes into one side to thread the playhead's wires through. Reattach the wires to the circuit board.

STEP 8 Drill two holes in the project box for the on/off switch's wires. Solder these to the wires that the play button formerly controlled (they were connected to the contacts removed in step 4). Glue the switch to the box.

STEP 9 Cut a larger hole on top of the project box and super-glue the tape recorder's original speaker in the box. Reconnect the speaker's wiring to the circuit board.

STEP 10 Put the battery holder inside the project box. Attach the holder's wires to the circuit board where its original battery terminals were connected.

STEP 11 Attach the project box to the back of the glove with Velcro. The wire leading to the playhead on your fingertip should allow for hand and finger movement. If necessary, splice in extra electrical wire.

STEP 12 Take apart a cassette tape and remove its tape from the spools. Arrange the tape on an interior wall.

STEP 13 Place batteries into the battery holder, turn the switch on, and run the playhead over strips of audio tape. Experiment with speed—nail the right tempo, and you'll hear the original recording.

Project box
containing
circuit board and
battery pack

Thimble
containing
playhead

Audio-tape design

Speaker

Glove

068 SCRATCH A PIZZA-BOX TURNTABLE

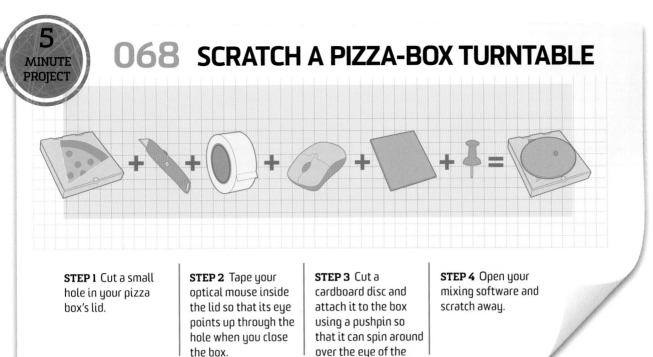

STEP 1 Cut a small hole in your pizza box's lid.

STEP 2 Tape your optical mouse inside the lid so that its eye points up through the hole when you close the box.

STEP 3 Cut a cardboard disc and attach it to the box using a pushpin so that it can spin around over the eye of the mouse.

STEP 4 Open your mixing software and scratch away.

069 PIRATE A VINYL RECORD

If you live in fear of scratching a super-rare record, this silicone mold is for you.

MATERIALS

Four wood boards 14¼ inches (36.5 cm) in length
Nails
Hammer
Glass plate
Caulking
Record
Dowel
Silicone rubber designed for mold making
Casting resin

STEP 1 Nail together the boards to make a square wood frame. Place the frame on the glass plate, and seal around the inside edge with caulking.

STEP 2 Put the record you want to copy inside the frame on the glass plate—the side you want to copy should be face up. Fit a dowel into the record's hole.

STEP 3 Prepare the silicone rubber and pour it into the mold. Let it dry overnight.

STEP 4 Peel off the silicone mold.

STEP 5 Mix the casting resin and pour it into the silicone mold. Once it's set, loosen the cast and remove.

STEP 6 Pop your repro record onto your record player and hit play.

070 CRAFT A BOOM BOX DUFFEL BAG

STEP 1 Create a simple image of a boom box, and draw or print it onto contact paper to create a stencil. The boom box's speakers should be more or less the same size as your speakers, which are best if they're of the cheap desktop variety.

STEP 2 Using a craft knife, carefully cut out the stencil.

STEP 3 Lay the duffel bag flat and remove the back of the contact paper. Smooth the contact paper over the fabric.

STEP 4 Squeeze out a line of paint at the top of the stencil, and use a piece of cardboard to spread the paint over it. Repeat until the paint is well distributed. Remove the stencil.

STEP 5 After the paint has dried, cut two holes slightly smaller than your speakers out of the design. These are the holes for the speakers.

STEP 6 Remove the speakers' backs and slide the speakers into the holes from the outside. Reattach the backs with the same screws, sandwiching the fabric.

STEP 7 Plug the speakers into your portable media player, shoulder up the bag, and pump some jams.

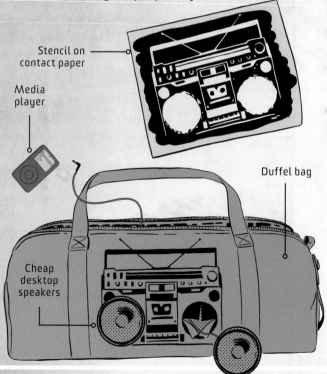

Stencil on contact paper

Media player

Duffel bag

Cheap desktop speakers

071 MAKE YOUR TIE GLOW IN THE DARK

STEP 1 Use a needle to poke a hole into the end of a tie where the EL (electroluminescent) wire will enter. It's best to use heavy-duty fabrics and to follow the seams.

STEP 2 Sew a piece of Velcro onto the tie and attach another piece to a battery pack. (We fit ours at the end of the tie.)

STEP 3 Draw a design, lay EL wire over the sketch, and tape it to the tie.

STEP 4 Measure heavy-duty fishing line that's more than twice the length of your EL wire. Thread a sturdy needle with the line and make a knot at its end.

STEP 5 Sew the wire down, securing it every 1/2 inch (1.25 cm). Remove the tape.

STEP 6 Plug the wire into the battery pack and never wear a boring tie again.

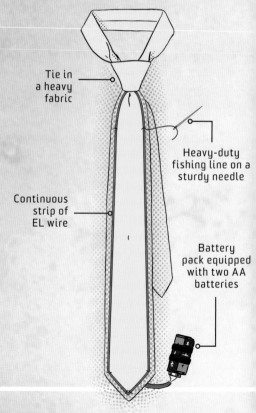

Tie in a heavy fabric

Heavy-duty fishing line on a sturdy needle

Continuous strip of EL wire

Battery pack equipped with two AA batteries

072 PUT HEADPHONES IN YOUR HOODIE

STEP 1 Use a craft knife to carefully detach the speakers from a headphone band, keeping the ear cushions and speakers (and the wire between them and the one that runs to a media player) intact.

STEP 2 Put on a lined hoodie. Safety-pin the ear cushions in place and test that they fit comfortably.

STEP 3 With a heavy-duty needle, sew four strips of Velcro onto each ear cushion's spot in the hoodie, and four more strips to the back of each ear cushion.

STEP 4 Cut a slit in the lower center of the hood where the speakers' wires will join and enter the lining.

STEP 5 Cut a slit into the lower corner of the hoodie's front where the cord will come out.

STEP 6 Check to make sure your wire is long enough to reach the incision in the jacket's front. If it's not, desolder the cord and solder on a longer one.

STEP 7 Attach the speakers to the Velcro and feed the cord into the hood's lining and out the front.

STEP 8 Pull up your hood and get skulking. To launder, detach the ear cushions and pull out the cord.

Adhesive Velcro

Sew-on Velcro

Lined hoodie

Ear cushions with intact speakers

Hole for cord entrance

Hole for cord exit

Media player

073 USE A GLOVE ON A TOUCH SCREEN

STEP 1 Thread a sturdy needle with 1 foot (30 cm) of conductive thread.

STEP 2 On the outside of a glove's pointer finger, sew a few stitches—enough to cover an area of about ¼ inch (6.35 mm) in diameter.

STEP 3 Turn the glove inside out, and sew three to five stitches. Allow some extra thread to dangle—this will ensure that your finger touches the conductive thread, completing a mini circuit and allowing the screen to pick up on your gestures.

STEP 4 Swipe and tap away. If you find that typing with your glove often results in hitting neighboring letters, pull out a few threads from the outside of the fingertip.

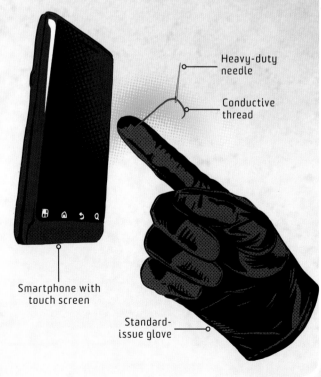

Heavy-duty needle

Conductive thread

Smartphone with touch screen

Standard-issue glove

074 PUMP JAMS THROUGH AN OLD-SCHOOL PHONOGRAPH

This phonograph probably hasn't played any new music since Stravinsky. Give it new life with this modernizing mod.

COST	$$$
TIME	☺ ☺ ☺
EASY ● ● ● ● ○ HARD	

MATERIALS

Wooden box
Drill with a hole bit
Felt
Miniature mono amplifier with tone control
Transformer for the amplifier
Two potentiometer knobs
3.5-mm stereo socket
Power plug
Power switch
Speaker
Soldering iron and solder
Electrical wire
Hot-glue gun
Brass horn from an old phonograph
Media player

STEP 1 Measure and cut two holes in the top of your box: one for the brass horn and a smaller one for the stereo socket.

STEP 2 Measure the box's inside and cut felt to those dimensions, then line the box with felt—it will make for better sound.

STEP 3 Set up the electronics according to the diagram, drilling holes for the power source, potentiometers, and power switch as you go.

STEP 4 Place the horn in its hole and hot-glue it in place. Sand and varnish the box, if you desire.

STEP 5 Close up the box, plug your media device into the stereo socket, and plug the contraption's power cable into an outlet.

STEP 6 Enjoy the sweet, sweet sound of anachronism.

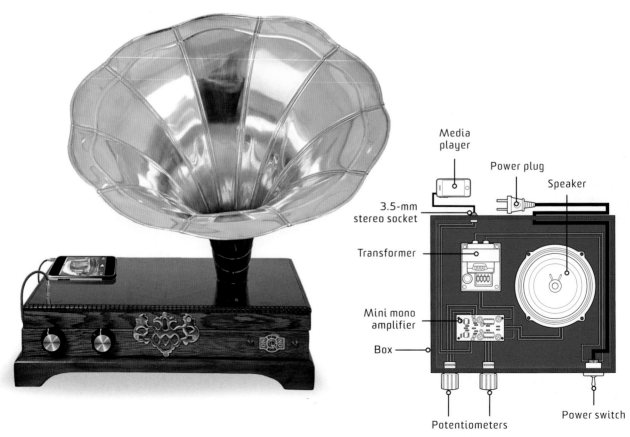

075 AMPLIFY MUSIC WITH PAPER CUPS

STEP 1 Turn one paper cup upside down and stick a toothpick through the bottom.

STEP 2 Put another cup on top of it so that it rests perpendicular to the first cup and is secured by the toothpick.

STEP 3 Cut a hole into the bottom of the top cup, and insert an earbud from your media player.

STEP 4 Repeat with the other two cups, then listen to your favorite tunes in stereo.

076 MAKE CUSTOM-FIT EARBUDS

Because anything you stick in your ear every day should be comfortable.

MATERIALS

Earbuds

Craft knife

Silicone putty

STEP 1 Use a craft knife to remove the stock tip (usually made of foam or rubber) that your buds came with.

STEP 2 Follow the instructions on your putty package to get the putty ready.

STEP 3 Pull up on the tip of an ear and, with your mouth open, press some putty in gently, folding in or removing the excess to create a flush, clean fit.

STEP 4 With the putty still in, insert the bud.

STEP 5 After the silicone has set (about 10 minutes), remove the mold by gently twisting it out of your ear.

STEP 6 Gently pull the bud out of the mold and use the craft knife to make a small hole in the mold to allow sound to come through. Reinsert the bud.

STEP 7 Repeat the entire process on the other earbud and enjoy a personalized fit.

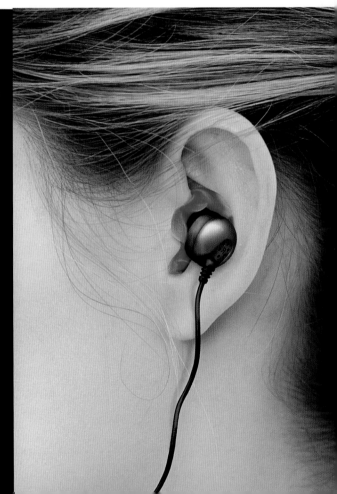

077 PUT A NEW SPIN ON AN OLD CD

In the age of MP3s, most people have a lot of old CDs lying around. Here's what to do with them.

EASY SPINNING TOP
Using a hot-glue gun, secure a large marble to the underside of a compact disc, right under the hole. Glue a plastic bottle cap to the top and give it a whirl.

BEER SPILL BLOCKER
Put a CD over your beer bottle so the bottle's neck sticks up through the CD's hole. Now when you knock the bottle over accidentally, the CD will prevent it from tipping all the way over—and spilling your brew.

ULTIMATE (COMPACT) DISC GOLF
This one's truly easy: Take an old CD and throw it around a disc golf course with some friends. Just don't throw it at your friends.

SUPERSHINY COASTERS
Cover compact discs with felt and use them as coasters. Make sure you cover the side with the artist's information on it—you don't want anyone knowing you once paid actual money for that Third Eye Blind CD, do you?

AIR HOCKEY IN A PINCH
Place a CD on a table about the size of, well, an air hockey table, and mark goal zones with tape. Stand across from your opponent, seize a CD spindle, and use it as an air hockey mallet to swat the CD back and forth.

078 GET YOUR AIR DRUM ON WITH ELECTRIFIED DRUMSTICKS

Now the masses can finally hear your brilliant air drumming.

COST	$$$$
TIME	☺ ☺ ☺ ☺
EASY	● ● ● ● ● HARD

This very cool DIY drumming setup uses an Arduino and a MIDI—that's short for "musical instrument digital interface"—device to create a drum kit sound without the drum kit price tag. Move the drumsticks to hit the snare or cymbal; tap your feet to hear the bass or hi-hat.

MATERIALS

Two 1½-inch (3.75-cm) wooden dowels, about 1 foot (30 cm) in length
Drill
Eight USB female type A connectors
Three ADXL335 accelerometers
Electrical wire
Wire strippers
Soldering iron and solder
Two 1½-inch (3.75-cm) vinyl end caps

Rubber-soled shoes you don't mind donating to the cause
Photocell
47k-ohm resistor
Four USB male-to-male type A cables
Arduino UNO
Five-pin DIN connector
5-volt DC-power supply with 2.1mm jack
USB-to-MIDI interface
Computer

STEP 1 Drill a hole through the two dowels—these will be your drumsticks. In each drumstick, widen the holes to fit a USB female connector at one end and an accelerometer at the other end.

STEP 2 Follow the circuitry diagram to solder together your cymbal and snare, housing their circuitry in the left and right drumsticks, respectively. Cover the ends of the dowels with vinyl end caps.

STEP 3 Make a hole through the rubber sole of each shoe, drilling from the heel to the toe. Widen the holes to fit a USB female socket at both heels, an accelerometer near the toe of the left shoe, and a photocell near the toe of the right shoe.

STEP 4 The left shoe will function as your bass drum pedal, while the right will work as a hi-hat pedal. Follow the circuitry diagram to attach their components.

STEP 5 Use the male-to-male USB connectors to attach both the drumsticks and the shoes to the remaining four USB female connectors. Attach these USB ports to the Arduino UNO and the drumsticks and shoes to the five-pin DIN connector according to the circuitry diagram.

STEP 6 Download the drum kit code from popsci.com/thebigbookofhacks. Program your Arduino with the code and start running it.

STEP 7 Plug your MIDI device into the DIN port, then connect the MIDI device to your computer. Plug the 5-volt DC-power supply into a wall outlet.

STEP 8 Slip the shoes onto your feet, pick up your sticks, and drum away. Head banging is encouraged.

079 Amuse Yourself with a Flipperdinger

Make uncles everywhere jealous with this dorky device, which makes a ball hover in midair.

MATERIALS

Putty
Long hollow reed
Knife
Smaller hollow reed

Acorn cap
Glue
Small, lightweight ball

STEP 1 Put putty into one end of the long reed, making an airtight seal. Near this end, make a hole through the reed. Stick the smaller reed into this hole, making a nozzle.

STEP 2 Remove the cup-shaped cap of an acorn and poke a hole in its center. Then fit the cup over the nozzle and secure it with glue.

STEP 3 Place the ball in the acorn cap and blow lightly but steadily into the open end of the reed. When done right, the ball rises slowly on a jet of air, hovering above the nozzle. As you ease off, the ball settles back into the cap, to the wonderment of all.

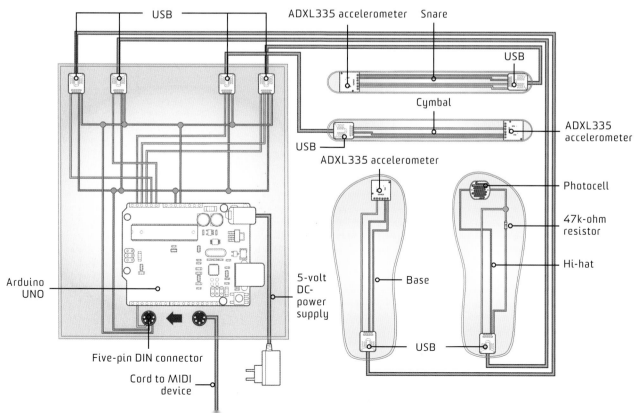

080 PLAY A POCKET THEREMIN

Throw together this pint-size, light-sensitive theremin for spooky sound effects on the cheap.

COST	$
TIME	🕐 🕐 🕐
EASY	● ● ● ● ○ HARD

MATERIALS

Two 555 IC timers
Two photocells
Two 0.01-mF capacitors
1k-ohm resistor
5k-ohm potentiometer
2-position PCB terminal
8k-ohm, 1-inch (2.5-cm) speaker

9-volt battery snap
Electrical wire
Soldering iron and solder
Drill
Project box
9-volt battery

Remember those eerie sci-fi soundtracks from the 1950s? Chances are those oscillating noises were generated by a theremin. Designed by Russian physicist Léon Theremin and popularized by Robert Moog, a full-fledged theremin will set you back $400. Or you can build this pocket-size version—it's light-sensitive, so play it in subdued lighting for the best sound effects.

ROCK ON
Léon Theremin, inventor, plays his creepy-sounding instrument circa 1919.

YOU BUILT WHAT?!

MAKING MUSIC WITH LASERS

Playing the harp isn't the most high-tech pastime—unless, like Stephen Hobley, you use lasers in place of the strings. Though not the first home-built laser harp, Hobley's creation is unquestionably the coolest. Played by disrupting the laser beams with the hands, it can produce just about any sound. Better yet, it's also a fully functioning controller for a version of *Guitar Hero*.

STEP 1 Wire your circuit according to the circuitry diagram below, soldering your connections. Keep the wiring loose enough that you can insert it into the box.

STEP 2 Drill nine holes in the sides of the project box, spaced to match the circuitry diagram.

STEP 3 Insert the circuit inside the project box. Thread the loose wires through the holes in the box.

STEP 4 Solder on the photocells, potentiometer, speaker, and battery snap.

STEP 5 Connect the snap to the 9-volt battery. You should immediately hear an eerie noise. If you don't, check your wiring for faulty connections.

STEP 6 Head to a spot with low light and, to produce a wide variety of sounds, move your hands over the theremin's photocells to vary the frequency and pitch of the output.

STEP 7 Now go film your own retro sci-fi flick; you've already got the sound effects in your pocket.

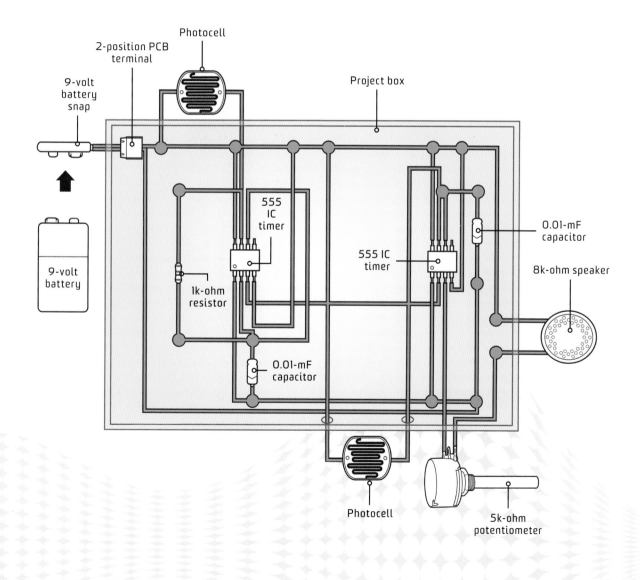

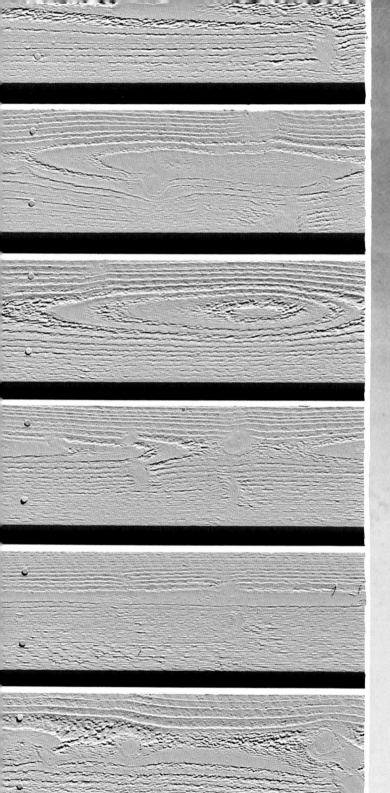

HOME IMPROVEMENTS

081 CUSTOMIZE YOUR WELCOME MAT

[mat] + [box cutter] + [stencil C] + [spray can] = **SCRAM!**

STEP 1 Use a box cutter to incise a 2-inch (5-cm) border in three welcome mats. Set the border aside.

STEP 2 Cut uniformly sized squares from each welcome mat.

STEP 3 Make stencils for each alphabet letter. Use spray-paint to stencil the squares with letters. Leave some blank.

STEP 4 Use one of the borders as a frame and fill it with letters and blank spaces of your choosing.

082 ORGANIZE YOUR ENTRYWAY WITH RECYCLED CANS

Make can cubbies for all those scarves, gloves, hats, and wallets.

MATERIALS

Assortment of cans
Drill

Several screws

STEP 1 Choose an assortment of can types and sizes—paint cans, soup cans, and so on. Clean them all well.

STEP 2 Use a drill to make two holes in each can's base, both directly across from each other. (If your can has a handle, be sure to drill your holes so the handle will hang down toward the floor.)

STEP 3 Mark stud positions on your entryway wall. Screw through each can's top hole first (larger cans will need to be attached to studs). Then straighten the cans and screw through the bottom holes.

STEP 4 Hang stuff on and put things inside the cans.

083 Give a Doorknob a New Spin

Despite the saying, a doorknob is only as dumb as you are. Repurpose this ubiquitous fixture for utility and fun.

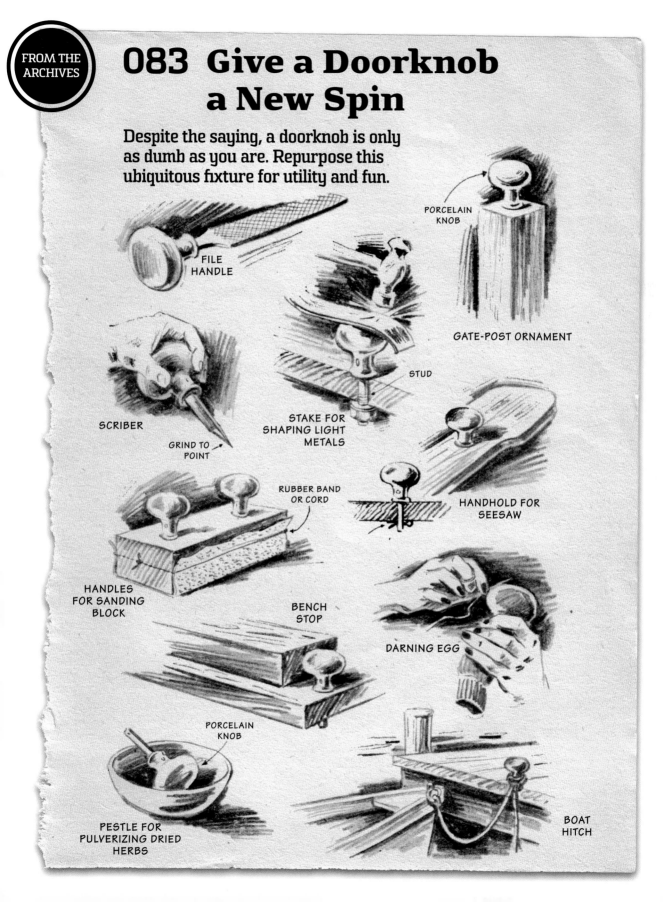

FILE HANDLE

PORCELAIN KNOB

GATE-POST ORNAMENT

STUD

SCRIBER

GRIND TO POINT

STAKE FOR SHAPING LIGHT METALS

RUBBER BAND OR CORD

HANDHOLD FOR SEESAW

HANDLES FOR SANDING BLOCK

BENCH STOP

DARNING EGG

PORCELAIN KNOB

PESTLE FOR PULVERIZING DRIED HERBS

BOAT HITCH

084 SET UP A SECRET DOOR

You don't have to be an action-movie character to have a private passage.

Contrary to what *Batman* would have you believe, building a hidden doorway isn't very hard. All you need is a room that leads into another room, three bookcases you don't mind modding, and a few pieces of hardware. Let the vanishing acts begin.

COST	$$$
TIME	🕐🕐🕐🕐
EASY	● ● ● ● ○ HARD

MATERIALS

Drill
Rolling caster
Three matching bookcases
Saw
Bolts
Drill

Three hinges with screws
Chalk
Two pieces of wood trim
Wood glue
Six magnets

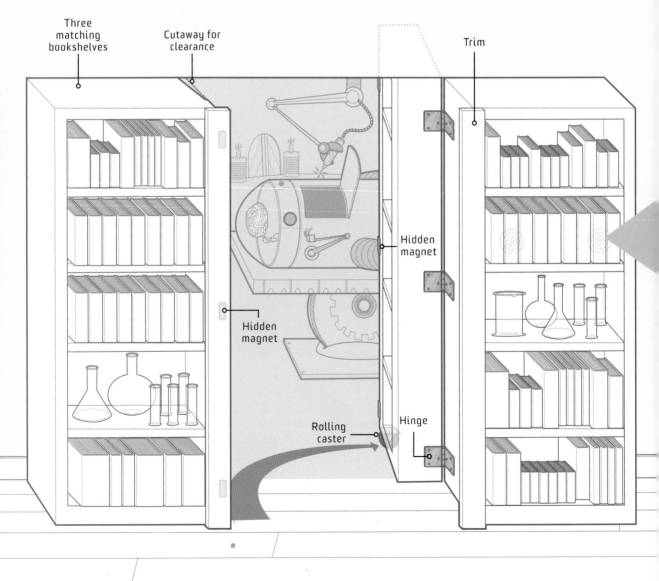

Three matching bookshelves

Cutaway for clearance

Trim

Hidden magnet

Hidden magnet

Rolling caster

Hinge

STEP 1 Using a drill, attach a rolling caster to the bottom left side of the bookcase that you plan on putting in the middle—the one that will swing back into your lair.

STEP 2 Once the caster is installed, check to see if the bookcase is the same height as the other two. If not, saw off some trim along the bottom.

STEP 3 Mount one of the other bookcases to the wall just to the right of the doorway, using multiple bolts and washers to secure it to the ceiling or through a wall stud.

STEP 4 Use three evenly spaced hinges to attach the swinging bookcase to the stationary case on the right. This bookcase should now cover the doorway completely and move backward into the hidden room.

STEP 5 Use a piece of chalk to trace the arc of the door's swing. Figure how much the door's movement will interfere with the shelf that goes on the left side, and use a saw to cut away a section in that case's right and back

side so that the door will swing freely, cutting all the way from the top to the bottom.

STEP 6 Line up the third bookcase on the wall next to the swinging bookcase and test it. If you need more clearance, continue to sand or saw down the back right corner.

STEP 7 Once the swing is perfect, bolt the third bookcase to the ceiling or a wall stud.

STEP 8 Glue a piece of matching wood trim to the front of each stationary case.

STEP 9 Glue two thin magnets to the center case's top and bottom left corners, and one more at its center.

STEP 10 On the left case, glue three thin magnets to the top, bottom, and center of the case's front left edge, lining them up with the magnets on the center case. This will allow the door to catch securely as it closes.

STEP 11 Secretly hang out in your hidden lounge.

085 MAKE INVISIBLE SPEAKERS

Sacrifice a few old books for a camouflaged sound source.

MATERIALS

Six hardcover books	Pin
Two desktop speakers	Hot-glue gun
Pencil	Drill
Jigsaw	Media player
Clamps	

STEP 1 Trace the profile of a speaker onto the cover of one book, then draw a square around it with 1/2 inch (1.25 cm) on all sides.

STEP 2 Drill a hole in the cover and then use a jigsaw to cut out this shape, piercing all the way through the book.

STEP 3 Trace the hole onto a second book's front cover, and onto a third book's back cover.

STEP 4 Cut this shape out of both books, cutting all the way to the unmarked cover without cutting through it.

STEP 5 On each book, fold the covers back and clamp them together. Use the jigsaw to cut away the page bits that are closest to the spine. (These will block sound.)

STEP 6 Drill holes into the spines' outsides.

STEP 7 Attach the speaker to the inside of the central book with hot glue, avoiding sensitive parts like the front. Then glue the three books together at their sides and clamp together; let dry.

STEP 8 Cover the edges of the inside cavity with glue.

STEP 9 Drill a hole into the back of the central book and run the speaker wire out to a media player. Repeat with the other three books, then hide your book speakers amid your favorite tomes.

Speaker cavity

Speaker

Holes in spines

086 MONITOR YOUR HOME WITH A LASER SECURITY SYSTEM

Everybody loves a good laser show . . . except maybe the thief caught in one.

COST	$$
TIME	☺ ☺ ☺
EASY ● ● ● ○ HARD	

MATERIALS

Two project boxes
Drill
Photocell
12-volt siren
5k-ohm variable resistor
2N3904 transistor
100uF capacitor
9-volt battery
Electrical wire
Wire strippers
Soldering iron and solder
Velcro
5-milliwatt red laser
Switch
Hot-glue gun
3.2-volt AC adapter
Small mirrors, if needed
Mounting putty, if needed

STEP 1 Drill two holes in the first project box: one for the siren, and one for the photocell. This will be the receiver.

STEP 2 Follow the circuitry diagram at near right, soldering together the components with electrical wire.

STEP 3 Install the assembled components inside the receiver project box. Mount the photocell and the siren on the box's sides and connect it to the interior wiring.

STEP 4 Drill two holes in the second project box: one for the switch, and one for the laser. Mount the laser and switch inside this box with hot glue.

STEP 5 Cut off and strip the ends of the AC adapter wires and run them into the box. Use electrical wire to connect them to the laser and switch, following the circuitry diagram at far right. Then close the box and test the laser.

STEP 6 Line up the laser box with the receiver box. Use the variable resistor to adjust the photocell's sensitivity so it can detect motion during daylight hours. When correctly tuned, the receiver box will not make sound when the laser is shining on it.

STEP 7 Attach Velcro to both project boxes. Mount the laser on the wall at about waist height beside the door you want protected. Plug in the AC adapter.

STEP 8 If you want to protect multiple doors and windows, use mounting putty to attach tiny mirrors to the wall at angles that bounce the laser's beam around the room. You may have to play with the mirrors' positions to get it right.

STEP 9 Once you're done with the mirrors, mount the receiver box so that the photocell lines up directly with the end of the laser beam. When the beam is broken, the alarm will sound.

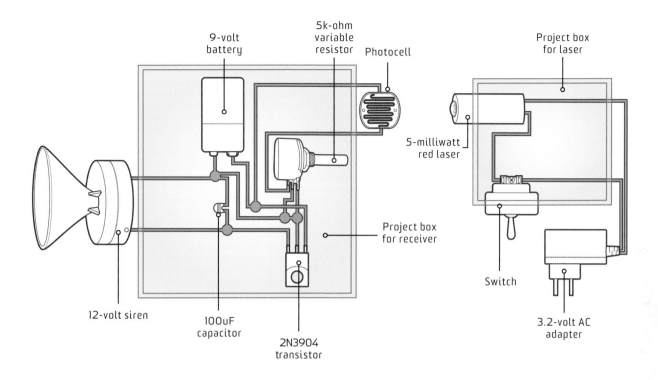

9-volt battery

5k-ohm variable resistor

Photocell

Project box for laser

5-milliwatt red laser

Project box for receiver

12-volt siren

100uF capacitor

2N3904 transistor

Switch

3.2-volt AC adapter

087 SNOOPER-PROOF YOUR WALLET

Foil RFID thieves with—well, aluminum foil, believe it or not.

MATERIALS
Wallet
Aluminum foil

Lurking inside your wallet's credit cards are radio-frequency identification chips (RFIDs), and lurking outside your wallet are goons who scan that info and make off with your identity.

STEP 1 Tear off a piece of aluminum foil about 6 inches (15 cm) in length.

STEP 2 Fold the aluminum foil to the size of a dollar bill.

STEP 3 Tuck the folded aluminum foil into your wallet's billfold, place your cards inside, and forget about those RFID scammers out there.

088 INSTALL AN ELECTRICAL-OUTLET WALL SAFE

Keep small valuables in a place no one would ever look—and hope burglars don't try to plug anything in.

COST	$
TIME	◔
EASY ● ○ ○ ○ ○ HARD	

MATERIALS

Cut-in box
Pencil
Drywall saw
Residential-grade volt receptacle
Roofing nails and washers
Faceplate
Screw
Screwdriver

STEP 1 Place the cut-in box on the wall where you want your safe and trace around it with a pencil. Cut the hole with a drywall saw.

STEP 2 Slide the cut-in box into the hole. Fill it up with small valuables.

STEP 3 The volt receptacle has two holes, one at its top and one at its bottom. Slide the roofing nails through the washers and then through these holes.

STEP 4 Attach the volt receptacle to the cut-in box by sliding the nails into the box's top and bottom holes.

STEP 5 Screw the faceplate onto the receptacle.

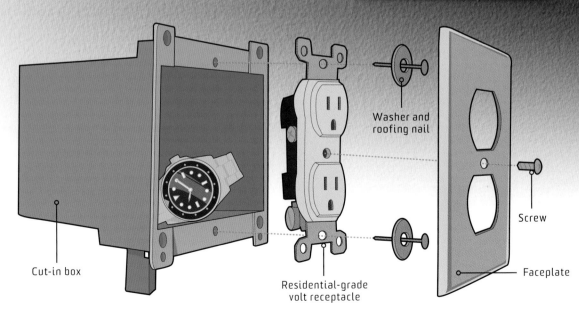

Cut-in box

Residential-grade volt receptacle

Washer and roofing nail

Screw

Faceplate

089 CARRY A FILM-ROLL KEYCHAIN

STEP 1 Drill a small hole into the spool hub of a 35mm film roll.

STEP 2 Insert a key-ring loop through the roll's hole.

STEP 3 Thread your keys onto the loop and carry them like an old-school film nut.

090 MAKE A MUSICAL STASH FOR YOUR CASH

Annoy would-be thieves with a safe booby-trapped with bad music.

MATERIALS

Musical greeting card
Craft knife
Double-sided tape
Box

STEP 1 Remove the noisemaker from a musical greeting card by opening the card and tearing off the paper over the noisemaker. Then cut out the speaker and circuit.

STEP 2 The speaker has a paper tab that, when unfolded, plays music. Use double-sided tape to adhere this tab so it straddles your box's hinge, and affix the speaker and circuit inside the box. When the box is opened and the paper tab is unfolded, it will sound the alarm.

STEP 3 Fill your box with treasure and listen for thieves.

Noisemaker speaker and circuit

Noisemaker paper tab

BUILD IT!

091 TURN YOUR HDTV INTO A MAGIC WINDOW

Tired of looking at the yard? Connect your TV to your laptop and gaze into space or deep sea instead.

COST	$$$
TIME	🕐
EASY ● ○ ○ ○ ○ HARD	

MATERIALS

Flatscreen TV with HDMI, DVI, VGA, or S-video port
Laptop with compatible port
Compatible cable
Converter box, if needed
Slideshow of your coolest photos

STEP 1 Assess your gear. Most flatscreens and laptops come with ports that allow you to hook the two devices together. The trick is making sure that both have the same connection type (HDMI, DVI, VGA, or S-video). If they don't, you'll need to purchase a small converter box.

STEP 2 Connect the laptop and the flatscreen with a compatible cable. Your computer screen should immediately appear on your TV. If it doesn't, go to the TV and cycle through the input devices until what's on your computer screen shows up.

STEP 3 Create a slideshow on your laptop and press play. Your backyard has never looked so good.

092 CRAFT A DIY DIGITAL PHOTO FRAME

Turn an old laptop into a digital frame that automatically displays new shots.

MATERIALS

Used laptop

Flickr account

USB adapter or PMCIA
  wireless card, if needed

Screwdriver

Custom frame and mat

Mounting board

Pin

Tape

Hot-glue gun

STEP 1 Before disassembling the laptop, download the Slickr screensaver from popsci.com/thebigbookofhacks and enter your Flickr account information.

STEP 2 Make sure the laptop is Wi-Fi enabled. If it's not, get a USB adapter or a PCMCIA wireless card (find either online or in tech retail stores).

STEP 3 Take apart enough of the laptop to get at the ribbon cable that connects the LCD (usually found under the keyboard), and carefully unplug it. Be careful when removing the plastic border from the screen—there are several thin cables, and if you rip one, the LCD is useless.

STEP 4 Measure the bare screen and order your frame, making sure it's deep enough to provide 1 inch (2.5 cm) of room behind the LCD so it can breathe. Skip the glass.

STEP 5 Cut two self-adhesive mounting boards—one to strengthen the frame's mat and one on which to mount the laptop bottom. Poke ventilation holes in the board that will go between the LCD and the laptop bottom.

STEP 6 Assemble the pieces in a sandwich—frame, mat, mounting board, LCD, mounting board, and laptop bottom—using tape. Hot-glue it all together.

STEP 7 Reattach the LCD cable to the laptop and reassemble the keyboard. Attach the second piece of board at an angle to the back of the frame as a stand.

STEP 8 Give it to Mom. Start it up. Add shots to your Flickr account for Mom to see.

093 GIVE AN OLD TV A RERUN

Resurrect an old TV as a monitor for an iPhone or an external display for a PC.

COST	$$
TIME	⏲ ⏲ ⏲
EASY	● ● ● ● ○ HARD

MATERIALS

Audio/video transmitter kit
Soldering iron and solder
Twin-lead cable
Wire strippers
Old television

A/V RCA cables
Media player
Converter cable, if needed
12-volt battery supply

STEP 1 Assemble the A/V transmitter kit you've purchased according to the instructions and circuitry diagram. This'll take some time—and some soldering.

STEP 2 Cut a length of the twin-lead cable and strip both ends of it. Solder one end to the antenna connector's pins on the underside of the transmitter kit's circuit board. Route the cable through the large hole in the kit's lid, and connect it to the TV's antenna screw terminals.

STEP 3 Attach the A/V RCA cables to your media player, and connect the other ends to the video- and audio-signal inputs on the transmitter kit. (For an iPod or iPhone, plug a converter cable into the dock connector and run the converter's video jack and one of the audio jacks into the kit's inputs.)

STEP 4 Connect the transmitter to a 12-volt battery, turn on your media player, and tune your television to UHF channel 21.

STEP 5 If necessary, tweak the picture and sound quality by adjusting the screws in the top of the A/V transmitter kit's case.

STEP 6 Choose a video from your media player's library, hit play, and enjoy your "relic's" new use.

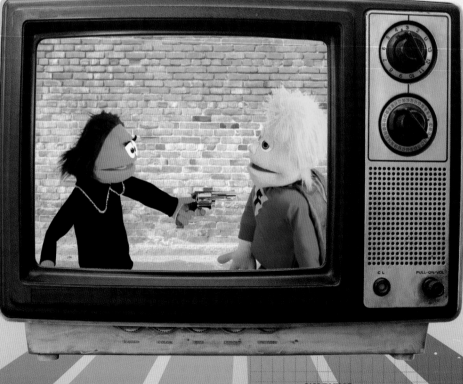

WARNING
The transmitter kit is designed to work wirelessly, but such use violates regulations, so we saved you the trouble. Plus, this solution is less likely to cause harmful interference.

094 HACK THE PERFECT GAMING CHAIR

Turn your old favorite recliner into your new favorite gaming chair.

MATERIALS

Old recliner

Plywood

Jigsaw

Sandpaper

Varnish

Heavy-duty swing-arm bracket

LCD monitor

Heavy-duty L-shaped bracket

Brackets with bolts and screws

Two speakers

Velcro, if needed

Superglue

Mousepad

Lightweight aluminum sheeting

Box cutter

Four magnets

STEP 1 Use a jigsaw to cut a piece of plywood the width of your recliner's arms to serve as a desktop.

STEP 2 Saw a U-shaped contour into the edge of the desktop that will face you, then sand and varnish it.

STEP 3 Attach the swing-arm bracket to one arm of your recliner using bolts or screws. (If necessary, remove the chair's stuffing or upholstery to find a panel or frame to which you can attach the hardware.) Secure the other end of the arm bracket to the desktop.

STEP 4 Attach the L-shaped bracket to the plywood desktop and mount your LCD monitor to it with screws.

STEP 5 Secure two speakers to the back of the chair using brackets and the appropriate screws or bolts. Again, dig through stuffing or upholstery to find a sturdy spot for mounting if necessary. For small, lightweight speakers, you could try adhesive Velcro.

STEP 6 Glue the mousepad to one side of the desktop.

STEP 7 With a box cutter, cut aluminum sheeting to the size of your keyboard and glue it to the plywood.

STEP 8 Glue magnets to each corner of your keyboard's underside to hold the keyboard to the aluminum.

STEP 9 Hook your speakers, monitor, mouse, and keyboard into your computer console and get gaming.

YOU BUILT WHAT?!

A WEARABLE LED TELEVISION

Electrical engineer David Forbes stunned everyone in the Detroit Metro Airport when he debuted his wearable TV—and, no wonder, with 160 circuit boards and enough electronics to start a data center strapped to his body. The vest features a sharp 160-by-120-pixel LED display, and it plays video signal from his iPod, all off battery packs he carries in his pockets. The charge lasts 90 minutes—just enough for three episodes of *The Simpsons*.

095 MAKE A TV OSCILLOSCOPE

STEP 1 Turn off and unplug a black-and-white TV.

STEP 2 Remove the TV's back and find the deflector coil assembly (the large coils looped around the glass tube). There are two pairs of wires on either side of the coil. Follow them to the TV's circuit board and desolder one, then plug the TV back in and turn it on. If the screen shows a horizontal line, you've cut a wire that enables the vertical coil. If the line is vertical, you've cut a wire that enables the horizontal coil. Keep this in mind.

STEP 3 Turn off and unplug the TV. Desolder the coil's remaining three wires, then resolder them so that the two that once plugged into the horizontal coil's input on the circuit board now go to the vertical coil's input.

STEP 4 Peel back an audio cord's end and strip its wires. Twist them with the wires that went to the vertical coil.

STEP 5 Replace the TV's back and plug the audio cord into a media player. Watch your music take shape.

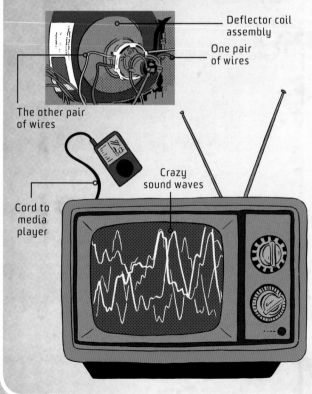

Deflector coil assembly

One pair of wires

The other pair of wires

Crazy sound waves

Cord to media player

096 HACK A TV CONSOLE INTO A SEAT

STEP 1 Make sure the TV is off and unplugged, then open up the console's backing. Gingerly remove the electronics, speakers, and television tube inside the TV. Be especially careful with the tube, which could break.

STEP 2 On the front of the console, locate the edges of the TV screen. Draw a line on both sides extending up over the lip and onto the console's top.

STEP 3 Using a jigsaw, cut down along the guides on the console's top until you reach the TV screen's frame. Remove this part of the console's top.

STEP 4 Gently remove the screen and its frame.

STEP 5 Return the console's backing; secure with nails.

STEP 6 Measure and cut two plywood pieces to cover the sides of the cavity. Stain or paint them so they match the rest of the console and nail them in place.

STEP 7 Measure and cut two pieces of foam to serve as bottom and back cushions for the seat. Cover them with material of your choosing. Glue them down inside the console.

STEP 8 Take a seat. You've earned it.

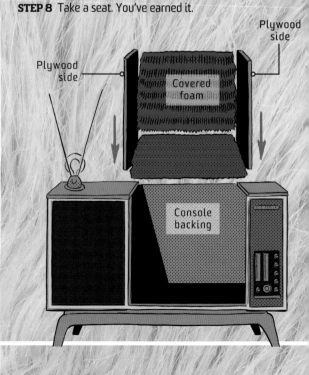

Plywood side

Plywood side

Covered foam

Console backing

097 INSTALL AN AQUARIUM IN AN OLD TV

STEP 1 Unplug the television, remove its back, and carefully pull out the electronics and television tube. Be especially careful with the tube, which is fragile.

STEP 2 Measure the height, depth, and width of the hole in the back of the TV. It should fit your run-of-the-mill 20-gallon (75-l) aquarium, hopefully with a little space left over for the filter, pump, heater, and power strip.

STEP 3 Place supports to hold the aquarium's weight and boost it up so it lines up behind the TV's screen. Leave space above it for a lightbulb.

STEP 4 Use a circular saw to cut off the console's top, then transform it into a lid with two hinges and a handle.

STEP 5 Mount a fluorescent bulb to the underside of the lid with small wood screws.

STEP 6 Place the tank inside the console, along with the power strip, filter, heater, and pump. Run the power strip's wire out of the lid and replace the console's back.

STEP 7 Fill the aquarium slowly. Add fish and accessories.

STEP 8 Plug all the components into the power strip, plug the power strip into the wall, and watch your fishies swim on the big screen.

098 BUILD A BOOB-TUBE BAR

STEP 1 Unplug the television and open up the console's backing. Using caution, take out the electronics, speakers, and glass tube inside the TV, and remove the screen.

STEP 2 Strip out any supports you won't be using on the inside, including unnecessary screws and nails. Sand the interior to remove splinters and old glue globs.

STEP 3 You need two shelves: one for booze that displays behind the TV screen's hole, and one for wine, which should be stored where the speakers used to be. If possible, reserve any plywood bases to use as shelves, or make new ones to fit inside your console and glue them in with wood glue.

STEP 4 Remove the existing grating and grill cloth that cover the speakers. Replace the grill cloth and remount the grating with hinges that allows easy access to the wine.

STEP 5 If you like, sand and paint or stain the outside.

STEP 6 Cut and insert two mirrors: one to fit over the shelf and one to fit on the back wall behind the window. Replace the console's backing.

STEP 7 Stock the bar with your preferred liquor and wine, and host a swanky party.

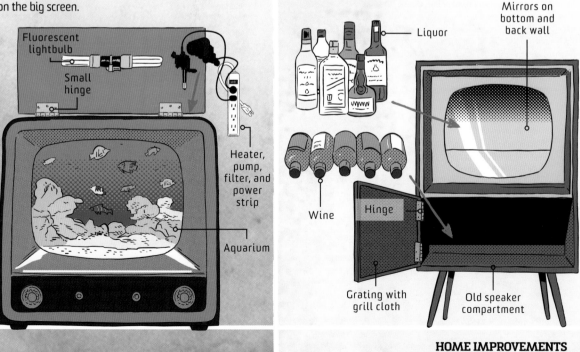

Fluorescent lightbulb

Small hinge

Heater, pump, filter, and power strip

Aquarium

Liquor

Mirrors on bottom and back wall

Wine

Hinge

Grating with grill cloth

Old speaker compartment

099 SET UP A DIY DRIVE-IN

Can't find an outdoor movie theater? Set up your own in your backyard.

COST	$$$
TIME	🕐
EASY ● ○ ○ ○ ○ HARD	

Seeing a movie outdoors used to be pretty simple. Drive a bit, pay at the entrance gate, find a parking space, and wait for the towering images to flicker into view. But finding a drive-in isn't easy these days. What to do if you yearn to experience the cinema outside? Create it yourself. Here's how to put together a cheap, portable screening for a group of friends.

Media player

Projector

Cords to power source and FM receiver

MATERIALS

White wall or sheet
Four grommets
Two tent stakes and twine
Battery-powered projector
Media player
Car cigarette lighter adapter
FM receiver

STEP 1 Use a white wall or a bedsheet as your backdrop. If using a sheet, put a grommet in each corner and secure the top grommets to trees or posts and the bottom grommets to the tent stakes using twine.

STEP 2 Hook a battery-powered, presentation-style projector up to your media player (a computer or an iPad).

STEP 3 Plug the projector into your car's cigarette lighter via an adapter to keep it juiced during the feature film.

STEP 4 Connect your media player's audio to an FM receiver. Set the receiver to the frequency of your choice.

STEP 5 Have your friends park within the specified range of the receiver and set their car radios to the same frequency as the receiver.

STEP 6 Hit play on your media player and be sure to pass the popcorn.

WARNING
Before starting this project, visit transition.fcc.gov/lpfm. This page details the FCC's regulations for low-power stations. Don't charge for attendance if you're showing a DVD, and get all proper permits if your DIY drive-in will be in a public place.

YOU BUILT WHAT?!

THE GRAFFITI LASER

Australian artist Chris Poole was driving around his native Perth when some curbside garbage caught his eye. Unlike the average scavenger, Poole wasn't searching for futons: He had his eye on an old slide viewer—a key component for his next project, a laser-based projector that could display photos (albeit with a green hue) to the entire town.

Thanks to his penchant for collecting, Poole already had the basic materials. To start, he rewired a tiny green laser—the kind used in a pointer—so it could work with a long-running battery pack he had lying around, which he had pulled out of an electric bicycle. Next he nailed an electronics-mounting frame to a wooden board 3 feet (1 m) in length and set the laser at one end, aimed down the frame. He snapped in a lens from a used disposable camera at the other end and set a makeshift slide holder and the scrapped slide viewer's lens in between. The viewer enlarges the beam so it covers the slide, allowing him to project an 8-by-10-foot (2.5-by-3-m) image of former *PopSci* editor-in-chief Mark Jannot from 100 feet (30 m) away.

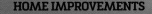

For cool mood lighting, combine off-the-shelf parts—and just add mineral oil.

Forget the lava lamp: This modern light source trades in the hippie-dippie vibe for an edgier, more industrial look. And you can make it yourself by filling a glass globe with mineral oil and hooking it up to an air pump for a bubbly effect.

| COST | $$ |
| TIME | ⊕ ⊕ |
| EASY ● ● ● ○ ○ HARD |

MATERIALS

Clear 1/4-inch (6.35-mm) PVC tubing
Craft knife
3-wire 18-awg SJOOW cord
Zip ties
3-prong male plug
Vapor-tight fixture with a 1/2-inch (1.25-cm) bulb
Nylon liquid-tight strain relief with flex fitting and threads that match the fixture
Wire strippers
Two 18-awg wire nuts
Rotary tool
Colored, clear 25-watt bulb
Mineral oil
Basic air pump

STEP 1 Measure and cut your clear tubing and electrical cord so that it will reach the power supply from your lamp. Tether them together with zip ties, then wire the male plug to the cord's end.

STEP 2 Remove the vapor-tight fixture's base from the cap.

STEP 3 Screw the strain relief into the threaded opening at the top of the vapor-tight fixture's cap.

STEP 4 Run the air tube and the electrical cord through the strain relief and into the cap. Strip the ends of the electrical cord and connect them to the vapor-tight fixture's leads with the wire nuts.

STEP 5 Use a rotary tool to drill a hole in the bottom of the vapor-tight fixture's base. Feed the clear tube through this hole, leaving about 8 inches (20 cm) below the base.

STEP 6 Screw the base back to the cap. As you do so, ground the fixture by twisting the green ground lead around one of the screws that connects the cap to the base.

STEP 7 Gently tighten the strain relief via its nut—don't overdo it, or you'll constrict the tubing.

STEP 8 Screw the clear, colored bulb into the socket.

STEP 9 Fill the glass globe about one-third full of mineral oil and screw the bulb to the base. Add the vapor-tight fixture's aluminum grill.

STEP 10 Hang your lamp, attach the air tube to the pump, plug in the pump and the light, and presto: bubble light!

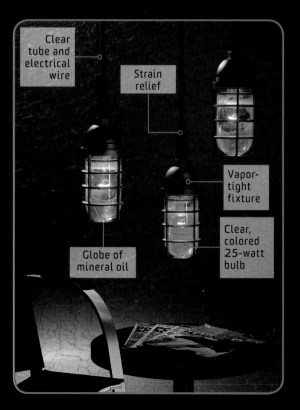

Clear tube and electrical wire

Strain relief

Vapor-tight fixture

Clear, colored 25-watt bulb

Globe of mineral oil

101 MOLD A RETRO LAMP BASE

Use one of those ubiquitous plastic bottles as a mold for a neat lamp base.

MATERIALS

Empty plastic water bottle with a relatively flat top
Craft knife
Drill
Petroleum jelly
Hacksaw
Hollow threaded rod
Hot-glue gun
Empty pill bottle
Plaster
Fine-grit sandpaper
Flat washer, lock washer, and nut
Lamp rewiring kit
Lampshade

STEP 1 Using a craft knife, cut off the bottom of the plastic bottle. Leave a slight rim so the mold has a rounded edge.

STEP 2 Drill a 1/2-inch (1.25-cm) hole into the center of the water bottle's cap.

STEP 3 Coat the inside of the water bottle and its cap with a thin, even film of petroleum jelly.

STEP 4 Use a hacksaw to cut a 1/2-inch (1.25-cm), hollow, threaded rod to the height of your water bottle, minus about 1/4 inch (6.35 mm).

STEP 5 With the cap screwed onto the bottle, thread the rod from the bottom so that 1/4 inch (6.35 mm) sticks out of the cap. Use a hot-glue gun to seal the area on the outside of the bottle where the threads meet the cap's top.

STEP 6 Find a pill bottle that's 75 percent smaller than your plastic bottle. Remove its lid and drill a 1/2-inch (1.25-cm) hole into the center of its bottom.

STEP 7 Coat the medicine bottle's bottom and halfway up its sides with petroleum jelly.

STEP 8 Holding both bottles with their bottoms facing each other, screw the medicine bottle onto the rod so it fits inside the larger plastic bottle, a bit past flush. (This creates a slight recess in the bottom of your lamp base.)

STEP 9 Place the entire apparatus upside down into a small glass so that the water bottle's cap points down inside the glass.

STEP 10 Mix then pour your plaster into the larger plastic bottle until it fills up to the rim of the larger bottle's bottom. Let set for a half hour or until the plaster sets.

STEP 11 Unscrew the bottle cap and the medicine bottle from the hollow threaded rod. Carefully peel the plastic bottle off the mold with a craft knife.

STEP 12 Once you've removed the bottle, sand the bottom flat and clean up any other rough surface areas.

STEP 13 Attach a flat washer, lock washer, and nut to the rod at the base of the lamp. Don't overtighten.

STEP 14 Drill a 1/4-inch (6.35-mm) hole through the side of the base into the slight recess in the lamp's bottom. Thread the lamp cord through the hole and into the rod.

STEP 15 Wire the socket and attach it to the rod at the top of the lamp base. Top it off with your shade of choice.

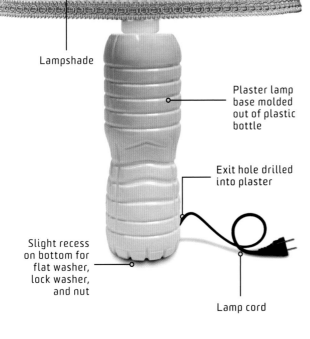

Lampshade

Plaster lamp base molded out of plastic bottle

Exit hole drilled into plaster

Slight recess on bottom for flat washer, lock washer, and nut

Lamp cord

102 CREATE A MESMERIZING PERSISTENCE-OF-VISION CLOCK

This clock uses optic trickery to make a moving display look like a static image.

In typical POV projects, your eye briefly continues to see an image after it disappears. But instead of showing one message, this model tells the time with a continuously updated rotating display. Neat.

COST	$$
TIME	⏱ ⏱ ⏱
EASY ● ● ● ● ○ HARD	

MATERIALS

Scrap wooden boards
Nails
Hammer
POV kit with LEDs in a color of your choosing
Soldering iron and solder
Two-pin right-angle connector
DC motor
Electrical wire
9-volt battery
10k-ohm potentiometer

100k-ohm resistor
470k-ohm resistor
10k-ohm resistor
10uF capacitor
LN914 diode
555 timer IC
Metal-oxide–semiconductor field-effect transistor (MOSFET)
Drill
On/off switch

STEP 1 Build the clock's backboard out of scrap wood (or whatever materials you have on hand).

STEP 2 Assemble the POV kit according to its instructions, then program its microcontroller with the software at popsci.com/thebigbookofhacks. (The software is preprogrammed to start at 12:00, but you can set it before programming the microcontroller.) Solder the two-pin right-angle connector to the POV kit's battery terminals.

STEP 3 Build the motor-speed controller using the circuitry diagram at right. Drill a hole slightly smaller than the motor's spindle in the clock, then mount the motor and controller to the clock's back. Tap the wood over the spindle so it sticks through the hole.

STEP 4 Mount another piece of scrap wood over the motor's spindle to act as a rotating arm. It should be large enough to accommodate your POV kit and battery pack.

STEP 5 Attach the POV kit and battery pack to the rotating arm so that their weight is evenly distributed.

STEP 6 Solder wires to the two-pin right-angle connector and then solder them to the battery pack's 9-volt battery snap. Turn on the motor's power supply, and adjust the motor-speed controller by turning the potentiometer knob until the POV display is readable.

Wire connecting the battery to the POV kit

Two-pin connector

Battery pack

Motor spindle

POV kit

Time displayed

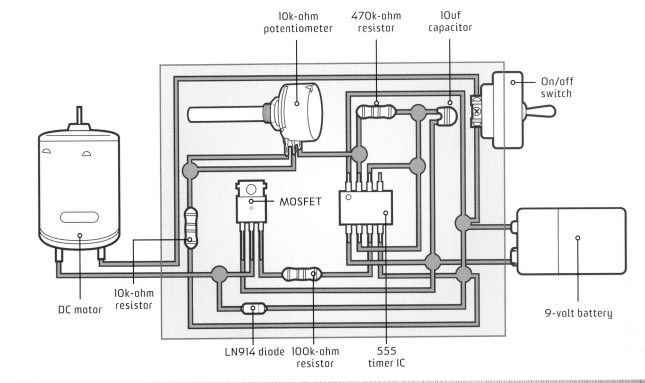

10k-ohm potentiometer

470k-ohm resistor

10uf capacitor

On/off switch

MOSFET

DC motor

10k-ohm resistor

LN914 diode

100k-ohm resistor

555 timer IC

9-volt battery

103 TELL TIME WITH A DART CLOCK

Bring the bar home with this dead-simple DIY timepiece.

MATERIALS

Dartboard

Battery-powered clock

Pencil

Drill

12 darts

Battery

STEP 1 Place the dartboard facedown and put the clock mechanism at its center. Trace the outline of the mechanism.

STEP 2 Mark the outline's center and double-check that it's the bull's eye. Drill a hole large enough to fit the chad that holds the clock's hands in place. Attach the clock to the board's back.

STEP 3 Push four darts into the board to represent the numbers 12, 3, 6, and 9.

STEP 4 Divide the area between each pair of darts into thirds. Mark these divisions, then place a dart at each mark.

STEP 5 Assemble the hands on the dartboard's front and screw on the chad that secures them.

STEP 6 Turn the board over, pop the battery into the clock, and set the hour and minute hands. Just don't confuse the time for the score.

104 Make a Modern Mag Rack

Magazines sure can pile up. House 'em in this fiberglass rack.

MATERIALS

1-by-2-foot (30-by-60-cm) polystyrene sheet
Ruler
Grease pencil
Box cutter
¾-inch (1.9-cm) thick wood
Jigsaw

Saw blade
Drill
Two wood dowels that are 9 inches (23 cm) in length
Wood glue
Six screws

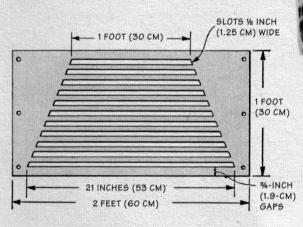

SLOTS ½ INCH (1.25 CM) WIDE

1 FOOT (30 CM)

1 FOOT (30 CM)

21 INCHES (53 CM)

2 FEET (60 CM)

¾-INCH (1.9-CM) GAPS

STEP 1 With a ruler and a grease pencil, draw the pattern at left onto the polystyrene.

STEP 2 Wearing a dust mask, use a rotary tool with a cut-off wheel to cut out all the ½-inch (1.25-cm) sections.

STEP 3 Use a jigsaw to cut the wood into two strips that are 2 ½ inches (6.35 cm) high and 1 foot (30 cm) long.

STEP 4 Create a groove ¾ inch (1.9 cm) deep in the top of the wood pieces with a saw blade.

STEP 5 Drill two indentations into the inside of each of the wood pieces. Slide the dowels into the holes so that they connect the wood pieces. Secure with wood glue.

STEP 6 Slide the polystyrene into one of the wood pieces' grooves. Secure it with three evenly spaced screws along one of the wood pieces.

STEP 7 Fold the polystyrene into a U shape and slide it into the second wood piece's groove. Secure with screws again.

105 SEW AN EASY EBOOK READER CASE

Protect your slick tablet with a felt case tucked inside an oversize book.

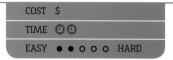

COST $

TIME ☺☺

EASY ●●○○○ HARD

MATERIALS

Tablet

Book 1 inch (2.5 cm) larger than your tablet on all sides

Box cutter

Felt

Scissors

Ruler

Hot-glue gun

Cardboard

Pencil

3 feet (90 cm) of ½-inch (1.25-cm) braided elastic

STEP 1 Using a box cutter, cut out the pages from the book. Glue a strip of felt to the inside of its spine.

STEP 2 Cut two pieces of cardboard to the size of the book's covers. Snip off the cardboard's corners.

STEP 3 Measure and cut two pieces of felt so they're 2 inches (5 cm) larger than the cardboard on all sides. Cut 45-degree-angle slits into the felt pieces' corners.

STEP 4 Position one of the cardboard pieces in the center of a felt piece. Fold the felt over the cardboard's corners and hot-glue it in place. Repeat with the other pieces.

STEP 5 Trace the tablet's outline on the back of one cardboard piece. On both sides of each of the outline's corners, use scissors to punch two holes large enough to fit your elastic. Each hole should be 1 inch (2.5 cm) from the outline's corner.

STEP 6 Cut four 4-inch (10-cm) pieces of braided elastic. Feed one from the back of the cardboard up through one of the holes and then back through the facing hole. Repeat with the other three strips and insert your tablet so that the strips go over the device's corners, holding it in place. If it fits, hot-glue the elastic pieces' ends to the cardboard.

STEP 7 Use scissors to cut two holes into the book's back cover near its outside edge. Thread the remaining elastic through one hole from the outside. Measure how long the elastic needs to be to encircle the book when it's closed with the tablet and cardboard tucked inside, then cut the elastic and glue its ends to the inside back cover.

STEP 8 Line up the felt-wrapped cardboard pieces with the book covers and hot-glue them together (the felt should be facing you, on the inside of the book).

STEP 9 Let the glue dry, slide the tablet under the elastic, and revel in being secretly high tech.

Elastic strips through the cardboard

Elastic strap

Felt-wrapped cardboard

Felt on book's spine

Old book with felt inside

TURN A PRINTER INTO A HIGH-VOLUME DOCUMENT SHREDDER

Got mail? Shred it and other sensitive documents with this hacked printer.

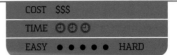

COST	$$$
TIME	☺ ☺ ☺
EASY ● ● ● ● ● HARD	

MATERIALS

Laser printer that prints 25 pages per minute

Screwdriver

Small Perfboard panel

Two LM3903 integrated circuits

Two 100uF, 6-volt electrolytic capacitors

Electrical wire

Wire strippers

Soldering iron and solder

6-volt, 60-mA DC motor

Drill

Glue

5-volt DC-power supply

Cheap, lightweight paper shredder (the kind that fits over a wastebasket)

STEP 1 Unplug and turn off your printer, then use a screwdriver to remove its rear-access panel. Take out the fuser, which bonds toner to paper and is a fire hazard.

STEP 2 Remove the printer's top and side panels and gut it: Take out any power supplies, computer processing units, motors, fans, laser units, toner cartridges, and related circuit boards and wiring. Leave in any solenoids (the long wire loops that control the printer trays) and the toner cartridge, which will control the drive for the trays. Reattach the top and side panels.

STEP 3 To make the controller, mount the two LM3903 integrated circuits onto Perfboard. Attach each capacitor to one integrated circuit, soldering the capacitors' positive leads to the integrated circuits' 2 pins, and their negative ones to the 1 pins.

STEP 4 Mount the controller in the case, then solder each of the printer's original solenoids to one of the two integrated circuits: The solenoids' negative leads go to the 8 pins, and their positive leads should go to the 6 pins.

STEP 5 Replace the printer's original motor with the 6-volt, 60-mA DC motor. Mount it inside the printer with the original motor's screws.

STEP 6 Take the 5-volt DC-power supply and glue it inside the case on a side panel near the original power supply's location. Then strip its output cord and connect its positive

and negative wires with the positive and negative wires of the power leads on the DC motor and the shredder. (The shredder's wires should run through the back of the printer at this point.)

STEP 7 Attach wires to the 5-volt DC-power supply's positive and negative leads, then connect them to the integrated circuits: The positive leads go to the 5 pin and the negative leads go to the 4 pin. Secure all the positive and negative connections with wire nuts.

STEP 8 Replace the side panel to cover the motor. (Cut a hole for clearance if parts stick out, but cover those later with panels to avoid injury.) Drill holes in the printer case's back, then secure the shredder to it with screws.

STEP 9 Load your trays with shreddables, and start making confetti out of your private information.

WARNING
Listen up: This project isn't for first-time tinkerers. If done incorrectly, it could result in fire, shock, or other nasty situations. Only attempt this project if you really know what you're doing, and even then, exercise extreme caution.

107 SORT MAIL WITH OLD CDS

STEP 1 Wearing safety goggles, use a blowtorch to bend a CD at a 90-degree angle about ¾ inch (1.9 cm) from the edge.

STEP 2 Repeat on two other CDs, this time bending the discs 1 ¾ inches (4.5 cm) away from the edge.

STEP 3 Glue the bent portions of the CDs to a base made of an un-molested CD. Glue the tallest CD in between the two bent ones.

STEP 4 Use the two sections to sort your mail into important and not-so-important stacks.

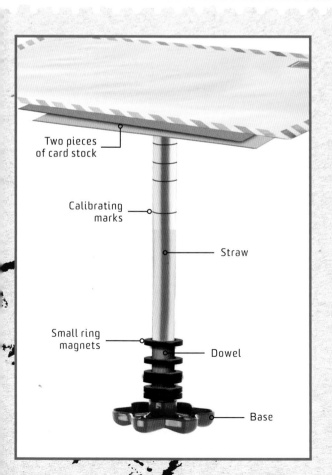

Two pieces of card stock

Calibrating marks

Straw

Small ring magnets

Dowel

Base

108 IMPROVISE A POSTAGE SCALE

This magnetic device says just how many stamps go on that envelope.

MATERIALS
Dowel
Handsaw
Improvised dowel base
Six small ring magnets
Two pieces of card stock

Straw
Scissors
Glue
Three objects with an array of masses

STEP 1 Use a handsaw to cut the dowel down to 6 inches (15 cm). Insert it into an object that works as a base. Slip the magnets over it with like poles facing each other.

STEP 2 Cut two card stock pieces. Make a hole in one that will fit your straw. Cut four slits into the straw's end, slide the straw through the hole, and fold the flaps back.

STEP 3 Glue the second card stock piece directly on top of the cardboard and straw. Slide the straw over the dowel.

STEP 4 Find objects measuring ½ ounce (15 g), 1 ounce (28 g), and 2 ounces (56 g). Put each on the card stock and mark where the straw hits the dowel.

STEP 5 Place a letter on the scale. Once you know its weight, you can determine its postage.

109 TURN YOUR ROOMBA INTO A SENTRY

Why? To patrol your home while you're away, capturing pics you can access from any mobile device.

COST	$$$
TIME	☺ ☺
EASY	● ● ● ○ ○ HARD

The Roomba vacuum is an incredibly sophisticated robot, especially for a gadget that costs less than $300. It scoots along at 1 foot (30 cm) per second, while its sensors detect and navigate obstacles. Here we've outfitted one with a webcam so you can keep tabs on your pad from afar.

MATERIALS

Wireless webcam

Video-streaming site account
  or dedicated website for video

Roomba

Strong Velcro

iPad or tablet, if needed

Mobile device for monitoring
  from afar

STEP 1 Get a wireless webcam that comes with its own free website for real-time broadcasting. If you want to use a wireless webcam you already own, set up an account for it on a video-streaming site.

STEP 2 Follow the camera's instructions to configure video capture and have it sent either to the website or to the streaming-video site.

STEP 3 Attach the webcam to your Roomba with Velcro, send it on its way, and head out the door. Any time that you want to check in on your 'bot's findings, load the video feed on your smartphone or a computer.

STEP 4 For extra deterrence, you can attach an iPad or a tablet PC to the Roomba, navigate to the streaming-video page, and display it on the screen. This way, would-be intruders will see what you're seeing in real time—and know they'd better put that Wii system down and scram.

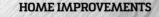

MAKE A ROBOTIC ARTISTE

Let your vacuum make a mess for a change—one that's worthy of any 22nd-century gallery.

MATERIALS

Large canvas	Glue or Velcro
Items to use as bumpers	Paint trays
Brushes and rollers	Paint

STEP 1 Lay a large canvas on your floor and—to keep your Roomba from painting areas you'd prefer left undecorated—arrange objects around the periphery to keep the Roomba within bounds. Place your charging station within that boundary.

STEP 2 Attach brushes and rollers with glue or Velcro to the front, back, and sides of the Roomba. For real drips, try repurposing an old chandelier, or cobbling together a paintbrush holder using a colander and kitchen utensils.

STEP 3 Set paint trays near the charging station so it can refuel with color after it recharges.

IT GETS EVEN BETTER
Any Roomba that's rolled off the assembly line since October 24, 2005, has a serial command interface (SCI), which is essentially an open platform for hackers to play with. This software allows your preprogrammed instructions to control your Roomba, making it an ideal ready-made base for any robotics project.

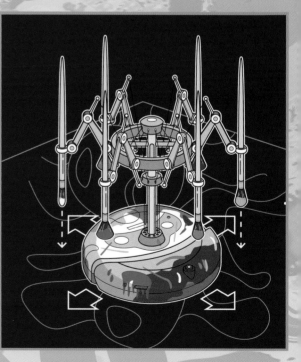

HOME IMPROVEMENTS

111 REMOVE RUST WITH ELECTRICITY

Blast away resistant rust with a bucketful of electrodes.

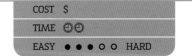

COST	$
TIME	◔ ◔
EASY ● ● ● ○ ○ HARD	

MATERIALS

5-gallon (19-l) plastic bucket

Five 18-inch (45-cm) sections of ½-inch (1.25-cm) non-stainless-steel rebar

Drill

5 feet (1.5 m) pliable rust-resistant wire

Pliers

5 feet (1.5 m) 12-awg insulated copper wire

Wire strippers

Five wire nuts

Box of washing soda

Water

Small board or other nonconductive object

One alligator clip

Nail

Hammer

Small battery charger

Wire brush extension mounted on a rotary tool

Antirust spray

STEP 1 Space the five rebar sections evenly inside the bucket. Use a drill with a ¼-inch (6.35-mm) bit to make two small holes in the bucket near each piece of rebar: one that's 2 inches (5 cm) down from the bucket's rim, and the second about 4 inches (10 cm) down from that.

STEP 2 To secure the rebar, thread rust-resistant wire through each hole, around the rebar, and back out again. Twist the wire tight and snip off the excess with pliers.

STEP 3 Once all rebar is in place, cut five 1-foot (30-cm) sections of copper wire and strip the ends.

STEP 4 On the outside of the bucket, connect rebar sections together with a piece of copper wire and cover with a wire nut. Leave the first and last rebar pieces unconnected, with the fifth section of copper wire loose.

STEP 5 Add 5 tablespoons of washing soda to the bucket and fill within 2 inches (5 cm) of the rim with clean water.

STEP 6 Secure a board (or any nonconductive object) across the top of the bucket.

STEP 7 With the battery charger turned off, attach its positive end to the rebar wire and nail its negative end to the nonconductive board. Then attach several alligator clips to the negative end and let them hang so that they almost touch or barely dip into the water.

STEP 8 Clean a small piece of your rusty object; attach this point to the alligator clips so that the object hangs inside the bucket. It should not touch the rebar.

STEP 9 Set the battery charger to a low setting (such as 6-volt 1.5 amp) and turn it on.

STEP 10 Bubbles will form and rust will begin to flake off. Leave your object in the water for anywhere from an hour to a couple of days. Then remove it and use a wire brush (and antirust spray, if necessary) to remove the remaining flaky rust.

Board or other nonconductive object

Alligator clips

Non-stainless-steel rebar

Battery's negative end

12-awg insulated copper wire secured with wire nuts

Pliable rust-resistant wire to battery charger

Battery's positive end

WARNING
We're serious about not using stainless-steel rebar for the electrodes. Stainless steel's chrome will leak during the electrolysis and form nasty compounds in your electrolyte.

112 CLEAN WITH A TOY-CAR BROOM

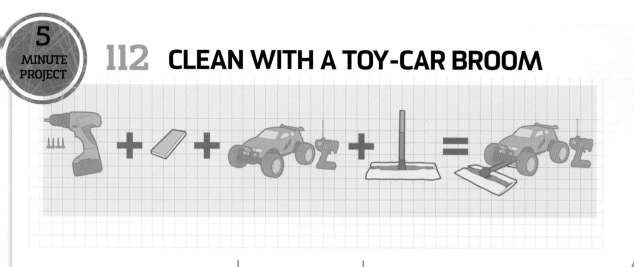

STEP 1 Use a drill and two screws to attach a very small board to the underside of a remote-controlled car.

STEP 2 Attach a disposable sweeper head to the board with a drill and two more screws. Make sure that the sweeper lies flat.

STEP 3 Use your remote to drive the dust away.

113 RIG A SUPERPOWERED SCRUB BRUSH

When elbow grease just won't cut it, add mighty power-tool action.

Bathroom brush with handle

Power saw with mini blade attachment

MATERIALS

Scrubber brush
Rotary tool
Power saw with mini saw blade
Clamps
Electrical tape

STEP 1 Cut a groove into the handle of a bathroom-style scrubber brush with a rotary tool.

STEP 2 Insert the power saw's mini saw blade into the groove and secure it with clamps.

STEP 3 Wrap the brush handle with electrical tape so that the clamps are secured in place.

STEP 4 Reattach the blade to the saw, turn it on, and polish your boat or scrub your tub. Just don't use it on your Benz.

HOME IMPROVEMENTS

114 TRACK YOUR FOOD'S FRESHNESS

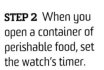 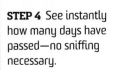

STEP 1 Remove the band from a basic digital watch.

STEP 2 When you open a container of perishable food, set the watch's timer.

STEP 3 Glue the watch face to the food item.

STEP 4 See instantly how many days have passed—no sniffing necessary.

115 MOD A CRUMB-COLLECTING CUTTING BOARD

Catch crumbs before they hit the floor with this cutting board mod.

MATERIALS
Router table
Cutting board
Sandpaper
Olive oil

STEP 1 Use a router table to cut ½-inch (1.25-cm) channels into the board, ½ inch (1.25 cm) apart.

STEP 2 Sand the surface of the board, including the edges of and inside the channels.

STEP 3 Wipe the board down with olive oil.

STEP 4 Cut bread, contain crumbs.

116 HARVEST FRIDGE MAGNETS FROM AN OLD HARD DRIVE

Get over that dead hard drive and pry out the superstrong magnets hiding in it.

COST $
TIME 🕐
EASY ● ● ○ ○ ○ HARD

MATERIALS

Computer with a dead hard drive

Torx screwdriver kit

STEP 1 Unplug your computer before you begin working.

STEP 2 Open up your case and locate the hard drive. There'll be a power cord attached to it; unplug that, and undo any screws holding the hard drive in place. Pull the hard drive out of the case.

STEP 3 Using a star-shaped Torx screwdriver kit, start unscrewing the many, many screws on the hard drive's case and remove it. You'll probably need to remove a lot of stickers in the process, too.

STEP 4 Once you're looking at the internal workings of the hard drive, locate the actuator arm (it's the part that protrudes over the disc-like thing, which is called a platter). Behind it is the actuator (aka, one of two big-deal rare-earth magnets that you're after). Unscrew its fasteners with a Torx screwdriver and pry it off.

STEP 5 Once you've got the first magnet off, you'll see a second one beneath it. Pry it out with a screwdriver, too, and use the magnets to spruce up the old fridge.

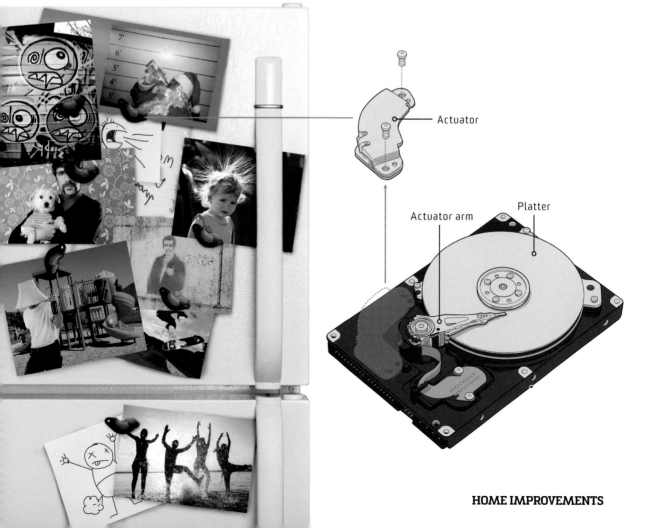

Actuator

Actuator arm

Platter

117 DO STUFF WITH BOTTLE CAPS

Next time you pop open a cold beer or soda,
pocket its cap and put it to use.

SOAP-SLIME KILLER
Twist a bottle cap into the bottom of a bar of soap—it prevents sticky crud from building up on your sink or tub surface.

FRIDGE MAGNET
Glue a small circular magnet inside a bottle cap with the nonmagnetic side facing the cap's back, then smack it on the fridge to hold up the number of that take-out joint you like so much.

TINY CANDLES
Place a wick in the cap's bottom, then pour hot wax to fill. You'll be well prepped next time the lights go out.

PLAYING PIECES
If you've got two 12-packs of different brands of beer, you're more than on your way to a good Friday night: You've got a full set of checkers pieces. Now all you need is a checkered tablecloth and a friend to play (and help drink).

MUD-ROOM MAT
Nail caps with their labels facing downward in a grid design onto a piece of wood. Place the mat in front of your door, and never track mud through the house again.

118 AVOID BURNING YOUR MOUTH WITH A SMART COASTER

Never burn your mouth on a hot drink again with this ingenious coaster.

COST	$
TIME	◔ ◕
EASY	● ● ● ○ ○ HARD

MATERIALS

LM324N (low-power operational amplifier)
Thermistor
Electrical tape
Empty metal shoe polish container
Rotary tool
Red LED
Hobby foam

Soldering iron and solder
1k-ohm resistor
10k-ohm resistor
10k-ohm potentiometer
Electrical wire
Wire strippers
3.7-volt battery
Mug

STEP 1 Clip off the unnecessary legs from the operational amplifier, keeping pins 1, 2, 3, 4, and 11.

STEP 2 Attach the thermistor to the inside of the metal container's lid with some electrical tape. Be sure to insulate both of the thermistor leads with tape.

STEP 3 Drill a hole into the side of the metal container for holding the red LED. Insulate the bottom of the container with some scrap paper or hobby foam.

STEP 4 Follow the circuitry diagram to make the circuit.

STEP 5 Fit the components inside the metal container, connect the 3.7-volt battery, and close the metal lid.

STEP 6 Check your LED light by putting your finger on the coaster lid. If it lights up, you're good to start calibrating it. If not, check your wiring.

STEP 7 Place your cup of fresh brew on the smart coaster and use the 10k-ohm potentiometer to adjust the thermistor's sensitivity. Turn the potentiometer until the LED glows and monitor the temperature of your beverage.

STEP 8 When the cup's temp has fallen to your desired drinking level, turn the potentiometer until the LED goes out. Your smart coaster is now calibrated for this mug. Remember, if you change mugs, you will have to recalibrate. Bottoms up.

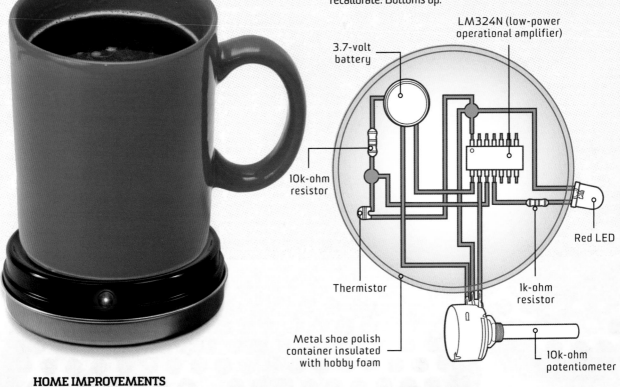

LM324N (low-power operational amplifier)

3.7-volt battery

10k-ohm resistor

Red LED

Thermistor

1k-ohm resistor

Metal shoe polish container insulated with hobby foam

10k-ohm potentiometer

119 Put an Old Coffee Can to Good Use

Long after the caffeine rush has worn off, coffee cans come in handy. Here's some clever stuff to do with your empties.

PIE TINS

LARGE-HUB REEL FOR EXTENSION CORD

DRILL SMALL HOLES

PUNCH HOLE UPWARD FOR COTTON WICK

CRANKCASE OIL

SOLDER WASHER

EMERGENCY FLARE TO BE ASSEMBLED ON THE ROAD

SMALL PARTS CLEANER SCREEN HOLDS PARTS, LETS SEDIMENT FALL TO THE BOTTOM OF THE CAN

COAT-HANGER WIRE

LINE MARKER FOR BADMINTON OR TENNIS COURT

DISPOSABLE PAINT PAIL

FIT WITH WIRE HANDLE FOR WIPING BRUSH

KEROSENE OR SOLVENT

ROLL-BACK TOY AS CAN IS ROLLED FORWARD, WEIGHT WINDS UP RUBBER BAND, CAUSING CAN TO TURN

PARCHMENT LACED OVER CAN

TOY BANJO USE GUT OR RUBBER BANDS FOR STRINGS

COVER FOR SNUFFER

2 INCHES (5 CM) SAND

OUTDOOR COOKER SAND SATURATED WITH GAS BURNS LONG AND CLEAN

120 DINNER TO GO NITROUS-INJE[...] DINING TABLE

The world's speediest piece of furniture, caught on film.

Why would a man spend a year and $7,000 const[...] a dining-room table that cruises at 130 miles per h[...] (210 km/h) and shoots flames up into the air as it s[...] away? Sheer competitiveness, as it turns out. A rec[...] the world's fastest furniture existed—92 miles per[...] (148 km/h) on a sofa—and Perry Watkins wanted[...]

Watkins, a sales director in Wingrave, England, ch[...] dining table as his furniture type because he thoug[...] would be easiest to mount onto a small, fast car. H[...] by buying an old two-seat Reliant Scimitar Sabre [...] convertible, ripping off the fiberglass panels, stripp[...] down to the chassis, and installing an off-the-shelf[...] oxide injection system for added power.

The resulting vehicle, dubbed Fast Food, smoked t[...] record, clocking an average speed of 113.8 miles pe[...] (180 km/h). But it was the trimmings that really w[...] onlookers. Watkins bolted dishware to the table, a[...] variety of authentic-looking foods, including gravy[...] fiberglass resin and tea kettles that puff flames 10[...] into the air. The helmeted diner is actually a mann[...]

Watkins is the real man behind the wheel, with his[...] barely visible underneath a plastic chicken on a pla[...] chicken is quasi-functional: Before kicking in, the n[...] system purges excess air through a tube leading to[...] fowl. "A 6-foot [1.8-m] plume of white smoke come[...] of the chicken's backside," Watkins says. He figure[...] probably a world record, too.

RAISE THE ROOF
Where's Watkins? He's in the driver's seat below the table, with his head poking from under a plated chicken.

121 IMPROVISE A SOUS-VIDE COOKER

Join the sous-vide craze with this el cheapo home-built model.

The trick to delicious, evenly cooked meat is keeping your water bath at a precise temperature by using a thermocoupler temperature sensor and a proportional-integral-derivative (PID) controller. Once you master this, play with other setups—a pot of water on an electric plate, an electric kettle, or a lightbulb in an insulated chamber.

MATERIALS

Cheap slow cooker or rice cooker with an on/off switch
Water
Thermocoupler temperature sensor

PID controller with auto-tuning feature
Vacuum sealer or zip-top plastic bag and straw
Food

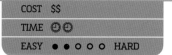

COST	$$
TIME	⏱⏱
EASY ● ● ○ ○ ○ HARD	

STEP 1 Fill your slow cooker with enough water to cover the food you'll be cooking.

STEP 2 Plug your slow cooker and thermocoupler into your PID controller, and your PID into a power outlet. (If you're feeling ambitious, there are several online tutorials on making your own PID from scratch. The model we use here will run you between $35 and $70—far cheaper than the $1,000 lab-grade immersion cooker on the market.)

STEP 3 Now it's time to vacuum-pack your food. If you don't have a vacuum sealer, try freezing your marinated meat and putting it in a sandwich bag, sticking the thermocoupler into your meat inside the bag, and partially sealing it up. Then suck the remaining air out with a straw and quickly seal it.

STEP 4 Set the desired temperature. The PID controller's LED display will show the thermocoupler's reading. Use the buttons to set how hot you need the cooker to get, based on the required temperature for your meat.

STEP 5 Place your meat in the slow cooker. Cook until the thermocoupler reading indicates that your meat has reached the desired temperature.

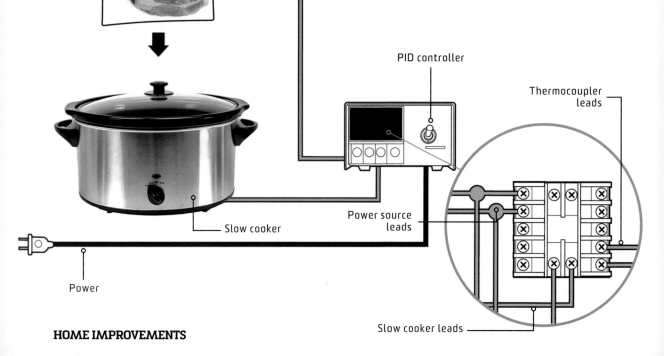

Thermocoupler temperature sensor

Deliciousness

PID controller

Thermocoupler leads

Power source leads

Slow cooker

Power

Slow cooker leads

122 BUILD A DIY SMOKER

This clay-pot cooking device gives food a wood-smoked taste.

MATERIALS

Hot plate

Large unglazed clay pot with base

Drill with masonry bit

Grill thermometer

Stainless steel saucepan without handle

Wood chips

Circular grill grate

STEP 1 Place the pot on blocks, then situate the hot plate inside the pot. Run the hot plate's wire through the drainage hole in the pot's bottom.

STEP 2 Attach a masonry bit to a drill and make a hole in the pot's base large enough to fit a grill thermometer.

STEP 3 Place a stainless-steel saucepan on top of the hot plate. (If you have one with a handle, remove it.)

STEP 4 Place wood chips in the pan, and a circular grill grate in the pot above the pan.

STEP 5 Throw some ribs on the grill grate and put the pot's base on the pot as a cover. Then place the pot in an open area, plug in your hot plate, and start cooking.

123 SET UP AN UMBRELLA SOLAR COOKER

What to do with an umbrella on a sunny day? Fry eggs on it!

MATERIALS

Umbrella with ribs

Hacksaw

Plastic or acrylic mirror sheets, mirror film, or heavy-duty aluminum foil

Newspaper

Pencil

Tape or glue

Soldering iron and solder

Metal plant stand

Small barbecue grill rack

Nonstick aluminum pot or frying pan

STEP 1 Cut the shaft off an umbrella with a hacksaw. Check that its ribs are in good shape, as they'll be supporting the reflective material that cooks your food.

STEP 2 Choose your reflective material, either mirror sheets (which are more durable but more costly and difficult to find) or aluminum foil, which will need to be replaced once you close the umbrella.

STEP 3 Using a piece of newspaper, create a template by tracing one of the triangular areas between the umbrella's ribs. Use this to cut enough reflective triangles to cover all of the umbrella's inside canvas.

STEP 4 Attach the reflective material to the umbrella with tape (or glue, if working with mirror sheets).

STEP 5 Solder the grill rack to a plant stand.

STEP 6 Place the umbrella on the ground in the sun and set the plant stand in the center.

STEP 7 Place an aluminum pot on the grill stand and watch the sun heat up your meal. Rotate the cooker at least twice an hour to keep it in the sun's strongest rays.

124 CONSTRUCT A TOILET-POWERED ZEN FOUNTAIN

Feel more relaxed with every flush of your commode.

COST	$
TIME	⏱
EASY ● ● ○ ○ ○ HARD	

MATERIALS

Plastic planter

Drill

4 feet (1.2 m) plastic tubing

Waterproof silicone

Shallow plastic dish

Gravel

Decorative stones

Hot-glue gun

STEP 1 Drill a hole near the bottom of the planter's side. Insert a piece of tube long enough to reach into the toilet tank, and seal around the tube with waterproof silicone. Let dry for 24 hours and test for leakages. (This tube will direct overflow water.)

STEP 2 Cover the planter's bottom with gravel so that the overflow tube is covered. Nestle a small plastic dish (into which the tiny waterfall will flow) among the gravel pieces, being sure not to obscure the dish.

STEP 3 Stack and hot-glue decorative rocks to create elevation for your tiny waterfall.

STEP 4 On this stack of stones, glue a second piece of tubing, which will act as your intake tube. Glue more stones on top to conceal it (along with any cool decorative stuff you want). Aim the tube toward the plastic dish.

STEP 5 Remove the cover from the basin of your toilet and connect your intake tube to the tube that feeds the water to your toilet (that'd be the one that's connected to the float ball). You may need to prop up the toilet basin cover to prevent crushing the plastic tubing.

STEP 6 Direct the overflow tube back into the toilet basin. Each time you flush, the water travels into your planter and overflows back into the toilet, completing the loop.

125 DOUBLE YOUR SHOWERHEAD ACTION

Why on earth should you do this? You know why, you sly dog, you.

MATERIALS

½-inch (1.25-cm) copper fitting union

5-foot (1.5-m) piece of ½-inch (1.25-cm) copper pipe

Copper-pipe cutter

½-inch (1.25-cm) copper T

Four ½-inch (1.25-cm) 90-degree copper elbows

½-inch (1.25-cm) 45-degree copper elbow

Blowtorch and solder

Two ½-inch (1.25-cm) male adapters

Two new showerheads

Wrench

Plumber's tape

STEP 1 Unscrew your existing showerhead. Screw one half of the ½-inch (1.25-cm) fitting union to the flange.

STEP 2 Using a copper-pipe cutter, cut the pipe into three pieces: one piece 2½ feet (75 cm) long, and two 1¼ feet (38 cm), from which the new showerheads will extend.

STEP 3 Attach the two equal-length pieces of pipe with the copper T to create the T-shaped framework.

STEP 4 Attach this T-shaped framework to the long piece of pipe with a 90-degree elbow and then a 45-degree elbow. Solder all joints.

STEP 5 To the end of the contraption that will connect to the wall, attach a 90-degree elbow and then the remaining half of the fitting union. Solder in place.

STEP 6 To the ends of the T-shaped framework, attach 90-degree copper elbows to point downward. Then attach the male adapters, then the showerheads. Solder in place.

STEP 7 Screw the two halves of the fitting union together to install the double showerhead. Use plumber's tape and a wrench to create a tight seal.

STEP 8 Scrub-a-dub.

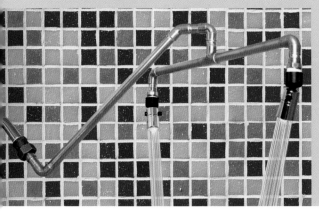

---

5 MINUTE PROJECT

126 CRAFT A TOILET-PAPER DISPENSER

STEP 1 Pull down the corners of a clotheshanger.

STEP 2 Bend one side inward to create a space for the toilet-paper roll. Straighten the bottom of the hanger to make a rectangular shape.

STEP 3 Add toilet paper and hang near the can.

127 HANG A MAGNETIC STUD FINDER

STEP 1 Tie a string to a strong magnet.

STEP 2 Dangle it against a wall, and mark where it clings to nails and screws embedded in the structure.

STEP 3 Look for a pattern in your marks—that's where the studs are, and where you should hang that trippy Magic Eye stereogram you found in your garage.

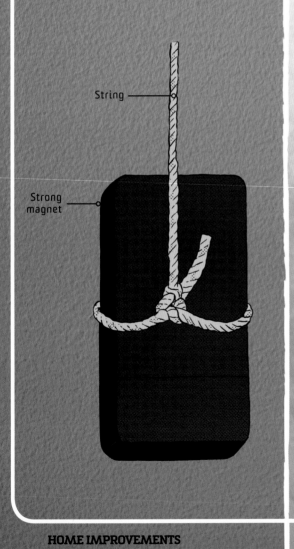

String

Strong magnet

128 TURN YOUR HARD DRIVE INTO A TOOL GRINDER

STEP 1 Peel off all the stickers on your hard drive and pry away its top cover, using a Torx screwdriver to remove any screws.

STEP 2 Strip out the fixings inside the hard drive with the Torx screwdriver. Remove the actuator (the magnets), the actuator arm, and the circuit board. Toss these or save them for later projects.

STEP 3 Remove the platter from the spindle and trace it onto the sandpaper. Then cut out the shape with a craft knife.

STEP 4 Glue the sandpaper to the platter and reinstall it onto the drive with the aluminum spindle's bottom under the platter and the spindle's round top over the sandpaper.

STEP 5 Attach a molex connector, plug the molex connector into a power supply, and grind away.

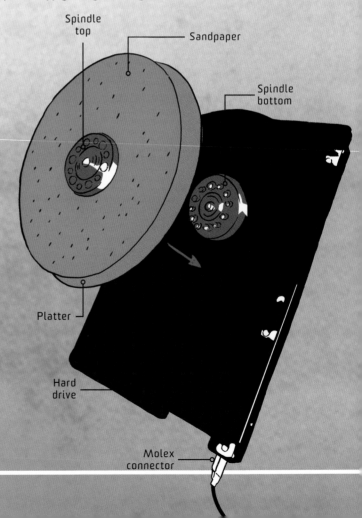

Spindle top

Sandpaper

Spindle bottom

Platter

Hard drive

Molex connector

129 CAPTURE SCREWS WITH A MAGNETIC WRISTBAND

STEP 1 Scrounge up some magnets from your home. You'll need one on the large side and several much smaller round magnets.

STEP 2 Use superglue to attach the smaller magnets to the larger magnet. You'll want to space them pretty evenly. Let dry.

STEP 3 Make a slit in the top of a terry-cloth wristband that's big enough to slide your larger magnet inside.

STEP 4 Slide the larger magnet inside the slit and sew it shut. When you're doing basic woodworking stuff, slip this wristband onto your arm and capture stray metal fasteners with its magnet.

130 RIG THE POOR MAN'S LASER LEVEL

STEP 1 Use a rubber band to secure a suction cup to a basic carpenter's level.

STEP 2 Use tape to mount a laser pointer onto the carpenter's level at a right angle.

STEP 3 Suction-cup the apparatus to a wall at the height that you want to hang your object, and turn on the laser pen.

STEP 4 Tilt the laser to make a level line and hang your Picasso.

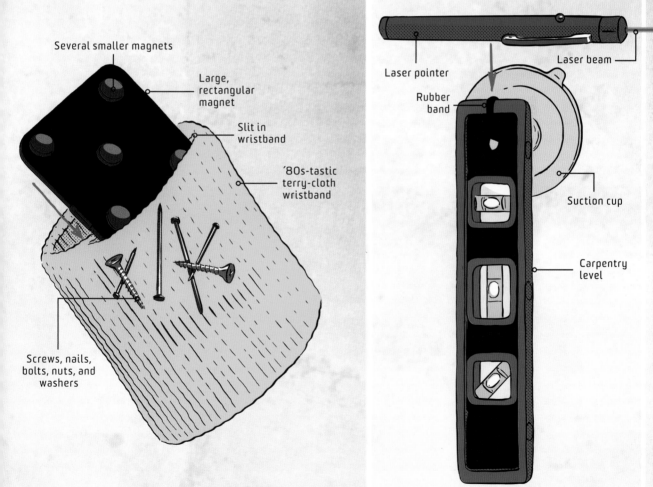

Several smaller magnets

Large, rectangular magnet

Slit in wristband

'80s-tastic terry-cloth wristband

Screws, nails, bolts, nuts, and washers

Laser pointer

Rubber band

Laser beam

Suction cup

Carpentry level

131 KIT OUT AN INSTANT-CHARGE SCREWDRIVER

Resuscitate a dead electric screwdriver with quick-charging supercapacitors.

COST	$
TIME	⊙ ⊙
EASY ● ● ● ○ ○ HARD	

MATERIALS

3.6-volt cordless rechargeable screwdriver
Phillips screwdriver
Soldering iron and solder
Four supercapacitors, 10F and 2.5-volt
Mini B USB cable
Breakout board for mini USB
Electrical wire

It's the do-it-yourselfer's version of Murphy's Law: Every time you need to sink some tough screws, the battery in your cordless screwdriver is dead. So forget those plodding batteries and shorten recharge time to a minute and a half.

STEP 1 Use a standard Phillips head screwdriver to open up the rechargeable screwdriver and remove the battery.

STEP 2 Desolder the barrel-shaped charge connector and the battery connection clip from the screwdriver's circuit board. Solder a red wire from the breakout board's VCC conductor to the positive pad on the circuit board, and a black wire between the ground connections of the boards.

STEP 3 Connect two capacitors in series with the positive lead of one soldered to the negative lead of the other. Repeat with another pair. Then join the two sets together in parallel (positive to positive, negative to negative).

STEP 4 Solder the positive leads from the power pack you just made to the red wires from the switch and the circuit board. Solder the pack's negative leads to the black wires.

STEP 5 Widen the charge port on the screwdriver case large enough to access a mini B USB cable. Fasten the breakout board to the inside of the screwdriver. Line up the port with the opening, and reassemble the case.

STEP 6 Plug the screwdriver into a USB port on your computer. The red LED should glow—when it goes out, in about 90 seconds, the screwdriver is charged.

STEP 7 Enjoy your new quick-charge screwdriver.

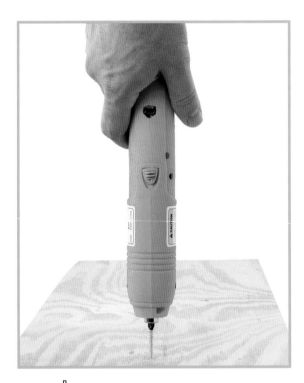

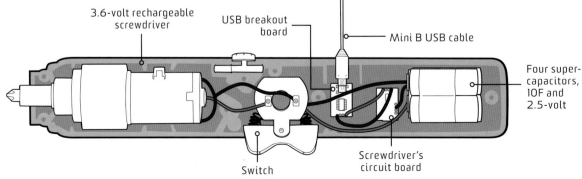

3.6-volt rechargeable screwdriver

USB breakout board

Mini B USB cable

Four super-capacitors, 10F and 2.5-volt

Switch

Screwdriver's circuit board

132 MAKE A MINI SCREWDRIVER

STEP 1 Drill a hole in the top of a glue-stick cap that's slightly smaller than the screwdriver bit.

STEP 2 Wiggle a drill bit through the hole in the cap.

STEP 3 Put a pencil eraser on the back of the drill bit to secure it in place.

STEP 4 Screw away.

133 REMOVE A STRIPPED SCREW WITH A RUBBER BAND

Stripped screws happen. Luckily, you've got that rubber-band ball to use up.

STEP 1 Place a wide rubber band across the head of the screw you want to remove.

STEP 2 Grab a screwdriver that's a size bigger than what the screw is made for.

STEP 3 Through the rubber band, apply hard, slow force to remove the stripped screw.

134 MAKE A RUBIK'S CUBE–INSPIRED CHEST OF DRAWERS

Everyone's favorite gaming cube gets transformed into clever furniture.

Each drawer swivels to mimic the cube's trademark maneuverability, while the colored patches are magnetized so you can peel them off and arrange them how you like. Cheating never felt so good.

COST	$$
TIME	◔ ◔ ◔ ◔
EASY	● ● ● ○ ○ HARD

MATERIALS

Table saw
Straightedge
Three sheets of ½-inch (1.25-cm) plywood
Three sheets of ¼-inch (6.35-mm) plywood
Three pairs of 22-inch (56-cm) full-extension drawer slides with runners
About 60 ½-inch (1.25-cm) flat head screws
Wood glue
Brad nails
Brad nailer
Orbital sander
Primer

White paint
Router with a V-shaped bit
54 ¼-by-1¾-inch (0.635-by-3-cm) dowels
Cordless drill with ⅜ inch Forstner bit
Bench saw
45 ⅜ inch (3.75-mm) steel washers
Epoxy glue
36 ⅜-inch (3.75-mm) rare earth magnets
Paint in five colors and black
Two 1-foot (30-cm) lazy Susan bearings

STEP 1 Using a table saw and a straightedge, cut pieces of the ½-inch (1.25-cm) plywood to make the cases (the boxes that hold the drawers). Start by measuring and cutting six 2-by-2-foot (60-by-60-cm) sheets for the tops and bottoms of the cases. Then cut six 24-by-7-inch (60-by-18-cm) sheets for the sides of the cases.

STEP 2 Still working with the ½-inch (1.25-cm) plywood, cut three 24-by-7¾-inch (60-by-19.75-cm) sections for the drawer fronts. Cut six 21-by-6-inch (54-by-16-cm) sections for the drawer sides.

STEP 3 Begin working with the ¼-inch (6.45-mm) plywood. First, measure and cut three 22-by-22-inch (55-by-55-cm) pieces for the drawer bottoms. Then, to make the backs of the drawers, cut three 22-by-6-inch (55-by-15.35-cm) pieces. For the backs of the cases, cut three 24-by-7¾-inch (60-by-19.75-cm) pieces.

STEP 4 Cut 54 6½-by-6½-inch (17-by-17-cm) pieces out of the ¼-inch (6.45-mm) plywood for the stickers.

STEP 5 Attach one of the drawer slides to each of the plywood case side panels with screws, leaving ¼ inch (6.35 mm) at the front edges, and making sure that the slides will be parallel to each other when the drawers are constructed.

STEP 6 Assemble the three cases with wood glue and brad nails, attaching top and bottom panels to side panels with the drawer slides on the inside. Let dry, then sand.

STEP 7 Prime, sand, and paint the drawers white.

STEP 8 Assemble the three drawers to fit inside these cases using the bottom, back, and side panels you cut for the drawers. Let dry and sand.

STEP 9 Attach the drawer runners to the outside of the drawers' side panels and check that they fit smoothly with the slides inside the cases.

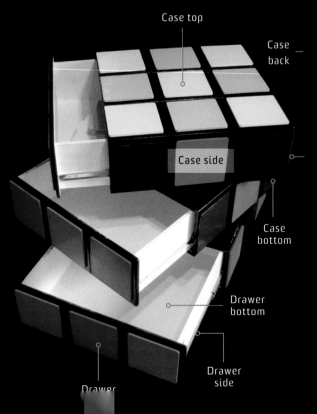

Case top

Case back

Case side

Case bottom

Drawer bottom

Drawer side

Drawer

STEP 10 Attach the faces of the drawers. Let dry and sand.

STEP 11 Use a router with a V-shaped bit and cut grooves in all the exposed faces, creating the look of cubes.

STEP 12 Drill two dowel-sized holes about three-fourths of the way through opposite corners of each of the 45 square "stickers." Using a Forstner bit, drill a shallow hole in the center of each sticker for the washer.

STEP 13 To cut the dowels in half, tape them to a piece of scrap plywood and run them through the bench saw.

STEP 14 Glue the half-dowels into the holes in the stickers, then epoxy the washers into the shallow holes in each sticker's center.

STEP 15 Prime, sand, and paint the stickers using a separate color for each set of nine.

STEP 16 Drill holes in all the exposed faces of the chest for the dowels and washers of the stickers.

STEP 17 Glue the rare-earth magnets into the center holes of the faces with epoxy. These should line up perfectly with the washers in the stickers, with enough clearance for the dowels on either side.

STEP 18 Rout out a thin layer of plywood from the bottom of the top case, the top and bottom of the center case, and the top of the bottom case and screw the lazy Susan bearings into them. Epoxy the bearings into place.

STEP 19 Attach the stickers to the sides and top, sliding the dowels into the holes.

STEP 20 Scramble the stickers or make it look solved, and move them around whenever the whimsy strikes you.

5 MINUTE PROJECT

135 **SAND TINY TRIM WITH A RAZOR**

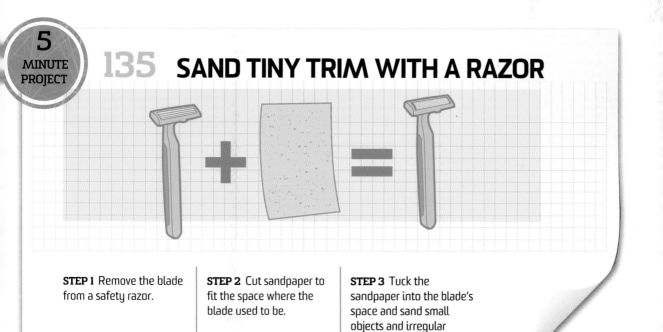

STEP 1 Remove the blade from a safety razor.

STEP 2 Cut sandpaper to fit the space where the blade used to be.

STEP 3 Tuck the sandpaper into the blade's space and sand small objects and irregular concave edges.

QUICK
HACKS

136 MAKE DUCT TAPE DO DOUBLE DUTY

Ah, duct tape. What can you do with it? A better
question may be, what *can't* you do with it?

ROPE IN A PINCH
Cut the length you need, then roll one edge inward for a pretty sturdy rope.

IMPROMPTU HINGE
Lay a small rectangle of duct tape across the gap between a cabinet's lightweight door and its frame, then close the door to fold the tape into a working hinge.

VACUUM HOSE EXTENDER
Sometimes the hose on your vacuum cleaner isn't long enough to get to out-of-reach places—like, say, your ceiling. Just add a length of PVC pipe to the hose and seal the seam with the good stuff.

TEMPORARY ROOF SHINGLE
Roof falling apart? Patch it with an improvised shingle of folded duct tape.

EMERGENCY SUNGLASSES
Fend off glare by folding a length of duct tape in half, cutting a slit in the center, and tying it around your head.

137 CREATE A LIFE-SIZE CARD-BOARD CUTOUT

STEP 1 Using a digital camera that shoots at least seven megapixels, snap a photo of a hilarious person.

STEP 2 Use photo-editing software to delete the background, turn any negative spaces gray or beige, and enlarge the image to life size.

STEP 3 Print the image out in sections and tape it together, or have a copy shop print out the image full size.

STEP 4 Trim the figure out of its background, leaving about a 2-inch (5-cm) border. Don't cut out the area between the figure's feet—a wide, solid bottom will help support it.

STEP 5 Attach cardboard pieces with spray adhesive to make a single piece that's big enough to fit your image.

STEP 6 Mount the image to the cardboard with the spray adhesive, and trim the cutout with a craft knife.

STEP 7 Cut out two cardboard supports and make slits in the bottom of your cutout. Slide the supports in to make it stand.

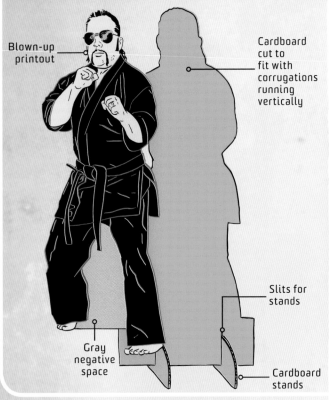

Blown-up printout

Cardboard cut to fit with corrugations running vertically

Slits for stands

Gray negative space

Cardboard stands

138 LOUNGE IN A CARDBOARD HAMMOCK

STEP 1 Cut cardboard into six strips 4 feet (1.2 m) long and about 1 foot (30 cm) wide, and two pieces 3 feet (90 cm) long and about 2 feet (60 cm) wide.

STEP 2 If you're recycling cardboard, patch holes and reinforce tears and weak spots with duct tape.

STEP 3 Duct-tape three of the six long strips together so their sides touch. Repeat with the other three, then tape the two sections together end to end.

STEP 4 Tape your remaining two pieces of cardboard over the center seam on the top and bottom to reinforce it. Use a lot of tape over each seam.

STEP 5 Make eight holes in the hammock, one at each corner and two near the center along each long edge.

STEP 6 Thread a piece of rope a little longer than the hammock through the holes along one side. Repeat on the other side.

STEP 7 Cut a broom handle in half and thread it through the two holes in the corners of the hammock's short sides. Reinforce with duct tape.

STEP 8 Drill two eyebolts at equal height into two nearby trees. Tie the hammock's rope to the eyebolts. Take it down if there's a chance of rain.

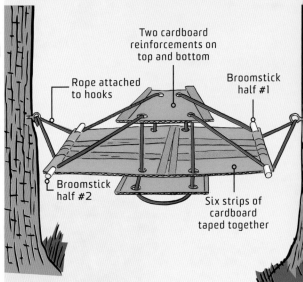

Two cardboard reinforcements on top and bottom

Rope attached to hooks

Broomstick half #1

Broomstick half #2

Six strips of cardboard taped together

139 CHAT ON A CARDBOARD TELEPHONE

STEP 1 Take an old phone apart, removing the casing around the electronics.

STEP 2 Cut out pieces of cardboard to fit around the electronics in your phone's handset. This will vary according to your phone—trace its case as a template.

STEP 3 Using a craft knife, cut out spaces in the cardboard handset through which you'll be able to access the keypad. Punch holes in the cardboard that will cover the speaker and the microphone.

STEP 4 Measure your cardboard handset and create a cardboard base that the handset can rest on. It should include a protruding piece of cardboard where the phone's depressor will hit, hanging up the phone.

STEP 5 Tape the electronics inside the cardboard handset and base, lining up all components with the various openings in the cardboard. Make a small opening in the base's bottom for the cord.

STEP 6 Dial someone up.

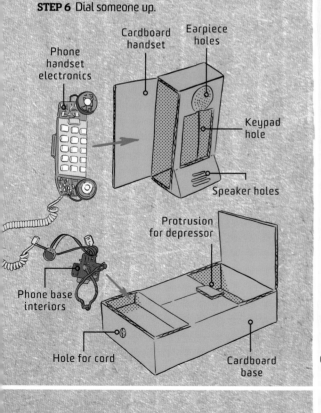

Phone handset electronics

Cardboard handset

Earpiece holes

Keypad hole

Speaker holes

Protrusion for depressor

Phone base interiors

Hole for cord

Cardboard base

140 HANG UP CARDBOARD BLINDS

STEP 1 Measure your window's height and width, then add about 20 inches (50 cm) to the height. Cut your cardboard to these dimensions, with its corrugations running horizontally.

STEP 2 Measure every 5 inches (12 cm) along the cardboard and mark these lines with a ruler. Using the back of a box cutter, score along the marks.

STEP 3 Flip the cardboard over and mark halfway between the scored lines. Score these marks in the opposite direction.

STEP 4 Accordion-fold the cardboard, firmly creasing every other line in the opposite direction.

STEP 5 With the cardboard all folded up, drill a hole through each end of the top all the way through to the bottom.

STEP 6 Thread a needle with twine and pull it through the holes on one side; knot it at the top. Repeat on the other side.

STEP 7 Drill two small eyebolts into the top of the window frame so that they line up with the string. Hang the blinds.

STEP 8 Fasten clothespins to the bottom of the twine lengths. When you want more light, push up the clothespins. For darkness, slide them down and let the cardboard unfold.

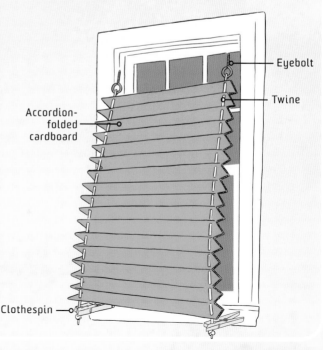

Eyebolt

Twine

Accordion-folded cardboard

Clothespin

141 MAN'S BEST FRIEND GETS A HIGH-TECH HOME

This dream doghouse comes complete with a solar heating system, LED lights, and a Wi-Fi security camera.

Former *PopSci* photographer John Carnett decided to make this pooch palace for Pearl, his labradoodle, after she dutifully watched him build a new house for three years. A standard model just wouldn't do, though, so he went a little overboard. After creating the design with computer-aided design (CAD) software, he added a solar hot-water radiant-heating system and made a green roof that retains rainwater, creates oxygen, and improves insulation. Then he decked it out with a few other touches, including some colored LED lights to brighten things up and a Web-enabled wireless video camera that lets him keep an eye on Pearl from his computer or phone. That's plenty of features for her, but the doghouse has one extra benefit for Carnett himself: The battery that powers it also powers all the low-voltage exterior lights on his property.

Carnett made a frame of 2-by-4-foot (60-by-120-cm) boards and walls made of insulated wood panels. The south-facing wall has a solar panel, which charges the gel battery mounted inside the house. A solar charge controller, switches, and other parts are inside a waterproof panel mounted on the exterior for easy adjustment. When the photovoltaic panels are exposed to sunlight, a pump circulates glycol fluid through evacuated tubes to a series of copper pipes underneath the floor. The pipes heat a concrete backing board below them, which in turn disperses heat through the hardwood floor into the house.

The porch ceiling contains a waterproof 12-volt LED light, and the two interior lights go on automatically when it gets dark outside. That way, Pearl always has a welcoming light on when she comes home at night.

142 MAKE AN AUTOMATIC PET FEEDER

Not around to feed your pet? Automate that action and fret about Fido no more.

MATERIALS

Screwdriver
Battery-operated clock
Metal dog-food bowl
Glue
Small, circular metal dish
Tape
Incredibly thin plywood
Saw
Drill
Hammer
Two nails

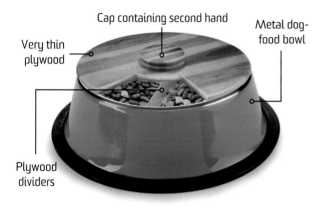

Cap containing second hand

Metal dog-food bowl

Very thin plywood

Plywood dividers

STEP 1 Using a screwdriver, remove the motor and the second and hour hands from an old clock.

STEP 2 Glue a small metal dish to the center of your pet's metal food bowl to form a central compartment. The dish should be big enough to hold the motor, and should be level with the bowl's top.

STEP 3 Tape the motor inside the central compartment and mount the hour hand to the motor.

STEP 4 Using a saw, cut four plywood dividers that will radiate out from the central compartment. Insert them.

STEP 5 Cut a piece of very thin plywood to fit over the bowl and cut away a quarter of it. Drill a hole into the top to accommodate the bit that extrudes from the motor.

STEP 6 Hammer two nails in the lid so that the hour hand is between them and, when it rotates, the lid goes with it. Trim so they don't get caught on the motor. Put the lid on.

STEP 7 Make a plywood cap that's large enough to cover the second hand. Tape the second hand to the cap upside down and mount it to the lid. It should rotate freely.

STEP 8 Fill the bowl with food. Every three hours, the lid will rotate and your pet can get more of the good stuff.

143 BUILD A CAT DOOR

Have the mewing beasts let themselves out for a change with this DIY cat hatch.

MATERIALS

Pencil
Jigsaw
Continuous hinge
Tin shears
Thin acrylic
Drill
1/4-inch (6.35-mm) bolts and nuts
Metal plate
Magnet

STEP 1 Sketch the opening on your door so it's 9½ inches (24 cm) wide by 8 inches (20 cm) high.

STEP 2 Cut the hole out with a jigsaw. (If your door is hollow, you'll need to secure pieces of thin wood to the top, bottom, and sides of the hole with glue and brads.)

STEP 3 Measure a piece of continuous hinge to the width of your hole and cut it with tin shears.

STEP 4 Measure and cut a piece of lightweight acrylic to fit over the opening. Drill holes into the acrylic that line up with the holes in the hinge, then attach the hinge with 1/4-inch (6.35-mm) bolts and nuts.

STEP 5 Mount the hinge right above the hole on the inside, making sure that it swings freely in both directions.

STEP 6 To keep the door from swinging, mount a metal plate to the hole's bottom ledge. Drill a hole into the acrylic and insert a magnet.

Magnet closure

Acrylic

Continuous hinge

Metal

144 PUT TOGETHER A HOMEMADE WIND MILL

Kiss those high energy bills goodbye with a backyard wind turbine.

COST	$$$
TIME	⏲ ⏲ ⏲ ⏲
EASY	● ● ● ● ○ HARD

MATERIALS

Two precut round steel plates 2½ inches (6.35-cm) in diameter
Hole saw
1-inch (2.5-cm) steel tubing
Arc welder
1-inch- (2.5-cm-) thick plywood
Jigsaw
Drill
Screws and wingnuts
4-inch (10-cm) PVC pipe
Aluminum sheeting

Epoxy
¼-inch (6.35-mm) metal rods
Sprockets and chain
Salvaged alternator
Lazy Susan bearing
3-inch (7.5-cm) steel tubing
Charge controller
Four car batteries
DC/AC inverter
Power cord

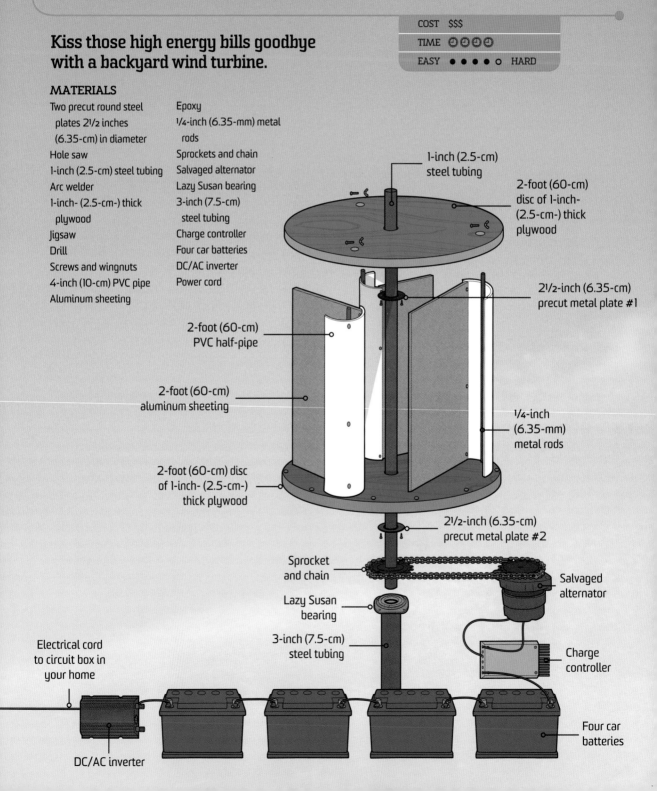

1-inch (2.5-cm) steel tubing

2-foot (60-cm) disc of 1-inch- (2.5-cm-) thick plywood

2½-inch (6.35-cm) precut metal plate #1

2-foot (60-cm) PVC half-pipe

2-foot (60-cm) aluminum sheeting

¼-inch (6.35-mm) metal rods

2-foot (60-cm) disc of 1-inch- (2.5-cm-) thick plywood

2½-inch (6.35-cm) precut metal plate #2

Sprocket and chain

Salvaged alternator

Lazy Susan bearing

3-inch (7.5-cm) steel tubing

Charge controller

Electrical cord to circuit box in your home

DC/AC inverter

Four car batteries

STEP 1 Using a hole saw, cut holes in the center of the steel plates that fit the 1-inch (2.5-cm) steel tubing.

STEP 2 Cut the steel tubing to 2 feet (60 cm) in length. Use an arc welder to connect it to the small plates, making an axle.

STEP 3 Using a jigsaw, cut the 1-inch- (2.5-cm-) thick plywood into two discs 2 feet (60 cm) in diameter. Drill a hole into their centers for the steel tubing. Slide the wood onto the axle, screwing the discs onto the steel plates.

STEP 4 Measure and cut sections of PVC pipe 2 feet (60 cm) in length; cut them into half-pipes.

STEP 5 Use a jigsaw to cut the aluminum sheeting into three sections 2 feet (60 cm) long and 1 foot (30 cm) wide.

STEP 6 Drill three evenly spaced holes into one edge of each PVC half-pipe and attach the aluminum sheeting with epoxy to form a J shape. Reinforce the J shapes with small screws.

STEP 7 Use epoxy to secure each J shape to the edges of the discs, with the flat face of the sheeting facing the axis.

STEP 8 Drill three holes in the wood discs so you can slide in metal rods at the center point of the half-pipes.

STEP 9 Weld a sprocket around the axle's end and a second sprocket to your alternator's spindle. Hook the two up with the chain.

STEP 10 Fit and weld the lazy Susan bearing to the top of the 3-inch (7.5-cm) steel tubing. Mount the entire assembly onto the lazy Susan bearing so it will swivel when the wind blows.

STEP 11 Hook your alternator to a charge controller, then connect its positive and negative lines to the first car battery. Connect all four car batteries in a row.

STEP 12 Hook the last car battery to DC/AC inverter, and then power your home's circuit box. Check with your local power-supply company for specifics, if needed.

145 HOOK UP A SOLAR CHARGER

Keep your gadgets powered even when you're off the grid.

MATERIALS

Plywood
Jigsaw
Drill
Nails
Hammer
Two 1-inch (2.5 cm) wood slats
5-watt, 12-volt solar panel
Hinge
Soldering iron and solder
1/4-inch (6.35-mm) plastic
  mono plug
Cigarette-lighter Y adapter
12-volt 12AH rechargeable
  battery
Solar DC charger controller
4 feet (1.2 m) of 18-gauge wire
15-amp DC panel meter
Two female terminal
  disconnects

STEP 1 Check online to discover your home's latitude. This is the angle at which you'll mount your solar panel.

STEP 2 Cut six pieces of plywood for the box. The lid should be slightly larger than the solar panel. Trim the top edges of the side, front, and back pieces to the appropriate angle. Cut the bottom to fit.

STEP 3 Drill a hole in each side panel for airflow: one in the back panel for the controller and battery cords, and one in the lid for the solar panel's cord. Then nail the wooden slats to the lid and mount the solar panel to it. Assemble the box with a hinge for the lid.

STEP 4 Snip off the cigarette-lighter plug and solder the 1/4-inch (6.35-mm) mono plug onto the Y adapter. Insert the mono plug into the controller's 12-volt output.

STEP 5 Connect all four power leads from the battery and the solar panel to the controller's input terminals. Hook up the 15-amp DC panel meter to the controller's input terminal for the panel.

STEP 6 Test all connections with the meter. Connect the red wire with a female-terminal disconnect to the battery's positive terminal, and connect the black wire to the negative terminal.

STEP 7 Place the station in the sun with the solar panel pointed south (north if you're in the southern hemisphere). Plug something in!

146 MAKE A GEODESIC DOME OUT OF PVC PIPE

COST	$$
TIME	☺ ☺ ☺
EASY	● ● ● ○ ○ HARD

It's a classic, and with good reason: It looks rad and is child's play to make.

Buckminster Fuller christened this structure in the 1940s, and it's been an icon ever since. You too can build its interlocking system of circles and triangles and know the glee of lightweight, modular housing.

MATERIALS

65 2-foot (60-cm) pieces of PVC pipe
Ten four-way pipe connectors
Six five-way pipe connectors
Ten six-way pipe connectors
Drill
130 3-inch (7.5-cm) bolt-and-nut sets
260 washers to fit the bolts
Four T-posts
Parachute
Ten bungee cords

STEP 1 Use ten lengths of pipe and the ten four-way connectors to hook together the circular base.

STEP 2 Fit two lengths of pipe into each four-way connector, pointing up. This should form triangles.

STEP 3 Hook five five-way and five six-way connectors, alternating the two types, to the tops of these triangles all around the first row of the dome.

STEP 4 Fit ten more lengths of PVC between these connectors, horizontally, for the second row of the dome.

STEP 5 Make another row of triangles by fitting 10 lengths of pipe into the upward-pointing openings of these connectors.

STEP 6 Connect five six-way connectors to the tops of these triangles.

STEP 7 Place 10 lengths of pipe horizontally between these connectors.

STEP 8 Position the last five lengths of pipe into these connectors so that they're pointing upward toward the top of the dome. Hook them into the last five-way connector.

STEP 9 If you like, remove one pipe near the bottom of the dome to create a doorway.

STEP 10 Drill holes through each connector and its pipes and secure these with washers, nuts, and bolts (with the bolts on the outside of the dome) to reinforce the frame. If you'd like to be able to take your dome down for transport, skip this step.

STEP 11 Drive four T-posts into the ground inside the dome so that they catch the bottom layer of pipe. This will add stability to the structure.

STEP 12 Cover the structure with a salvaged parachute or other piece of fabric, tying it to each of the bottom row's four-way connectors with bungee cords.

STEP 13 Decorate your geo dome and veg out.

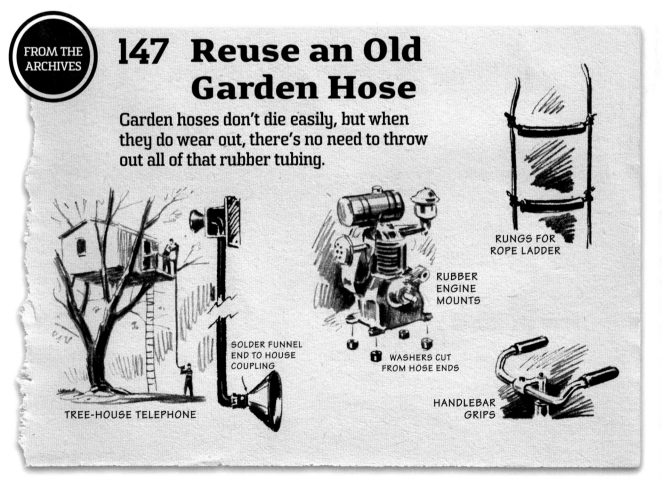

FROM THE ARCHIVES

147 Reuse an Old Garden Hose

Garden hoses don't die easily, but when they do wear out, there's no need to throw out all of that rubber tubing.

RUNGS FOR ROPE LADDER

RUBBER ENGINE MOUNTS

SOLDER FUNNEL END TO HOUSE COUPLING

WASHERS CUT FROM HOSE ENDS

TREE-HOUSE TELEPHONE

HANDLEBAR GRIPS

148 MAKE THE LAZY MAN'S MOWER

Mowing the lawn used to suck. Now it kind of rules.

Grass—it'd be great, if you didn't have to cut it. Luckily, you can rig this simple self-propelled lawnmower so it goes in a circle all on its own, doing most of the work for you while you enjoy a brewski on the porch.

COST	$$
TIME	☺☺
EASY ● ● ○ ○ ○ HARD	

MATERIALS

Lawnmower	Nails
Two rebar posts	Hammer
Drill	Twine
Wooden block	6-foot (1.8-m) wooden dowel
2x4	Clamps

STEP 1 Locate a good spot in your lawn with equal clearance on all sides so that the mower can go in a circle without running into any permanent fixtures.

STEP 2 Drill two holes into a large wooden block, and pound the rebar into the ground through those holes. Cap it off by nailing a 2x4 on top of the wooden block.

STEP 3 Measure and cut enough twine to reach the outer perimeter of the area you wish to mow, leaving a bit of excess.

STEP 4 Knot one end of the twine to one of the rebar posts in the ground.

STEP 5 Knot the other end to the mower and position it as far away from the posts as possible. The mower will work its way inward as it moves in circles, winding the twine around the posts as it goes.

STEP 6 Place a clamp on the mower's gas lever to keep it moving. Measure and cut a 6-foot (1.8-m) dowel and secure it to the clamp. If the mower gets too close to a structure, the dowel will knock off the clamp, and the engine will shut down.

A GOLF CART POWERED BY THE SPIRIT (AND ENGINE) OF A TRUCK

One day, Bill Rulien decided he'd had enough of people boasting about how they had modified their golf carts with hot-rod paint jobs or monster-truck tires. "I thought, I'm gonna build something that will say, 'Well, top this.'"

Rulien owns several golf-cart sales shops, so he had his choice of bodies. What he needed was a bigger engine. He picked out a cart that he'd been selling for parts and yanked the electric motor, transmission, and drivetrain. Then he bought an old truck for its V8 engine, drivetrain, steering, and transmission, and began cutting up its chassis to fit the tiny cart's body. He shortened the truck's driveshaft as well, but he still had to connect the two vehicles. With steel he had lying around, he fabricated a frame that joins the cart's body with the truck's chassis.

The finished cart clears 120 miles per hour (193 km/h) and can tear up even the deepest sand traps. Rulien is waiting until golf season to really push the vehicle, but it has already made an impression. When a truck driver eyed the beast, he declared, "Jeez, that's overkill!" And thus was she christened.

149 SET UP DIY GROW LIGHTS

Create a light system to keep houseplants thriving during winter's short days.

Setting up specialized grow lights that mimic the sun's rays is a good solution, but you can get similar results with LEDs. We connected three inside a clear plastic tube to make a "light spike" that you can stick into a pot for direct exposure, and added a controller that adjusts the brightness.

| COST | $$ |
| TIME | 🕐🕐 |
| EASY ● ● ● ○ ○ HARD |

MATERIALS

Project box
Drill
2.1-mm power-connector jack
10-position header
100k-ohm slide potentiometer
Soldering iron and solder
Electrical wire
10k-ohm resistor

Wire strippers
White LED design kit
Five clear plastic tubes with endcaps
Five two-position connectors
15-volt 1A wall-mount power supply

STEP 1 Drill six holes in your project box to accommodate the various components, then assemble the controller by mounting the power-connector jack inside the box and the 10-position header and the 100k-ohm slide potentiometer on the box's sides.

STEP 2 Wire the box according to the circuitry diagram.

STEP 3 Cut the wire inside the LED design kit into five equal lengths. Attach the red wire to the red connector, and the black wire to the black connector, on each LED strip. Slip each strip inside a clear tube, and seal it with the endcaps so that it's watertight.

STEP 4 Add the two-position connectors that will hook up the tubes and the box. Attach each one to the red and black wires from each LED strip.

STEP 5 Press a spike into your plant container. Keep all wiring, electrical connections, and the LED strips away from soil and moisture.

STEP 6 Plug the spikes' two-position connectors into the control box's 10-position header, and connect the power supply to turn the LEDs on.

STEP 7 Adjust the slide potentiometer to control the brightness of the spikes, and watch your garden grow.

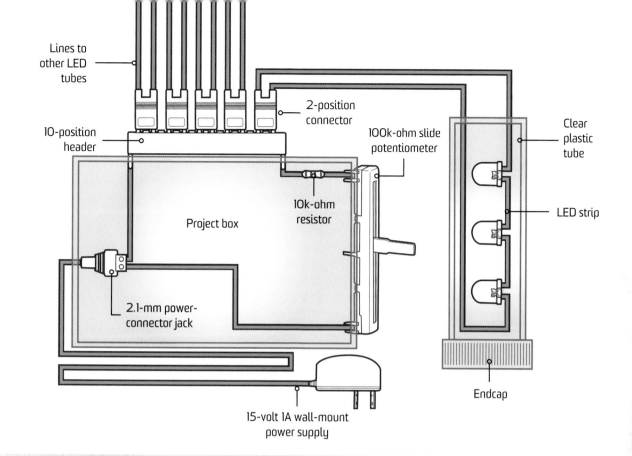

Lines to other LED tubes

10-position header

2-position connector

100k-ohm slide potentiometer

Clear plastic tube

LED strip

10k-ohm resistor

Project box

2.1-mm power-connector jack

Endcap

15-volt 1A wall-mount power supply

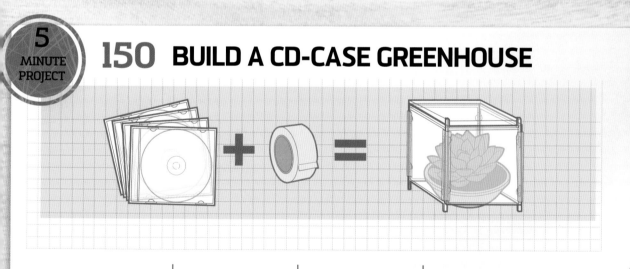

150 BUILD A CD-CASE GREENHOUSE

STEP 1 Remove the front panels from three plastic CD cases.

STEP 2 Tape the three plastic panels together to make a box with three sides.

STEP 3 Open a fourth CD case and tape it to the box to make the last side and a lid with a functioning hinge.

STEP 4 Place it over a small plant and set in the sun.

151 THE ULTIMATE SNOWBLOWER

Keep your driveway clear of the white stuff with this eight-cylinder blaster.

When Kai Grundt announced he was building a snowblower from a discarded V8 engine, a friend just laughed. So a year later, instead of showing him the finished product, Grundt showed him what it could do. He buried the man's truck under 7 feet (2 m) of snow. From two houses away.

Since Grundt, a metal fabricator in Muskoka, Ontario, started with the huge engine from his old Chevy truck, he knew power wouldn't be a problem. The problem would be making the 800-pound (362-kg) machine easy to handle. He didn't want the snowblower racing away when he revved the blades that suck up the snow—the V8's crankshaft spins them up to 6,200 rpm—so he chose to run its tank-like tracks via a different system. Powered by the 412-horsepower V8, a hydraulic pump feeds a pair of hydraulic motors that each turn one track. This allows him to give the blades a boost while keeping the machine moving at a safe pace.

Moving snow can be a frigid business, so Grundt installed a remote-start system to get the machine warmed up before he steps outside. The blower doubles as a heater, too. He faced the engine's radiator toward the back; an electric fan blows excess heat right at his legs.

And what about noise control? Twin custom-designed pipes ensure that there's no exhaust streaming into the driver's face during operation. Grundt also gave the pipes a series of interior channels that reroute and slow down the expelled air, dampening the noise. Cutting down on the decibel level also keeps the neighbors happy.

THAR SHE BLOWS
Using controls built into the handlebars, Grundt can turn one track forward and the other in reverse, spinning the rig in place. These handlebars are hollow, and the coolant fluid flows through them, keeping his hands toasty.

GADGET UPGRADES

152 RIG A DIY POLYGRAPH TEST

If you suspect somebody's putting you on, monitor him with a lie detector test.

COST	$
TIME	⏱
EASY ● ● ● ○ ○ HARD	

MATERIALS

Scissors
Adhesive Velcro
Aluminum foil
Electrical wire
Wire strippers
Arduino UNO
10k-ohm resistor
USB cable

STEP 1 With scissors, cut a strip of Velcro and a strip of aluminum foil so that they are equal in length and long enough to wrap around a finger.

STEP 2 Strip the end of a piece of wire, put it on the foil's center, and place the adhesive Velcro on top to secure it, sandwiching the wire between the foil and the Velcro.

STEP 3 Flip the foil over and adhere a small piece of Velcro to this side, so that you can secure it around a finger with the aluminum foil inside—this is an electrode. Repeat this process so you have two electrodes.

STEP 4 Wire the electrodes to the Arduino UNO according to the circuitry diagram.

STEP 5 Connect the Arduino to your computer using the USB cable. Then download the "Graph" code found at popsci.com/thebigbookofhacks onto the Arduino, and run the processing program on your computer.

STEP 6 Find a person you want answers from. Put the electrodes on one finger of each of the person's hands.

STEP 7 A graph pops up. The more the person sweats, the more conductive his skin becomes, and the higher the line of the graph goes. Skyrocketing right along with it, of course, is the likelihood that he is lying.

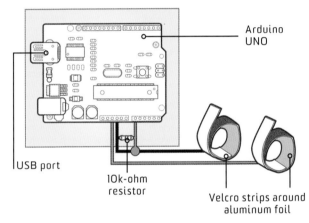

Arduino UNO

USB port

10k-ohm resistor

Velcro strips around aluminum foil

153 LISTEN IN WITH A FOXHOLE RADIO

When your radio is dead, this throwback device will do the trick.

Prisoners of war once cobbled together these makeshift radios so they could get the news. Now you can use one to pick up that final radio station that hasn't started online streaming yet.

MATERIALS

Large safety pin
Toilet-paper tube
Magnet wire
Wood pencil stub
Stripped cat 6 cable for
    antenna and ground
Radiator or metal coat hanger
Wood board
Metal thumbtacks
Blued or rusty razor blade
Earphones

STEP 1 Use a safety pin to poke a hole in the toilet-paper tube, and secure the magnet wire to the tube by tying one end through the hole.

STEP 2 Create a coil by wrapping the magnet wire tightly around the tube 120 times, making sure that the wire is packed closely together as it coils. The number of coils affects what radio stations you'll pick up, so experiment with their arrangement if you aren't hearing your desired station clearly.

STEP 3 Make a "cat whisker" by poking the safety pin into the graphite of a pencil stub's dull end.

STEP 4 Hang the antenna cable far out the window and attach a ground cable to a metal radiator inside your home. If you don't have a radiator, attach the ground cable to a metal coat hanger and stick it in the ground outside.

STEP 5 Place the toilet-paper tube and a blued razor blade onto the wood board and push in two thumbtacks next to the tube and two next to the razor blade. Wrap the antenna wire around the components according to the diagram, twisting wires together when excess is needed.

STEP 6 Peel back the insulation on your headphones' audio jack. Use stripped wire to connect the safety pin in the pencil to one of the audio jack's wires, and connect the other wire to the ground.

STEP 7 Don your earphones, and touch the pencil lead to the razor blade. Move the pencil until you pick up the smooth tunes you desire.

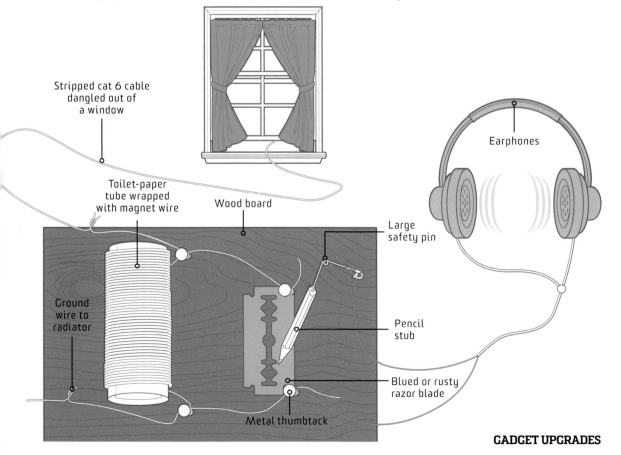

Stripped cat 6 cable dangled out of a window

Toilet-paper tube wrapped with magnet wire

Wood board

Earphones

Ground wire to radiator

Large safety pin

Pencil stub

Blued or rusty razor blade

Metal thumbtack

154 TACK UP A DIPOLE ANTENNA

STEP 1 Use wire cutters and pliers to snip a coat hanger and stretch it into a length of about 52 inches (132 cm).

STEP 2 Make a small U-shaped loop on each end of the coat hanger's wires. Sand the loops to remove paint or coating.

STEP 3 Cut a piece of plywood to 1 inch (2.5 cm) in width and 1 foot (30 cm) in length. Screw two ½-inch (1.25-cm) sheet-metal screws about ¼ inch (6.35 mm) into the wood.

STEP 4 Hook the U-shaped wire loops around the screws.

STEP 5 Slide the U-shaped tabs of a 75- to 300-ohm matching transformer under the metal screws on the plywood, one per screw. Tighten the screws until the wire ends and the transformer tabs are held together against the wood.

STEP 6 To connect a coaxial cable, screw the cable's F-type connector into the transformer.

STEP 7 Connect the coaxial cable to the FM radio, turn the receiver on, and position the antenna for the best signal.

STEP 8 Use a mounting bracket and screws to mount the antenna where it works the best.

155 CRAFT A CELL-PHONE "CANTENNA"

STEP 1 Use a can opener to remove the bottom of a lidless, empty can that's 4 inches (10 cm) in diameter.

STEP 2 Solder the open end of another lidless, empty can to the first can. The total height should come to 1 foot (30 cm).

STEP 3 Solder a short piece of copper wire to an antenna connector, and drill a hole for it 3¾ inches (9.5 cm) from the closed end of the cylinder. Secure it in place with a nut on the inside.

STEP 4 Screw a passive antenna adapter cord to the antenna connector.

STEP 5 Attach the adapter cord to the back of your phone. (Don't have a smartphone? Try a basic pigtail adapter—choose one that works for your specific phone.)

STEP 6 Enjoy improved reception. Hear what people have to say for a change.

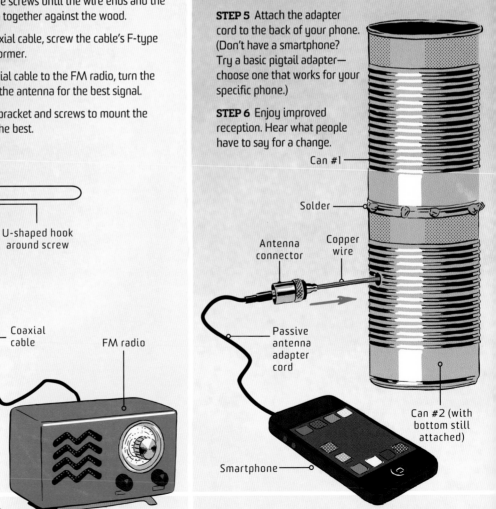

Hanger

U-shaped hook around screw

75- to 300-ohm matching transformer

Coaxial cable

FM radio

Plywood strip

Mounting bracket

Can #1

Solder

Antenna connector

Copper wire

Passive antenna adapter cord

Can #2 (with bottom still attached)

Smartphone

156 BOOST WI-FI WITH A STEAMER

STEP 1 Use tin snips to remove the steamer's center post and to make a hole about 1/2 inch (1.25 cm) long for the USB modem's connector end.

STEP 2 Insert the USB modem into the hole with the connector end facing downward. Superglue it in place and let it dry.

STEP 3 Zip-tie two sets of two of the steamer's leaves together so that all the leaves stay open.

STEP 4 Plug the USB modem's connector end into the USB extension cable, and plug the other end of the extension cable into your laptop's ethernet portal.

STEP 5 Start picking up Wi-Fi signals from far, far away.

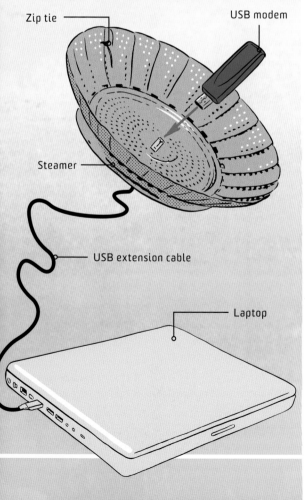

Zip tie

USB modem

Steamer

USB extension cable

Laptop

157 HANG HDTV-ANTENNA ART

STEP 1 Strip 14-gauge copper wire, then cut and bend it into eight V-shaped pieces. Place these wires onto a picture frame so that the peaks of the V shapes are 5 3/4 inches (14.5 cm) apart, then drill a small hole on each side of both V ends.

STEP 2 Strip 22-gauge enameled wire, then attach the V shapes to the frame by threading the enameled wire through one of the holes, crossing it over the copper wire, pulling it through the second hole, and twisting it in back.

STEP 3 Cut two lengths of copper wire to 20 inches (50 cm) in length, then bend them as shown. Lay them down the center of the picture frame so that they are 2 inches (5 cm) apart.

STEP 4 Attach the two vertical wires to the V-shaped pieces with more stripped enameled wire. Make a hole on each side of the two vertical wires' ends, then attach them to the frame as you attached the V-shaped pieces.

STEP 5 Wrap stripped enameled wire around the main vertical wires where they are bent so that they nearly touch.

STEP 7 Solder two pieces of stripped enameled wire to the bottom vertical copper wires. Connect these two wires to the matching transformer, and then connect the transformer to your TV using a coaxial cable.

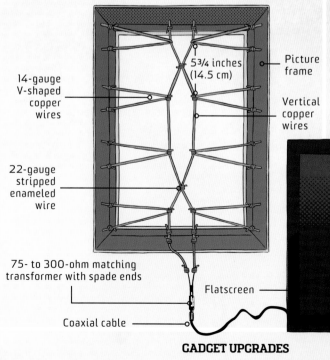

5 3/4 inches (14.5 cm)

Picture frame

14-gauge V-shaped copper wires

Vertical copper wires

22-gauge stripped enameled wire

75- to 300-ohm matching transformer with spade ends

Flatscreen

Coaxial cable

Left button

Foam gasket

Right button

Left thumbstick

Face buttons

Home button under face button

Smartphone

Holes for speaker

Audio cord concealed inside here

Bottom plate

Female audio jack hidden in battery compartment

Charger cord concealed inside here

Xbox 360 controller

158 MOD AN XBOX 360 CONTROLLER INTO A SMARTPHONE CASE

Why choose between gaming on a smartphone and gaming on a console?

If you've gotten addicted to the feel of a controller in your hands, this smartphone case mod is for you. The phone's home button is cleverly concealed behind one of the face buttons, and both the charging and audio cords are neatly concealed inside the controller shell.

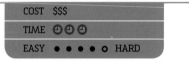

COST	$$$
TIME	⏲ ⏲ ⏲
EASY ● ● ● ● ○ HARD	

MATERIALS

Xbox 360 controller
Torx screwdriver
Phillips screwdriver
Smartphone
Rotary tool
Scissors
Superglue

Foam
3.5-mm audio-jack extension cable
Smartphone wall charger with USB cable
Pliers

STEP 1 Turn over your controller and pull off the battery compartment's plastic cover. Peel away the serial-number sticker inside the battery compartment case and use the Torx screwdriver to remove the screw underneath it.

STEP 2 Remove the other screws on the controller's back. Lift the back off, and remove the bottom plate.

STEP 3 Lift out the circuit board. The thumbsticks, triggers (the buttons on the back below the left and right bumper buttons), and rumble pack motors (the cylindrical bits that dangle) will come right out with it.

STEP 4 Peel away the rubber pads that were behind the circuit board. Then turn the controller upside down and let all the buttons fall out.

STEP 5 Turn the controller back over and remove the screws on the directional pad. Use a screwdriver to release

159 MAKE A PHONE "BOUNCEABLE"

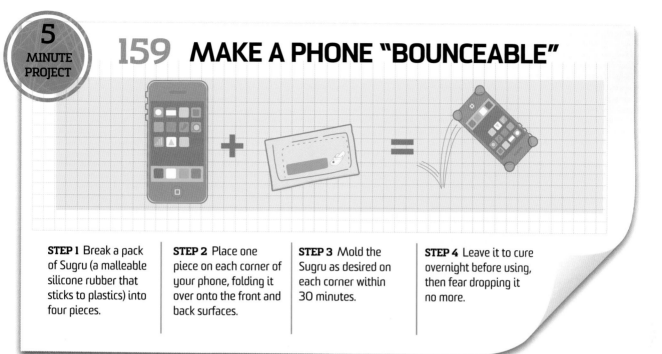

STEP 1 Break a pack of Sugru (a malleable silicone rubber that sticks to plastics) into four pieces.

STEP 2 Place one piece on each corner of your phone, folding it over onto the front and back surfaces.

STEP 3 Mold the Sugru as desired on each corner within 30 minutes.

STEP 4 Leave it to cure overnight before using, then fear dropping it no more.

the tabs in the directional pad's center. Then remove the directional pad's front and back.

STEP 6 Pull the top shelf (the upper part with the right and left bumper buttons) off the circuit board.

STEP 7 To pry the triggers from the circuit board, apply pressure to the long rod and pop up the triggers, then pinch their sides, pull out the springs, and turn them gently to pry them free. Pull the left thumbstick off the circuit board while you're at it.

STEP 8 Turn your attention to the controller. Measure a space to fit your smartphone inside it so that your smartphone's home key is as close as possible to a button on the controller. (This may be the green button, or it may be the left thumbstick.) Cut out this hole with a rotary tool.

STEP 9 Use a rotary tool to drill multiple small holes in the controller over your smartphone's speakers.

STEP 10 Use scissors to cut the rubber pad that was behind the face buttons, only leaving contacts for functioning buttons. (In the case of an iPhone, this is the green button.) Reinstall the rubber pad inside the console shell with the functioning button lined up with its contact.

STEP 11 Glue all the nonfunctioning buttons back in place, along with the left thumbstick.

STEP 12 Measure and cut foam to pad the inside of the controller's upper shell, with a window the same size

as your smartphone's screen. Glue the foam inside the console's hole.

STEP 13 Use a rotary tool to drill a hole in the bottom of the battery compartment. It should be big enough for the female end of your audio jack to stick out.

STEP 14 Drill a second hole in the inside wall of the battery compartment that's large enough so you can thread through the audio jack's male plug. Pull the male end through this hole and into the main compartment.

STEP 15 Use a rotary tool to cut another hole in the battery compartment's back wall, this time large enough to fit the USB end of the smartphone's charger cable.

STEP 16 Use a rotary tool to remove the plastic casing from the smartphone's charging cable, reducing its size so it will fit inside the controller. Glue this end inside the controller's main compartment, oriented so it will plug into your phone. Then thread the USB end through to the battery compartment and coil the cord.

STEP 17 Place your smartphone inside the shell, attaching it to the charging socket and plugging the male end of the audio jack into its audio input.

STEP 18 Close the upper shell over the smartphone and secure with screws.

STEP 19 Use your phone as you normally would, and watch people do a double take.

160 Build a Hands-Free Phone

Ever wonder what people did before speakerphone? They built this gadget, which lets you hang up and still hear.

MATERIALS

Perfboard
A-4705 microphone-to-grid transformer
A-3329 output transformer
Microphone
2-inch (5-cm) magnet speaker
Two CK721 transistors
0.01-mF ceramic capacitor
5-mF, 8-volt midget electrolytic capacitor
1-megohm carbon resistor
75k-ohm carbon resistor

Four AA batteries and holder
On/off switch
Electrical wire
Metal panel for electrical grounding
Wood paneling
Foam rubber
Glue
Screws
Soldering iron and solder
Saw
Screwdriver
Rotary tool

STEP 1 Assemble the electronics on the perfboard according to the circuitry diagram. Leave wire so you can later attach the on/off switch, speaker, and microphone.

STEP 2 Measure and cut wood to form the sides and bottom of a box that's large enough to fit the perfboard, then secure the box with wood glue and line the interior with foam rubber to act as a sound insulator. Glue in place.

STEP 3 Use a rotary tool to make holes on the box's sides for the speaker and on/off switch.

STEP 4 Place the assembled electronics in the box and secure the perfboard with screws. Thread the speaker and on/off switch to their openings on the sides of the box, and screw or glue them into place.

STEP 5 Cut paneling to form the box's lid, shaped to fit your phone's handset. Cut holes for the mouthpiece and earpiece.

STEP 6 Cut and glue foam rubber so that the earpiece and mouthpiece fit the lid snugly. (These pieces will insulate against outside sound and feedback.)

STEP 7 Mount the lid on top of the box and glue the microphone into the opening for the earpiece under the foam rubber.

STEP 8 Place the setup near your phone. When you receive a call, place the handset on top of the box with the phone's earpiece next to the microphone. Then go about your business while Aunt Marge rattles on.

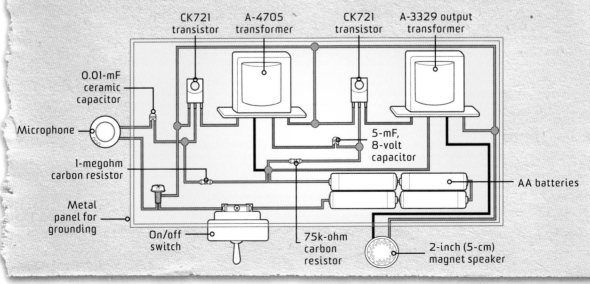

161 MAKE A REMOTE DISPLAY FOR YOUR COMPUTER

This stylish DIY display scrolls scores, news, weather, and anything else your computer feeds it.

COST	$$
TIME	⏱ ⏱ ⏱
EASY ● ● ● ● ○ HARD	

MATERIALS

Lithium-polymer ion battery
100-mAh lithium-polymer charger
Soldering iron and solder
Electrical wire
5-volt DC-to-DC step-up circuit
On/off switch
Bluetooth modem
1-by-16-character vacuum fluorescent display (VFD)
Custom case (such as a vintage radio case)
LCD Smartie software

STEP 1 Set your soldering iron to below 350°F (176°C). Solder the lithium-polymer ion battery to the charger.

STEP 2 Solder the lithium-polymer charger's output to the input of the 5-volt DC-to-DC step-up circuit. Solder an on/off switch to the step-up circuit for controlling power.

STEP 3 Connect the step-up circuit's positive and negative terminals to the Bluetooth modem and the 1-by-16-character display. Then connect the Bluetooth modem's TTL serial output to the VFD's TTL serial input.

STEP 4 Build a box to your liking, using a salvaged radio case or pieces of scrap wood.

STEP 5 Use your computer's Bluetooth software for pairing and connecting the computer to the Bluetooth modem. Set the Bluetooth port for 9600, 8, N, and 1 communication parameters.

STEP 6 Download LCD Smartie. Select the test display device driver, and enter the Bluetooth COM port number and communication parameters. Set the screen size to 1-by-16-characters and apply your changes to LCD Smartie.

STEP 7 Choose the data that you want to stream and go about your business. Just stay within 50 feet (15 m) of your computer to ensure a Bluetooth wireless connection.

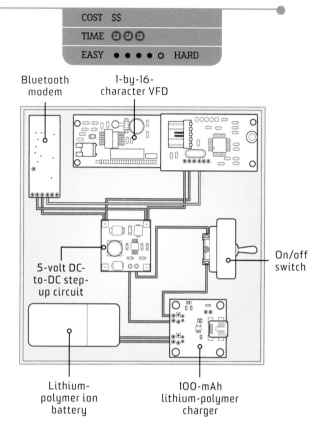

Bluetooth modem
1-by-16-character VFD
On/off switch
5-volt DC-to-DC step-up circuit
Lithium-polymer ion battery
100-mAh lithium-polymer charger

You have 1 email

Beam your phone's image onto a wall for an instant big screen.

COST	$$
TIME	⏱
EASY ● ● ○ ○ ○ HARD	

MATERIALS

Narrow cardboard box
Box cutter
Fresnel lens
Audio cord
Speakers
Hot-glue gun
Modeling clay
Smartphone

STEP 1 Start with a narrow cardboard box (a shoebox does just fine) and cut a hole that's a little smaller than your Fresnel lens into one of the smaller ends.

STEP 2 Poke a smaller hole into the opposite end of the box that's big enough to allow you to run the audio cord from your phone to the speakers.

STEP 3 Using the hot-glue gun, firmly adhere the Fresnel lens over the larger hole inside the box.

STEP 4 Place modeling clay on the side of your smartphone, then position it on that side inside the box with the screen facing the lens. (The modeling clay helps to stabilize your phone in the box, but you can still adjust its position to get a better picture.)

STEP 5 Select your entertainment of choice, then set your phone's preferences to display in landscape orientation.

STEP 6 Connect your phone to the speakers, threading the audio cord through the smaller hole.

STEP 7 Close up the box, aim the lens at a blank wall, and switch off the lights. Then grab some Milk Duds and kick back with a downloaded movie or the latest episode of *The Daily Show*. Your screen should display at a nice 8¹/₂ by 11 inches (22 by 28 cm).

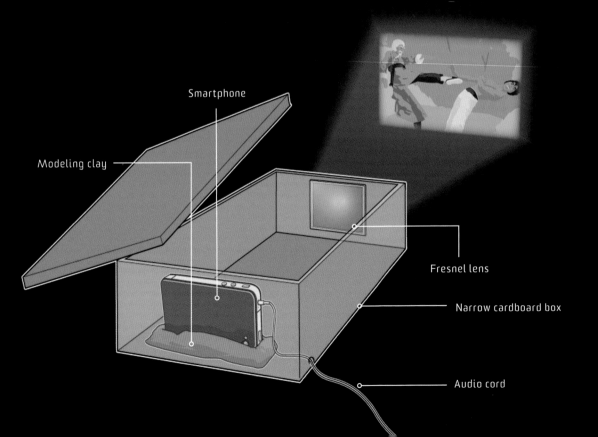

Smartphone

Modeling clay

Fresnel lens

Narrow cardboard box

Audio cord

163 CHARGE A PHONE WITH SOLAR RAYS

Harness the sun's rays to keep your phone juiced on the go.

MATERIALS

Two 3-volt, 20-mA mini solar panels
Wire strippers
Small heat-shrink tubing
Heat gun
Soldering iron and solder
Cell-phone charger
Large heat-shrink tubing
Double-sided tape
Mint tin

STEP 1 Cut the wires on both mini solar panels to 1 inch (2.5 cm) in length; strip ¼ inch (6.35 mm) of the plastic coating off each wire.

STEP 2 Cut the small heat-shrink tubing into four 1-inch (2.5-cm) pieces. Cover the solar panels' two positive wires with the tubing; heat to shrink with the heat gun.

STEP 3 Solder the negative lead of one solar panel to the positive lead of the other. Cover with a piece of small tubing; heat to shrink with the heat gun.

STEP 4 Cut off 2.5 feet (75 cm) from your charger cord. Strip 2.5 inches (6.35 cm) from the loose end.

STEP 5 Cut ¼ inch (6.35 mm) off the wires inside the cord to make leads. Cover with the large tubing; heat.

STEP 6 Solder the negative leads of the charger cord wires and the solar panels together; repeat with the positive leads. Slide large tubing over them and heat.

STEP 7 Cover the backs of the solar panels with double-sided tape; secure them inside the tin.

STEP 8 Tuck the wires into the tin and close it. To use, open up the tin and let the solar panels juice up.

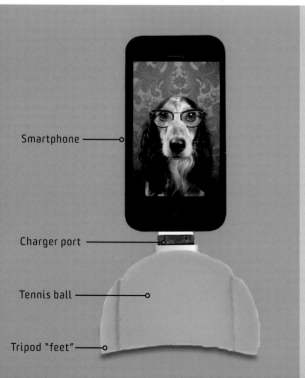

Smartphone

Charger port

Tennis ball

Tripod "feet"

164 MAKE A SMART-PHONE TRIPOD

Take steady smartphone shots with a sporty improvised tripod.

STEP 1 Cut a tennis ball in half.

STEP 2 With a pen, mark three "feet" on the bottom. (These will allow the tennis-ball half to balance.) There should be about 2 inches (5 cm) between each foot.

STEP 3 Cut slight arches between the tripod feet.

STEP 4 Make a slit in the top of the tennis ball and insert a charger port.

STEP 5 Plug your phone into the port and snap away.

165 TURN YOUR OLD NETBOOK INTO A TOUCHSCREEN TABLET

Forget dropping big bucks on a fancy new tablet—just hack your own.

COST	$$
TIME	🕐🕑
EASY ● ● ● ○ ○ HARD	

MATERIALS

Netbook
Screwdriver
Putty knife
Touchscreen overlay
Epoxy

Moldable silicone, if needed
Flash drive
Keyboard
Mouse
Retractable stylus

STEP 1 Turn off and unplug your netbook, then use a screwdriver to remove its bezel and the display's backing so that the LCD panel and its cables are exposed. Then remove the keyboard and trackpad. (This may involve removing screws from the base of the netbook and prying off the top case with a flat tool, such as a putty knife.)

STEP 2 Place the netbook's exposed LCD panel over the area where the keyboard and trackpad used to be, taking care to avoid damaging the panel's cables. Don't cover any areas that the netbook uses for ventilation.

STEP 3 Remove the paper on the back of the touchscreen overlay to reveal the adhesive backing. Place it over the LCD panel.

STEP 4 Plug the touchscreen overlay's USB cable into the netbook's USB port. It will be either an internal port on the motherboard, or an external port as on most computers.

STEP 5 Reattach the bezel to the front of the converted netbook with epoxy. If parts of the bezel cover the touchscreen, remove them before reattaching. If there is too much space between the bezel and the base of the netbook tablet, fill the gap with moldable silicone, sealing the two parts together. Let dry for 24 hours.

STEP 6 Copy the drivers that came with the touchscreen overlay onto a flash drive and plug the drive into the newly modified netbook tablet. Connect a keyboard and mouse to the tablet and install the drivers.

STEP 7 Run the calibration tool and use the stylus to calibrate the touchscreen overlay.

STEP 8 Touch away on your new ad hoc touchscreen tablet, and chuckle at suckers who spent a bundle on a brand-new one.

Netbook base with keyboard and trackpad removed

Screen bezel

LCD panel covered with touchscreen overlay

🐟 ×50

166 FASHION A DIY STYLUS FOR YOUR TOUCHSCREEN DEVICE

Cobble together a stylus and keep your greasy fingers off that tablet.

MATERIALS

Small scissors

Conductive foam

2-mm drafting lead holder

Plastic ink tube from a ballpoint pen

STEP 1 Use the small scissors to cut a piece of conductive foam to a cube shape about ¼ inch (6.35 mm) in length on all sides.

STEP 2 Trim the conductive foam down further to create a rounded tip.

STEP 4 Drop the piece of foam into the lead holder and use the plastic ink tube from a ballpoint pen to push the foam down until it protrudes just out of the tip of the holder. Discard the ink tube.

STEP 5 Pinch the holder's tip to secure the foam in place. Try it out on a tablet near you.

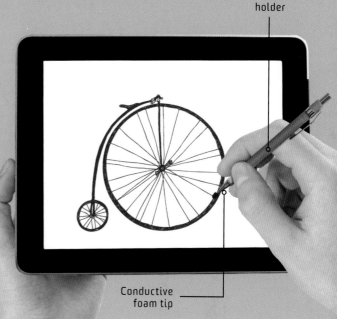

Drafting lead holder

Conductive foam tip

---

5 MINUTE PROJECT

167 PROTECT YOUR TOUCHSCREEN WITH THIN VINYL

STEP 1 Measure and cut a piece of thin, nonadhesive vinyl sheeting to cover the phone's touchscreen.

STEP 2 Wipe away any dust on the vinyl and on your phone's screen.

STEP 3 Line up the vinyl with the touchscreen and slowly apply it, smoothing out air bubbles as you press it down.

168 STASH A FLASH DRIVE IN A CASSETTE

STEP 1 Using a small screwdriver, pry off the USB drive's plastic casing.

STEP 2 Decide where you want the flash drive to poke out of the cassette. Then trace the flash drive's connector end onto that spot.

STEP 3 Remove the small screws holding the cassette together with the small screwdriver.

STEP 4 Cut out the traced area with a rotary tool.

STEP 5 Wind the tape so that it's on the spool farther away from the hole for the flash drive.

STEP 6 Tape the flash drive down inside the cassette with electrical tape so that its end sticks out through the hole.

STEP 7 Reassemble the cassette, load up the flash drive with a playlist of songs, then gift it as a throwback "mix tape."

169 MAKE A PINK-ERASER FLASH DRIVE

STEP 1 Remove the flash drive's plastic casing.

STEP 2 Find two erasers of the pink, parallelogram variety. Cut off the end of one, starting where the end begins to slant down. Cut the other to roughly one-third the original length.

STEP 3 Use a craft knife to hollow out both erasers. Test to make sure the flash drive fits nicely.

STEP 4 Stick the drive inside the larger eraser, then cap it off with the smaller one. There you have it: a discreet flash drive that holds your top-secret documents—almost as if they've been "erased."

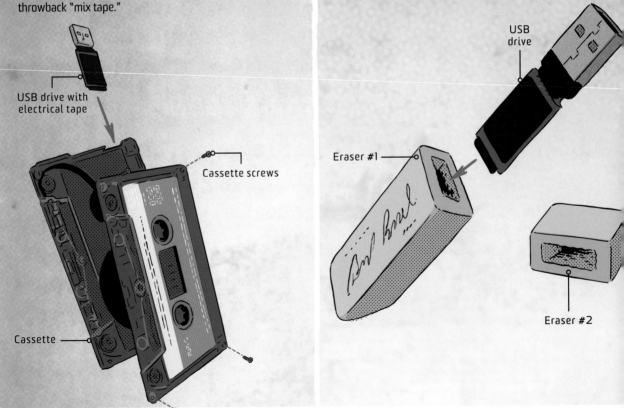

USB drive with electrical tape

Cassette screws

Cassette

USB drive

Eraser #1

Eraser #2

170 FAKE IT WITH A SAWED-OFF FLASH DRIVE

STEP 1 Peel off the plastic cover of the USB drive. (It helps to pick a flash drive that's on the smaller side.)

STEP 2 Use a craft knife to make deep cuts in the casing along both sides of the connective end of a USB cord, piercing to the metal shell underneath. Peel off the plastic casing to get at the inner parts.

STEP 3 Use a small screwdriver to pry apart the metal shell. Remove the "lid."

STEP 4 Underneath this lid are a few wires and miscellaneous plastic bits. They're in your way, so go ahead and cut them out with a craft knife.

STEP 5 Grab the flash drive, and protect its back (where there are metal parts that require insulation) with electrical tape.

STEP 6 Apply epoxy to the inside of the opening you've made in the end of the cord, then slide the USB drive inside.

STEP 7 Hack the cord, fray the wires as desired, and plug it into your computer. Await sounds of horror.

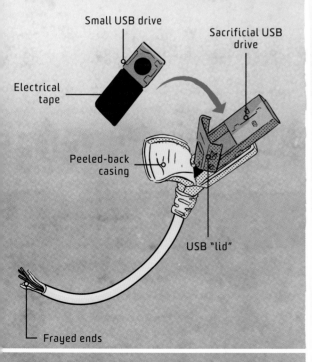

Small USB drive

Electrical tape

Sacrificial USB drive

Peeled-back casing

USB "lid"

Frayed ends

171 HOUSE A FLASH DRIVE IN A LEGO

STEP 1 Peel off the plastic casing on the flash drive.

STEP 2 Find a LEGO brick large enough to house the drive (a 2x6 one is ideal). Using a rotary tool, scrape out the brick's insides.

STEP 3 Measure the USB connector to get the dimensions that you'll need for the hole in the LEGO. Keep in mind that the hole should fit the USB snugly, allowing the business end to protrude and plug into your computer.

STEP 4 Draw a rectangle of these dimensions against the small end of the brick. Cut the shape out with a rotary tool.

STEP 5 Use the rotary tool to remove the top from a second LEGO of the same size and color.

STEP 6 Tape the flash drive to the top's underside with electrical tape.

STEP 7 Glue the LEGO top to the hollowed-out LEGO, allowing the USB connector to stick out the end.

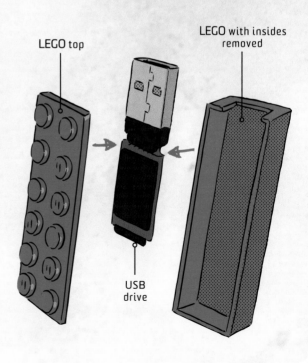

LEGO top

LEGO with insides removed

USB drive

HACK A FOOT-OPERATED MOUSE

Take some strain off the old wrist with a funny foot-powered mouse.

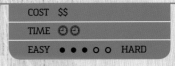

COST	$$
TIME	☺ ☺
EASY	● ● ● ○ ○ HARD

MATERIALS

½-inch (1.25-cm) PVC sheet
Bedroom slippers
Two roller lever switches
Optical mouse
Rotary tool
Small hand file
Soldering iron and solder
Electrical wire
Metal brackets
Nuts, bolts, and washers
Screwdriver
Metal wire
Screws and nails
7 feet (2 m) of ¾-inch (1.9-cm) clear plastic tubing
Rubber doorstops

STEP 1 On the PVC sheet, position and trace your slippers the way your feet would rest while you're seated. Mark places for the left- and right-click roller lever switches near the left slipper, where your foot will operate the mouse, then outline the mouse slightly to the left of the right slipper's top.

STEP 2 Using the rotary tool, channel out holes for the roller lever switches and a hole for the mouse. Use the file to smooth the edges of the holes.

STEP 3 Remove the mouse's top cover from the base. Lift out the circuit board and remove the scroll wheel.

STEP 4 On the bottom of the circuit board, locate where the mouse's switches once connected to its buttons. Solder a length of electrical wire to each of the mouse's outboard solder connections.

STEP 5 Put the circuit board back inside the mouse cover. Solder the lead wires from the outboard solder connections to the left and right roller lever switches—the wire from the original left-click switch to the new left switch, and the right to the right.

STEP 6 Secure two metal brackets to the mouse with two nuts, bolts, and washers. Screw the brackets into the underside of the PVC sheet so that the mouse is belly up.

STEP 7 Thread small pieces of metal wire through the mounting holes in each roller lever switch. Bend the ends and use nails to secure the switches under the PVC sheet.

STEP 8 Screw plastic tubing around the edges of the PVC sheet and in between where your feet go to create bumpers that help guide your feet.

STEP 9 Trim four rubber doorstops to work as risers, propping the PVC sheet up off the floor and providing clearance for the mouse. Screw one to each corner of the footboard.

STEP 10 Plug the mouse's USB connector into your computer and scroll with your feet.

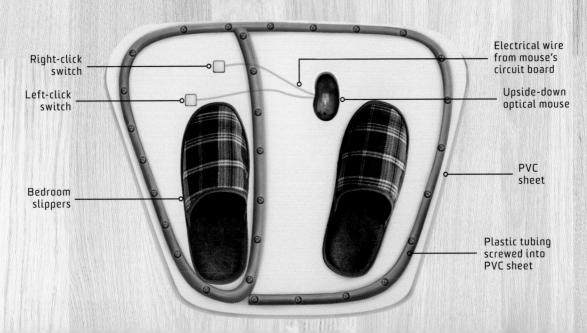

Right-click switch

Left-click switch

Bedroom slippers

Electrical wire from mouse's circuit board

Upside-down optical mouse

PVC sheet

Plastic tubing screwed into PVC sheet

173 TRICK OUT YOUR COMPUTER TOWER WITH ENGRAVING

This is one tower mod that doesn't belong hidden under your desk.

MATERIALS

Paper and pencil or printer
Computer tower
Screwdriver
Spray paint
Plexiglas sheet
Masking tape

Safety goggles
Rotary tool
Small engraving bits
Screws and bolts
Fluorescent strip, if needed

STEP 1 Draw or print your design on a sheet of paper to fit the tower's side panel.

STEP 2 Unscrew the metal side panel from your computer tower and set it aside for later.

STEP 3 Spray-paint a sheet of Plexiglas with a color to match your case so only the engraved design will be visible later. Let dry.

STEP 4 Tape the drawn or printed design onto your Plexiglas sheet, being sure to tape it over the painted side.

STEP 5 Put on your safety goggles and, using the rotary tool, begin engraving. Follow the lines of your design on the paper and etch it on the Plexiglas beneath. Work carefully and slowly to avoid ruining your design.

STEP 6 Remove the taped-on template and wipe down the engraved Plexiglas.

STEP 7 Measure and cut a hole slightly smaller than your Plexiglas in the metal panel.

STEP 8 Drill four holes into the corners of the Plexiglas and the case. Attach the etched panel to the metal frame with screws small enough that it will fit inside the case.

STEP 9 If your machine lacks a fluorescent strip, install one, either plugging it into the power supply or directly to the circuit board. (Which you choose depends on the bulb you've purchased, and what sort of machine you have.)

STEP 10 Use the original bolts and screws to reattach the metal panel with the Plexiglas inside the tower.

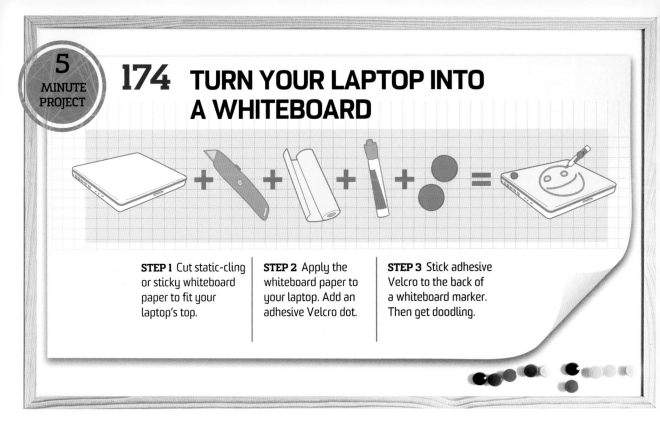

174 TURN YOUR LAPTOP INTO A WHITEBOARD

STEP 1 Cut static-cling or sticky whiteboard paper to fit your laptop's top.

STEP 2 Apply the whiteboard paper to your laptop. Add an adhesive Velcro dot.

STEP 3 Stick adhesive Velcro to the back of a whiteboard marker. Then get doodling.

175 DYE YOUR LAPTOP

Fight the monotony of boring case colors with a laptop dye job.

MATERIALS

White plastic laptop
Small screwdriver
Sandpaper
Denatured alcohol
Paper towel

Rubber gloves
Deep pan
8 cups (2 L) water
Fabric dye
2 tablespoons table salt

STEP 1 Carefully take apart your laptop. You'll likely need a small screwdriver to remove the screws that hold the case, battery, and other parts in place. Separate the plastic parts (the ones you'll be dyeing) from the metal and electronic parts.

STEP 2 Sand down the plastic pieces to remove the glossy layer, which prevents dye from absorbing quickly and evenly. Leave it if you don't want a matte laptop, but the process takes longer and results in splotchiness.

STEP 3 Clean all the parts with denatured alcohol and a paper towel, then let them dry.

STEP 4 Wearing rubber gloves, fill your deep pan with 8 cups (2 L) of water. Add the dye to the water along with 2 tablespoons of table salt. Stir together.

STEP 5 Place the pan on the stove and heat. When the water starts to boil, submerge the part you wish to dye.

STEP 6 Add water if the liquid boils off, and stir every once in a while. Larger parts require more time.

STEP 7 Once you're satisfied with a part's dye distribution, remove it from the bath, wipe it down, and rinse it with cold water. Dry thoroughly.

STEP 8 Reassemble your laptop. Resume being awesome.

176 MAKE A STEAMPUNK-INSPIRED LAPTOP CASE

Give your high-tech machine an old-school Victorian vibe.

COST	$
TIME	☺ ☺ ☺
EASY ● ● ● ○ ○ HARD	

MATERIALS

Laptop
Tracing paper
Double-sided heavy-duty adhesive sheet
Wood veneer sheeting
Sandpaper
Craft knife
Hot water
Masking tape
Paint and paintbrushes
Polyurethane
Superglue
Miscellaneous embellishments

STEP 1 Lay tracing paper over the back of your laptop and trace where the wood veneer will go, leaving holes for plugs, fans, and hatches that allow you access to the computer's insides.

STEP 2 Open up your laptop and, using the same method, create patterns for the frame around the screen and the area surrounding the keyboard.

STEP 3 Apply a heavy-duty adhesive sheet to the blank side of the wood veneer sheeting.

STEP 4 Sand the veneer for a smooth look and feel.

STEP 5 Tape the tracing paper onto the wood veneer and cut it out using a craft knife. Cut out the veneer pieces to go around the screen and keyboard, too.

STEP 6 In the corners of the veneer, cut diagonal slits so that you can fold the veneer over the laptop's corners.

STEP 7 Soak the veneer in hot water to make it pliant. Be sure to dry off excess water before applying the veneer to your computer—for extra security, remove the battery before placing the veneer on the laptop.

STEP 8 Use masking tape to secure the wood to the laptop. Let it dry so it can mold nicely to the computer's shape, then remove it and set it aside.

STEP 9 On your laptop, use tape to mask off any areas that the veneer won't cover, including the hinge. Then paint those areas a color of your choosing.

STEP 10 Peel away the veneer's adhesive backing and apply the veneer to the laptop, starting with the inside pieces. Don't press down until you've got it lined up perfectly, then go slowly and press out air bubbles as you apply it. Cut away any excess material.

STEP 11 Mask off areas that aren't covered with veneer, then coat the veneer with polyurethane.

STEP 12 Add any desired embellishments with superglue. Apply another coat of polyurethane to make it for keeps.

Steampunk touches

Painted hinge

Wood veneer sheeting

177 TURN ON YOUR COMPUTER WITH A MAGNET SWITCH

Dupe would-be information thieves with a handy on/off switch mod.

MATERIALS

Screwdriver

Computer tower with plastic front panel

Wire strippers

Reed switch

Steel or iron nut

Electrical tape

Small magnet

STEP 1 Open your computer tower and remove the front panel, exposing the wires attached to the power button. Cut one of the wires, and strip both ends.

STEP 2 Place the reed switch between the two wire ends and twist them together, sandwiching the reed switch.

STEP 3 Tape the reed switch to the inside of the front panel of your computer and tape or glue the steel or iron nut next to it. Close the computer back up.

STEP 4 To turn on your computer, push the power button and stick a magnet to the case where the reed switch is located—the nut should hold the magnet in place. If someone tries to turn your computer on without the magnet, they'll have no luck.

178 PRINT SECRETS WITH INVISIBLE INK

Bet the CIA sure wished it had come up with this printer hack.

MATERIALS

Inkjet printer

UV invisible ink

Syringe

UV lamp

STEP 1 Open up your inkjet printer and extract one of the ink cartridges. Remove its cap and pull out the sponge.

STEP 2 Rinse out the sponge and the inside of the cartridge until the water runs clear, then put the clean sponge back inside the cartridge.

STEP 3 Use a syringe to inject invisible ink into the sponge. Replace the cartridge's cap and put the cartridge back inside the printer.

STEP 4 Adjust your computer's settings to print using only the color that you've replaced with invisible ink.

STEP 5 View the secret info on the documents by holding

179 FAKE OUT THIEVES WITH A DESKTOP HACK

Deter computer raiders with a wallpaper that looks just like your desktop—but isn't.

STEP 1 Take a screenshot of your computer's desktop, then set the screenshot as your wallpaper.

STEP 2 Hide the real icons in another folder.

STEP 3 Sit back and watch people try to open your desktop's unclickable folders.

Private

Secrets

Confidential

More secrets

Don't look!

Embarrassing

180 SHIELD YOUR SCREEN FROM PRYING EYES

Sick of snoops looking at your screen? Improvise your own privacy monitor.

MATERIALS

LCD monitor
Craft knife
Paintbrush
Paint thinner
Paper towels
Piece of plastic
Old glasses
Tape
Superglue

STEP 1 Unplug an old LCD monitor and remove the plastic frame around it.

STEP 2 Use a craft knife to cut around the screen's edge, then peel back both the polarized and the antiglare films. Hang on to the polarized layer and remember its orientation.

STEP 3 Apply paint thinner to loosen the glue on the monitor's screen—don't drip it on the monitor's frame. Then wipe it off with paper towels and scrape off the softened glue with a piece of plastic.

STEP 4 Reassemble your monitor. At this point, when you turn it on, the screen looks white and blank. If you hold up the polarized film, you should see images on the screen.

STEP 5 Pop the lenses out of a pair of old glasses. Tape the lenses to the polarized film and trace around them.

STEP 6 Hold the polarized film lenses up as though you were wearing them, and look at the monitor. If you can see the images on the screen, cut out the lens-shaped film pieces with your craft knife.

STEP 7 Glue the polarized lenses onto your glasses. Put them on, and enjoy the invisible images on your screen.

181 SET UP A LAPTOP COOLING SYSTEM

Chill down your machine with copper's thermal conductivity.

MATERIALS

Rotary tool
Paper
Scissors
Sheet of 0.5-mm copper plating
Tin snips
6-mm center-tapped lip and spur drill

Two pieces of 6-mm copper tubing, each 2 inches (5 cm) in length
Solder and soldering iron
Plastic tubing
Rubber tubing
Bilge pump

STEP 1 If necessary, use the rotary tool to cut away at your laptop's plastic casing until the fins of your computer's internal radiator and heat sink are exposed.

STEP 2 Experiment to determine how big the fins of your heat extractor should be. Try inserting strips of paper between the fins of your computer's heat sink, cutting them down until they fit perfectly. For maximum cooling, the fins should fit as deep into the heat sink as possible.

STEP 3 Once you've determined the necessary measurements for your copper heat extractor's fins, clean the copper sheet with soap and water. Using one of your paper fins as a template, trace seven copper fins.

STEP 4 Trace two holes 6-mm in diameter along one of the short edges in each fin, positioning the holes 5/8 inch (16 mm) apart. The 6-mm copper tubing should fit snugly through these holes, once you've drilled them.

STEP 5 Cut out the copper fins with tin snips and use the lip and spur drill to cut out the holes. Set the drill to a slow speed and do your drilling on a flat surface to prevent the copper sheet from warping.

STEP 6 Thread the fins onto the two lengths of copper tubing. You can temporarily place coins between the fins to help space them evenly so that they'll line up with the heat sink's indentations. Solder the tubes and fins together.

STEP 7 Cut a piece of plastic tubing to a length of about 1 1/2 inches (3.75 mm). Heat it until you can bend it to fit over both pieces of copper tubing on one side of the fin-and-tubing contraption. Insert the contraption into your computer's heat sink.

STEP 8 Hook two lengths of rubber tubing to the bare pieces of copper tubing that are plugged into your computer's heat sink. Connect these two lengths of rubber tubing to a bilge pump filled with water. Power it up and the water will circulate, carrying heat from the heat skink and keeping your computer cool.

Line to bilge pump

Copper tubing and fins

Plastic tubing

Heat sink

Laptop that tends to overheat

182 CONTROL YOUR MOUSE FROM AFAR

Direct your mouse with a simple laser pointer.

MATERIALS

Optical mouse
Laser pointer, less than 10 mW

STEP 1 Lean your mouse against your computer monitor so that it's propped upright with its belly facing out.

STEP 2 Identify your mouse's sensor, which looks like a tiny bubble tinted black.

STEP 3 Shine the laser pointer directly at the sensor. Once you get a lock on the sensor, you can move it around in the mouse's vicinity to control your computer's cursor.

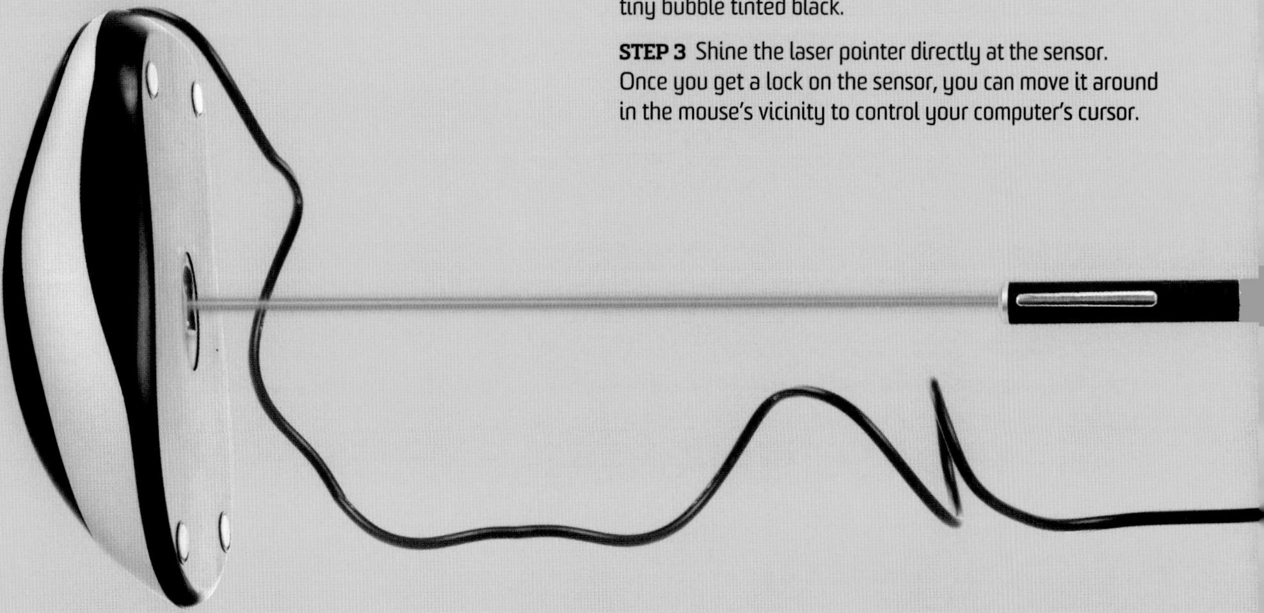

---

5 MINUTE PROJECT

183 MAKE AN EXTERNAL HARD DRIVE

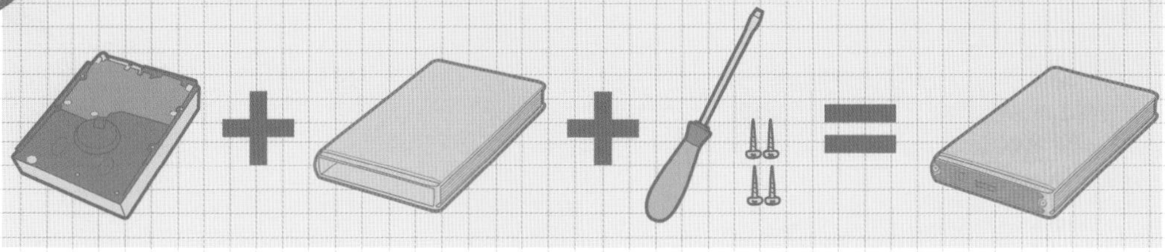

STEP 1 Salvage a working hard drive from a laptop or a computer tower.

STEP 2 Locate the ports on a hard drive case's baseplate, then attach them to the hard drive.

STEP 3 Line up the holes in the drive and baseplate and screw them together.

STEP 4 Slide these parts inside the case. Screw on the faceplate, lining up its holes with the ports to keep them accessible.

184 ADD KEYBOARD THUMBTACKS

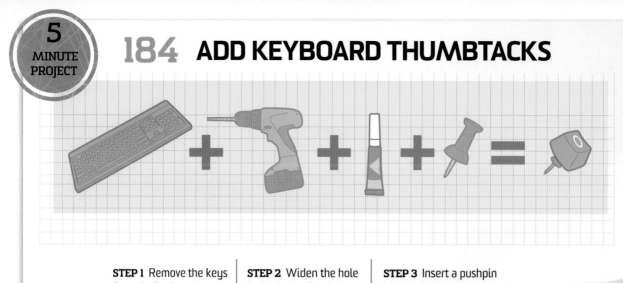

STEP 1 Remove the keys from the keyboard, and cut off the excess plastic on the back of each key with a rotary tool.

STEP 2 Widen the hole in the back of each key using a rotary tool. Put a dab of glue in the hole.

STEP 3 Insert a pushpin into the hole, pointy end facing out. Pin up something important.

185 RIG A SUPERPORTABLE KEYBOARD

Cut a keyboard to get to the touch-sensitive membrane inside.

MATERIALS

USB keyboard
Screwdriver
Transparent contact paper
Superglue
Adhesive stickers

STEP 1 Use a screwdriver to deconstruct the keyboard. The good stuff is in the middle: It's the three-layer membrane and the attached control board, which feeds the USB wire.

STEP 2 Remove and reserve the membrane's control board and switch pad (the rubber pad that presses the control board's contacts to the membrane).

STEP 3 Using the switch pad, board, and nuts and bolts, reassemble the membrane to the control board. The traces of the membrane should line up with the traces on the control board. (If your keyboard had a socket and ribbon cable, reinsert the cable.)

STEP 4 Cover both sides with transparent contact paper, and apply glue to the edges to keep the three membranes in place.

STEP 5 Apply adhesive stickers for each key, taking care to place the stickers on the keys' contacts. (For instance, the space bar is huge, but the contact is small, so you'll want to be sure that you put the sticker directly on the contact—just not on the key.)

STEP 6 Roll it up and be ready to type anywhere.

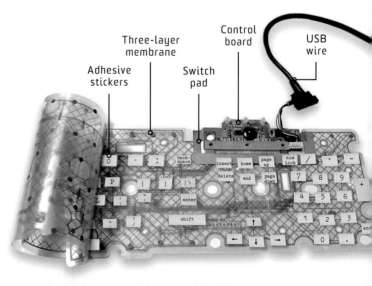

Three-layer membrane

Control board

USB wire

Adhesive stickers

Switch pad

Brighten up your all-night gaming sessions with this LED-lit mousepad.

COST	$
TIME	⊙ ⊙
EASY	● ● ● ○ ○ HARD

MATERIALS

Safety goggles
Plexiglas
Tablesaw with a glass-cutting blade
Rotary tool with glass-safe bit
Two small white LED lights

Electrical wire
USB connector
Clear tape
Printed design, if desired

STEP 1 Decide what size and shape you'd like your mousepad to be. Then, wearing safety goggles, use a table saw with a glass-cutting blade to cut the Plexiglas to size.

STEP 2 Fit your rotary tool with a glass-safe bit, then use it to round the Plexiglas's edges and wear them down. The more surface area that you make opaque, the more light your mousepad will emit.

STEP 3 Use your rotary tool to carve a channel into the Plexiglas, starting from the top center of the glass and forking into two channels about 1 inch (2.5 cm) down.

STEP 4 Use the rotary tool to extend the two channels parallel to the glass's top edge, ending 1 inch (2.5 cm) from the Plexiglas's edges.

STEP 5 Attach pieces of electrical wire to the LEDs' leads, then peel back the plastic on your USB cord. Attach the two positive wires and two negative wires on the LEDs to the USB cord's positive and negative wires.

STEP 6 Place the LEDs and wires into the carved channels and secure them with clear tape. Cover the mousepad with a design, if you like.

STEP 7 Plug the USB into your computer, dim the lights, and get your game on.

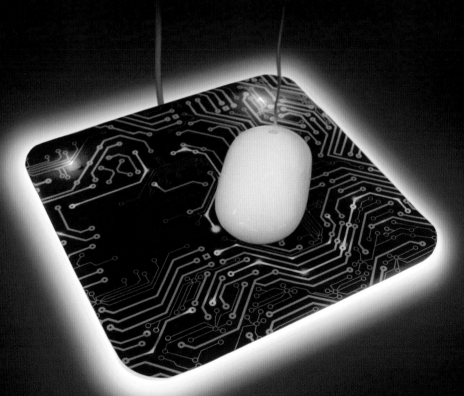

187 UPCYCLE AN OLD CIRCUIT BOARD

So a gadget's circuit board is down for the count.
There are still countless things you can do with it.

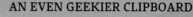

AN EVEN GEEKIER CLIPBOARD
Use a heat gun and pliers to strip off all the solder and bits and bobs, then apply laminate to make it smooth. Swap the clip from an old clipboard onto your new, high-tech version.

NERDTASTIC GUITAR PICK
Use a soldering iron to remove any electrical components on the circuit board, then use a rotary tool to cut out a guitar pick shape. Sand it until it's smooth and start picking.

META MOUSE PAD
Desolder a circuit board so that it's bare and cover both sides with vinyl. Plop your new mousepad on your desk and get your scroll on.

LIGHT UP THE CIRCUIT
Form a box shape with four stripped circuit boards and drill holes in their corners. Fasten them together with zip ties, and hook this box up to a hanging light-socket assembly for some nice spotlight action.

188 MAKE A LAPTOP STAND FROM A BINDER

STEP 1 Using a metal saw, cut a piece of aluminum rail so it's the length of a ring binder. Then use a metal file to round the rail's edges so you don't get scraped.

STEP 2 Place double-sided tape on the inner side of the rail.

STEP 3 Drill two sets of two holes big enough for bolts—one set through the rail and one set through the binder.

STEP 4 Line up the holes and attach the rail and binder with the bolts, securing them with a nut on the underside. Cover these bolts with tape to avoid scratches on the laptop.

STEP 5 Measure and cut a strip of no-skid felt to the dimensions of the rail, then adhere it to the inner side of the rail. Measure and cut a larger sheet of felt so that it covers the top of the binder and secure it with adhesive. It will prevent your laptop from sliding around.

STEP 6 Use a rotary tool to cut a hole into the binder's corner for cords to pass through.

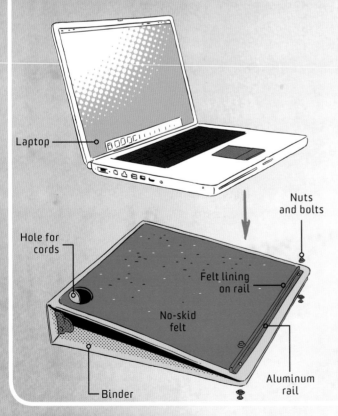

Laptop

Nuts and bolts

Hole for cords

Felt lining on rail

No-skid felt

Binder

Aluminum rail

189 BUILD A USB HUB INTO YOUR DESK

STEP 1 Remove your computer, cords, and other electronics from your work station to protect them from sawdust.

STEP 2 Measure your hub and mark a spot for it on a wood desktop using a pencil and ruler.

STEP 3 Use a jigsaw to cut out the opening, tracing your marked lines. It's better to cut it slightly smaller than your hub (you can always sand it) than too big (you'd have to fill any gaps with caulking).

STEP 4 Remove the plug of wood and insert your USB hub to make sure it fits. Use sandpaper to adjust and smooth the opening.

STEP 5 Use epoxy to attach the USB hub to the inside of the hole; let dry.

STEP 6 Run the input cord from the USB hub up behind your desk to your computer.

STEP 6 Next time you need to plug something in, forget reaching around your monitor: Just plug it into the hub on your desk.

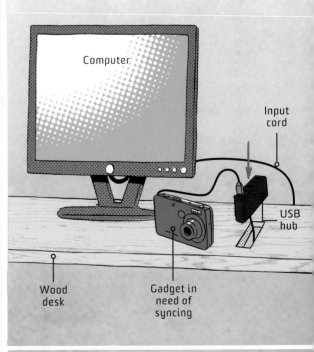

Computer

Input cord

USB hub

Wood desk

Gadget in need of syncing

190 STASH YOUR PRINTER IN A DRAWER

STEP 1 Remove the front panel of a drawer and drill a hole into the back panel for cables. (It's better to do this in a lower drawer so that the weight of your printer doesn't stress the structure.)

STEP 2 Measure and cut two evenly spaced recessed areas for the utility hinges on the front edge of the bottom panel. This way, the bottom and front panels will line up neatly when you reattach the front.

STEP 3 Line up the front and bottom panels and screw on the utility hinges.

STEP 4 With the front panel lowered, screw the support hinges to the drawer's side panels and then to the front panel.

STEP 5 Place your printer in the drawer and feed the cables through the hole in the back to attach it to your computer (or, if it's wireless, to a power source).

191 MOUNT STUFF BEHIND YOUR MONITOR

STEP 1 If you have limited desk space, use the back of your monitor for storage. Apply double-sided tape or adhesive Velcro strips to your computer monitor's back, or purchase plastic hooks with suction cups or Velcro backing.

STEP 2 Begin attaching office supplies you need—tape, tissues, notecards, a stapler, or a holder for pens and scissors—and maybe some you don't. (Hey, candy and headphones can make the workday go faster.)

STEP 3 Be sure to use lightweight materials so that your monitor doesn't tip over. Also, keep the fan clear of obstacles. Otherwise, your machine could overheat, which is much more inconvenient than not having any drawers.

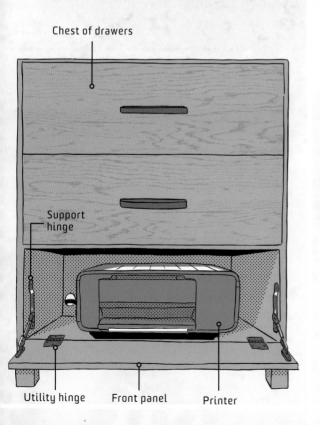

Chest of drawers

Support hinge

Utility hinge   Front panel   Printer

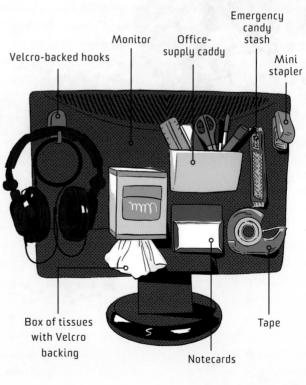

Emergency candy stash

Monitor   Office-supply caddy

Velcro-backed hooks

Mini stapler

Box of tissues with Velcro backing

Notecards

Tape

192 ORGANIZE LOOSE CABLES

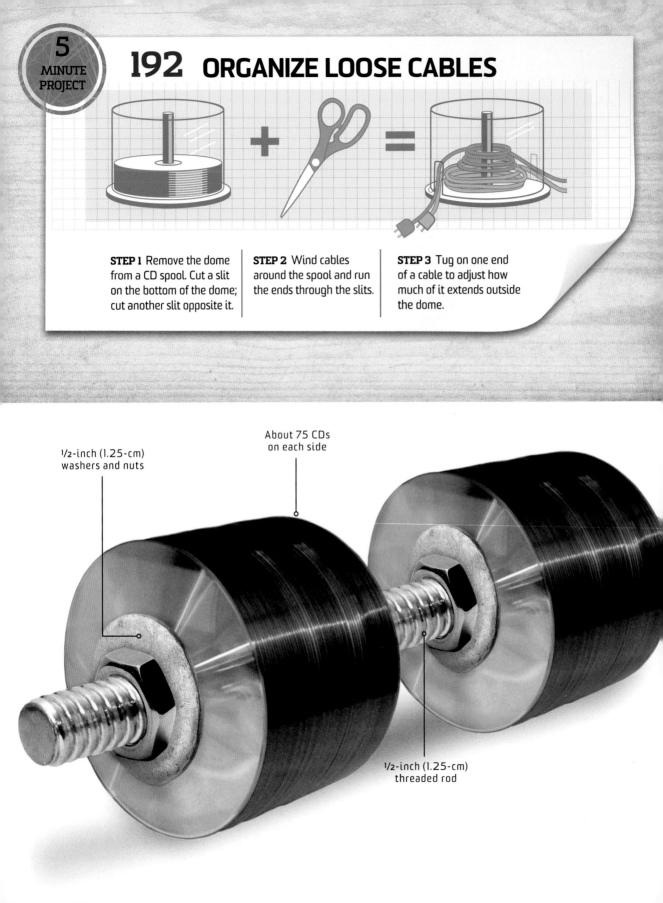

STEP 1 Remove the dome from a CD spool. Cut a slit on the bottom of the dome; cut another slit opposite it.

STEP 2 Wind cables around the spool and run the ends through the slits.

STEP 3 Tug on one end of a cable to adjust how much of it extends outside the dome.

½-inch (1.25-cm) washers and nuts

About 75 CDs on each side

½-inch (1.25-cm) threaded rod

193 MAKE A FLOPPY-DISK BOX

Solve the double problem of a messy desk and a surplus of useless floppies with one simple DIY craft.

MATERIALS

Five floppy disks
Drill

Twelve zip ties
Scissors

STEP 1 Locate the tiny dimples on the back of each floppy disk. Drill through these dimples, repeating until you have holes in each corner of four of your five disks.

STEP 2 Place two of the four floppies in front of you so that their holes are aligned. Thread a zip tie through the two holes at the bottom, and then another zip tie through the two holes at the top.

STEP 3 Repeat with two more disks, then connect the four floppies into a box shape.

STEP 4 Drill four holes in the fifth floppy, this time slightly above the dimples. This is the box's bottom.

STEP 5 To secure the bottom floppy to the box, line it up with one of the sides at a 90-degree angle. Thread a zip tie through the bottom's holes and the holes in the side.

STEP 6 Close the box and thread zip ties through the remaining holes in the bottom and side pieces. Cut off the ends of the zip ties.

STEP 7 Tighten and trim the zip ties, then stock the box with pens and revel in your newfound tidiness.

194 GET PUMPED WITH A CD DUMBBELL

CDs are pretty much obsolete. But having jacked arms never gets old.

MATERIALS

1/2-inch (1.25-cm) solid threaded rod
Ruler
Permanent marker
Table vise

Reciprocating saw or hacksaw
Four 1/2-inch (1.25-cm) washers and nuts
About 150 CDs
1/2-inch (1.25-cm) wrench

STEP 1 Measure and mark 6 inches (15 cm) from one end of the rod. (This is where the first CD stack will end.)

STEP 2 Place one hand on the rod, leaving about 1/2 inch (1.25 cm) of clearance between your hand and the mark. Make a second mark about 1/2 inch (1.25 cm) from the opposite side of your hand.

STEP 3 Measure and make a third mark 6 inches (15 cm) from the second mark for the second CD stack.

STEP 4 Place the rod in a table vise. Saw off any excess at the third mark with a reciprocating saw or a hacksaw.

STEP 5 Thread a nut onto both sides of the rod to the marked lines in the center. Add a washer on both sides.

STEP 6 Put about 75 CDs on each end, and slide on a washer and nut on both ends. Tighten with a wrench.

STEP 7 Pop your new 10-pound (4.5-kg) dumbbell out of the vise and do a few reps—you might not get ripped, but you're well on your way to getting sculpted biceps.

195 ASSEMBLE A CEREAL-BOX SPECTROMETER

See the rainbow inside everyday light sources with this easy setup.

MATERIALS

Safety glasses
Thick gloves
CD
C-clamp

Craft knife
Cereal box
Tape
Light source

STEP 1 Wearing a pair of safety glasses and thick gloves, clamp a CD down on a surface edge. Score it across the center with the craft knife, then break it in half.

STEP 2 Make a horizontal slit about 1 inch (2.5 cm) in length in one side of a cereal box, near the box's top. It should be about the width of a coin.

STEP 3 In the opposite side of the box, straight across from the first incision, make another slit. Then extend this cut to the front and back of the box, sloping down at a 45-degree angle with your craft knife. It should be deep enough for the CD half to at least partially slide into. Secure the CD in place with tape.

STEP 4 Cut a 1/2-by-1/2-inch (1.25-cm-by-1.25-cm) square hole in the box above the CD slice.

STEP 5 Hold the box up with the slit facing your light source. Look through the viewing hole at the top to see the rays of light separated on the CD inside the box.

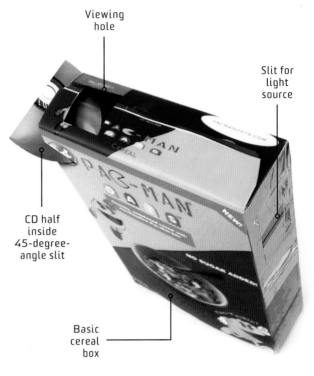

Viewing hole

Slit for light source

CD half inside 45-degree-angle slit

Basic cereal box

A PORTABLE X-RAY MACHINE

Late one night, Adam Munich found himself talking with two guys online: one who complained of rolling electricity blackouts and one who had broken his leg in Mexico and said his local hospital couldn't find an X-ray machine. The two situations fused in Munich's mind; he wondered if a cheap, reliable, battery-powered X-ray machine existed. After discovering that the answer was no, he spent two years building one himself out of nixie tubes, old suitcases, chain-saw oil, and electronics from across the globe. It was an incredibly ambitious project for anyone, let alone a 15-year-old.

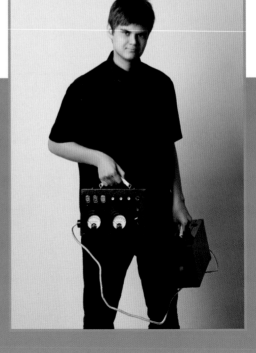

196 RIG A SUPERSIMPLE RADIATION DETECTOR

Fear fallout no more with a device that tells you when radiation levels are high.

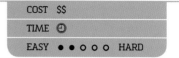

COST	$$
TIME	⏱
EASY ● ● ○ ○ ○ HARD	

Radiation is all around us in small doses, and most of it isn't harmful for you—it's really the ionizing, DNA-scrambling stuff that we have to look out for. Enter this chamber–in-a-can, which lets you see if an object's radiation levels are off the charts.

MATERIALS

Aluminum can
Craft knife
NPN Darlington transistor
Electrical tape
Electrical wire
9-volt battery and snap

4.7k-ohm resistor
Soldering iron and solder
Aluminum foil
Rubber band
Multimeter

STEP 1 Make a hole in the can with a craft knife. Bend the transistor's base leg down into the can and tape it in place.

STEP 2 Use electrical wire to attach the transistor's collector leg to the negative pole of the battery snap. Keep the transitor's leads sticking up, away from the can.

STEP 3 Solder one lead of the resistor to the base of the can, near the edge. Attach the other lead to the positive pole of the battery snap with a piece of wire.

STEP 4 Tape the battery snap to the side of the can and hook the battery up to the snap.

STEP 5 Cover the can's open end with aluminum foil. Pull the foil taut, then secure it with a rubber band.

STEP 6 Attach one probe of the multimeter to the transistor's emitter leg, and the other to the wire between the resistor and the battery.

STEP 7 Turn on the multimeter. Allow the reading to stabilize—avoid touching the can or moving around near it. Once it stabilizes, you'll have the baseline reading for the radiation in the room. Keep the can away from power sources, which could confuse its reading.

STEP 8 To measure the radioactivity of an object relative to the baseline, simply place it beside the can's end and observe the changed reading on your multimeter.

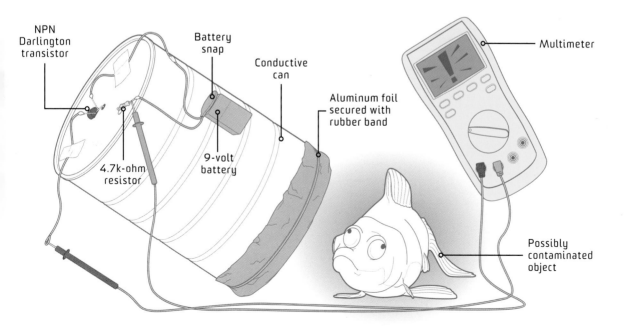

NPN Darlington transistor

Battery snap

Conductive can

Aluminum foil secured with rubber band

Multimeter

4.7k-ohm resistor

9-volt battery

Possibly contaminated object

197 SET UP A PLASMA GLOBE INSIDE A SIMPLE LIGHTBULB

Make a miniature Tesla coil inside this ubiquitous household fixture.

COST $$
TIME 🕐 🕐
EASY ● ● ● ● ● HARD

MATERIALS

Ferrite-core flyback transformer (salvaged from an old CRT television)
Wire strippers
Screwdriver
Hacksaw
18-gauge wire
22-gauge wire
Electrical tape
Rotary tool
Project box
60-watt or higher clear lightbulb
24-volt DC-power supply
On/off switch
Superglue
Electrical wire
Lightbulb socket
2N3055 transistor and heat sink
5-watt, 27k-ohm resistor
5-watt, 240k-ohm resistor
Soldering iron and solder

Decades ago, famous mad scientist Nikola Tesla invented what he called the "inert gas discharge tube" to conduct various experiments in electricity and magnetism.

These days, you can use the same technology to create an entertaining display piece that generates static and responds to your touch by arcing electricity to your fingertips. With a few salvaged materials, you too can harness the power of high-frequency alternating current—and be well on your way to becoming a mad scientist yourself.

STEP 1 Salvage a transformer from an old CRT television. To do this, turn off the television and unplug it, then open up its back and locate the transformer. (It's the bulky square metal ring with two cylindrical "cores" on it, bolted into the television's circuit board.)

STEP 2 Remove the transformer by clipping away the wires (leaving extra wire on the transformer itself) and unscrewing the bolts holding it to the circuit board.

STEP 3 There are two sets of windings on the transformer's primary and secondary core, both encased in plastic. Use a hacksaw to cut through the plastic around the windings on the smaller primary core. Then cut through and remove the windings.

STEP 4 Wind 18-gauge enameled wire around the spot where the windings used to be about five times. Then wrap 22-gauge wire four times next to the 18-gauge windings. Secure both wires with electrical tape.

STEP 5 Use a rotary tool to make three holes in a project box: one for your lightbulb socket, one for the power supply, and one for the on/off switch. Super-glue these parts in place on the top and side of the box, and place the transformer inside the box.

STEP 6 On the secondary core, there is another set of windings. Pry the two loose ends off the core and twist them to the connectors on the lightbulb socket.

STEP 7 Take one end of the 18-gauge wire wrapped around the transformer and connect it to the transistor's case post, and connect the other end to the power switch.

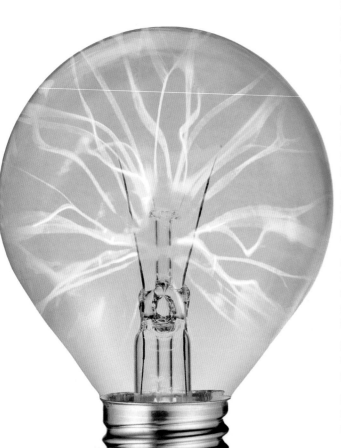

STEP 8 Take one end of the 22-gauge wire and attach it to the transistor's base post. Attach the 22-gauge wire's other end to a wire between the 27k-ohm resistor and the 240k-ohm resistor.

STEP 9 Complete the rest of the circuit as shown below using electrical wire, then screw your lightbulb into the socket, plug in your power supply, and turn on the switch.

STEP 10 Kill the lights and watch your plasma globe glow.

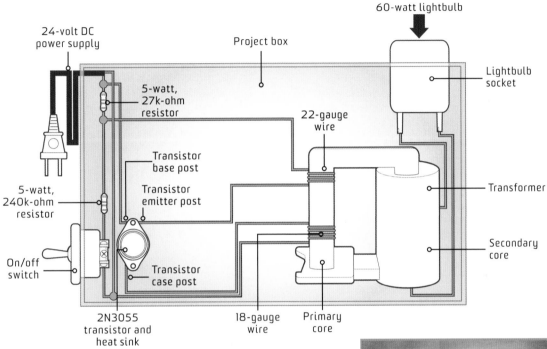

24-volt DC power supply · Project box · 60-watt lightbulb · Lightbulb socket · 5-watt, 27k-ohm resistor · 22-gauge wire · Transformer · Transistor base post · Transistor emitter post · 5-watt, 240k-ohm resistor · Secondary core · On/off switch · Transistor case post · 2N3055 transistor and heat sink · 18-gauge wire · Primary core

YOU BUILT WHAT?!

A HOMEMADE SCANNING ELECTRON MICROSCOPE

Ben Krasnow went looking for a challenge and decided to try his hand at the toughest one he could imagine: a homemade scanning electron microscope, fashioned from an old oscilloscope, a glass bell jar, and a refrigerator magnet to focus the electron beam. His completed microscope delivers about 50x magnification—a far cry from commercial SEMs' 1,000x or more—but experts say that doesn't lessen the accomplishment. William Beaty, a research engineer who had hoped to build the first DIY SEM, put it simply: "D'oh!"

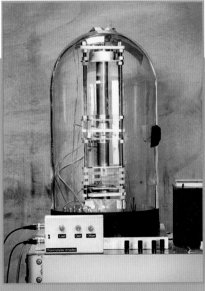

198 ILLUMINATE SKETCHES WITH HOMEMADE CONDUCTIVE INK

Write it, wire it up, and see it in lights.

MATERIALS

2.5 ml ammonium hydroxide
Two pipettes
Test tube
1 gram silver acetate
Centrifuge
0.2 ml formic acid
Syringe

Syringe filter
Glass vial
Glass to paint on
Thin paintbrush
9-volt battery
LEDs

STEP 1 Use a pipette to measure the ammonium hydroxide into a test tube, then add the silver acetate. Place the tube in the centrifuge; let it mix for 15 seconds.

STEP 2 Using a second pipette, transfer 0.2 ml formic acid into the test tube solution one drop at a time, mixing it in the centrifuge between each drop.

STEP 3 Set the test tube aside for 12 hours.

STEP 4 Pull the plunger out of the back of a syringe and add a filter to the syringe, then decant the solution in the test tube into the syringe.

STEP 5 Open the glass vial and place it under the syringe, then place the plunger back into the syringe and force the liquid through the filter and into the vial.

STEP 6 Using the liquid in the vial, draw or write something on glass with a thin paintbrush, leaving gaps for the leads of the power source and the LEDs.

STEP 7 Heat the glass in an oven set to 200°F (93°C). Wait 15 minutes, then remove it. It should have a conductive silver coating.

STEP 8 Once you've placed the battery and LEDs on the glass, your circuit art will light right up.

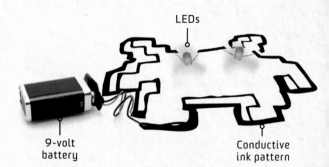

LEDs

9-volt battery

Conductive ink pattern

---

199 HACK INFRARED GOGGLES

STEP 1 Unscrew the eyepieces from a pair of welding goggles. Remove the dark green welding lenses, leaving just the clear plastic.

STEP 2 Use a green welding lens as a template to cut out eight circles of blue gel sheet and two circles of red gel sheet.

STEP 3 Add four blue gel sheet pieces to each eyepiece, screw them back onto your goggles, and enjoy the crazy spectrum.

STEP 4 Add a red gel sheet piece for a different effect. Whatever you do, just don't look at the sun.

200 DECIMATE STUFF WITH A DIY LASER CUTTER

It used to be lasers were just for scientists. Now they're for anyone who can harvest a few parts from an old PC.

COST	$$
TIME	☺ ☺ ☺
EASY ● ● ● ● ○ HARD	

MATERIALS

Old computer with a DVD burner
Soldering iron and solder
Knife
Vise
Metal file
Pliers
Tweezers
AixiZ module
LM317 regulator
3k-ohm resistor
Wire strippers
Drill
Thermal glue
Laser safety goggles

STEP 1 Unplug the computer and open its case. Locate and remove the power supply, heat sinks, and DVD burner.

STEP 2 Open the DVD burner, lift the circuit board, and remove the sled underneath (the part with the laser diode).

STEP 3 To extract the laser diode from its heat sink, first load your soldering iron with enough solder so it will make contact with both of the diode's soldered pins. Slide a knife under the diode's ribbon, and pull up on it as you touch the solder to the diode's pins to remove the ribbon.

STEP 4 Place the laser diode in a vise and file through its heat sink. Once you've weakened the heat sink, hold it with pliers and wedge a knife under the lip of the top. Use tweezers to extract the diode from the heat sink.

STEP 5 Unscrew the AixiZ module (a laser housing unit) and place the top facedown on your workspace. Drop the laser diode in it with the laser facing down, carefully pressing it so the diode's back is flush with the module.

STEP 6 Attach two long leads to the diode's negative and positive pins and reattach the back of the AixiZ module, threading the leads through the hole in its back.

STEP 7 Solder a 3k-ohm resistor across the LM317 regulator's adjustable and output voltage pins, then solder the laser diode's positive lead to the adjustable pin on the LM317 regulator.

STEP 8 Clip the wire connectors off the ends of the wires attached to the power supply, then clip and strip the black and green wires and solder them together.

STEP 9 Solder the diode's negative lead to the power supply's red (negative) wire, and the power supply's yellow (positive) wire to the regulator's input pin.

STEP 10 Drill a ½-inch (1.25-cm) hole through the large heat sink that you harvested from your computer.

STEP 11 Slide the AixiZ module into the large heat sink, making sure it doesn't protrude. Secure with thermal glue.

STEP 12 Use thermal glue to attach the small heat sink to the LM317 driver you wired.

STEP 13 Put on safety goggles that are specifically designed to protect against lasers. Burn and cut things.

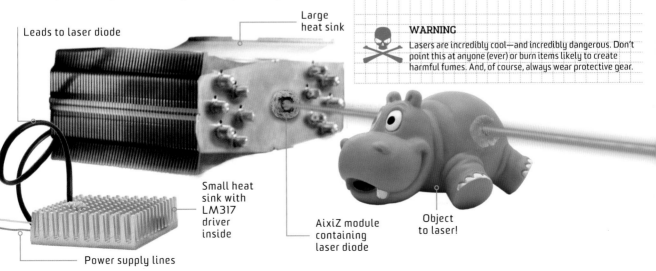

Leads to laser diode

Large heat sink

Small heat sink with LM317 driver inside

Power supply lines

AixiZ module containing laser diode

Object to laser!

WARNING
Lasers are incredibly cool—and incredibly dangerous. Don't point this at anyone (ever) or burn items likely to create harmful fumes. And, of course, always wear protective gear.

201

A 3D PRINTER THAT RUNS ON SUN AND SAND

This bizarre-looking contraption turns the desert's resources—a whole lot of sun and sand—into glass.

When design student Markus Kayser wanted to test his sun-powered, sand-fed 3D printer, he knew the gray skies outside his London apartment wouldn't do. So he shipped the 200-pound (90-kg) device to Cairo, Egypt, hoping to find plenty of sun and sand that could, in conjunction with a large lens, produce glassware.

How does this machine work? Two aluminum arms, holding the lens at one end and solar panels at the other, can pivot from straight overhead down to a 45-degree angle to chase the sun. Sensors detect the shadows and feed the data on their position to Kayser's computer, which directs the motorized frame to adjust to properly align the lens. Two photovoltaic panels, one on either side of the machine, keep the printer powered. Since the panels are attached to the same arms as the lens, they also benefit from the sun tracking, ensuring that they always get direct light.

Kayser first designs the object he wants to print in a computer-assisted design (CAD) program. His computer sends instructions to the printer, which works from the bottom up. After a layer has cooled into glass, he adds more sand to the sandbox in the center of the machine and flattens it out, and the printer begins heating the next layer. Kayser's first major piece, a bowl, took about four and a half hours to print.

PRINTING A BETTER BOWL
Kayser has printed a glass bowl and several sculptures. He admits they're not perfect; he says he could have used more complicated optics. But, he adds, perfection wasn't the point: "This is about showing the potential."

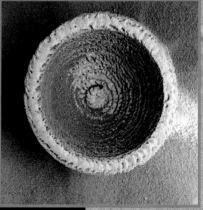

202 SHINE A MINI FLASHLIGHT

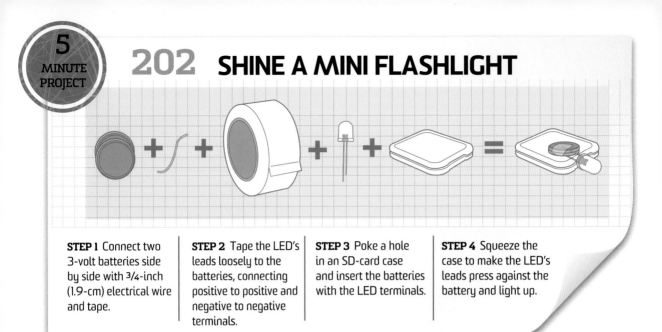

STEP 1 Connect two 3-volt batteries side by side with ¾-inch (1.9-cm) electrical wire and tape.

STEP 2 Tape the LED's leads loosely to the batteries, connecting positive to positive and negative to negative terminals.

STEP 3 Poke a hole in an SD-card case and insert the batteries with the LED terminals.

STEP 4 Squeeze the case to make the LED's leads press against the battery and light up.

203 BRIGHTEN UP A STANDARD-ISSUE FLASHLIGHT

Turn an average flashlight into something much, much brighter.

MATERIALS

Small industrial flashlight
Rotary tool
Krypton bulb
Three lithium 3-volt batteries

STEP 1 Twist off the bottom of the flashlight canister. Remove and discard the batteries.

STEP 2 Unscrew the top. Take out the factory-issue bulb and recycle it or reserve it for another project.

STEP 3 Use a rotary tool to remove the ridges inside the battery housing that hold the batteries in tightly.

STEP 4 Insert the krypton bulb and put the top of the flashlight back in place.

STEP 5 Insert the 3-volt batteries into the case where the standard batteries once were.

STEP 6 Close the flashlight and cast a brighter beam.

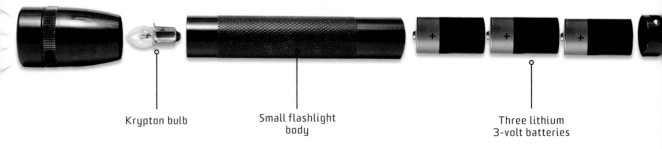

Krypton bulb

Small flashlight body

Three lithium 3-volt batteries

BEAM A BATMAN-STYLE SPOTLIGHT

Send up a tiny desktop signal whenever you're in need of big-time assistance.

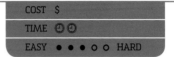

COST	$
TIME	⊘ ⊘
EASY ● ● ● ○ ○ HARD	

MATERIALS

Large translucent flip-top
  bottle cap from a detergent
  or shampoo bottle
Craft knife
Aluminum foil
Scissors
Double-sided tape
USB laptop light

Wire cutters
Soldering iron and solder
Hot-glue gun
Clear plastic sheet
Cap from a sports bottle
Loose change
Foam board or cardboard
Black paint

STEP 1 Use a craft knife to cut off the top of the large flip-top bottle cap; discard it. Wrap the bottle cap in strips of aluminum foil, leaving small gaps between strips and adhering them with double-sided tape.

STEP 2 Cut the USB plug off the USB laptop light using the wire cutters; pull out the LED and its attached wires.

STEP 3 Flip the bottle cap over so that the exit hole is on the bottom and the cap's neck becomes the top. Crumple up aluminum foil, form it into a rough bowl shape, and place it inside the cap.

STEP 4 Punch a hole in the aluminum foil with a craft knife. Thread the LED wires through it and out the exit hole of the large cap, nestling the LED in the bowl shape.

STEP 5 Use a craft knife to make a slit in the covering of the USB lamp's detached USB plug, and peel the covering off. Then take apart the metal case and solder the wires that once went to the LED encased in the lamp back on to the LED's relevant pins.

STEP 6 Use hot glue to secure the wires in place. Reattach the metal case and then the rubber outer housing.

STEP 7 Cut a piece of plastic sheet to fit over the cap, with three tabs around the edge to fit down into the bottle cap. Fold down the tabs and apply glue to them, then press the plastic "lens" in place.

STEP 8 Cut a tiny logo out of aluminum foil and glue it onto the lens.

STEP 9 Use the cap from a sports bottle to make the base. Glue a couple of coins into the cap's bottom to weight it.

STEP 10 Cut a support piece out of foam board or cardboard for the spotlight to rest in. Be sure to make a slender bottom point that will fit into the small hole in the sports-bottle-cap base. Paint the base and support black.

STEP 11 Glue the foam support to the small sports-bottle-cap base, then glue the spotlight to the support.

STEP 12 Send your signal.

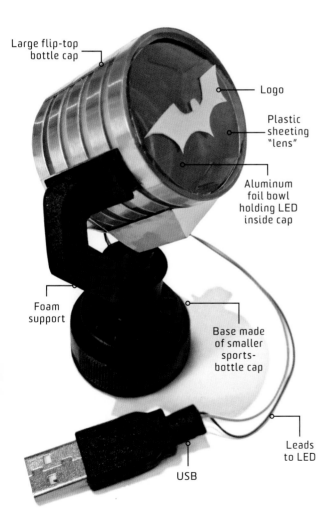

Large flip-top bottle cap

Logo

Plastic sheeting "lens"

Aluminum foil bowl holding LED inside cap

Foam support

Base made of smaller sports-bottle cap

USB

Leads to LED

205 REPURPOSE FOIL FOR TECHIE USE

Dig this stuff out of a kitchen cupboard and
make the most of its conductive properties.

DO-IT-YOURSELF CAPACITORS
Cut a 2-foot (60-cm) length of aluminum foil, and three lengths of plastic wrap to match. Cut the foil in half lengthwise and tape a piece of electrical wire to each sheet, then put the pieces of foil on top of each other with plastic wrap in between. Put more plastic wrap on top of and below the foil, then roll it all up and hook the wires to a battery charger. Charge stuff up.

SECURE LOOSE BATTERIES
Sometimes, batteries don't quite connect with the springs inside your devices. So fold up a piece of aluminum foil and slide it between the battery terminals and the springs.

CELL-PHONE–SIGNAL BLOCKER
To stay under cover and prevent people from picking up your GPS coordinates, tightly wrap your phone in multiple layers of aluminum foil. To test it, try calling your phone. If it goes straight to voicemail, the signal to and from your phone is successfully blocked, and your coordinates are protected.

DIY LIGHT REFLECTOR
Wrap a large piece of cardboard in foil to create a quick and cheap light reflector for photography.

206 IMPROVISE A TRIPOD

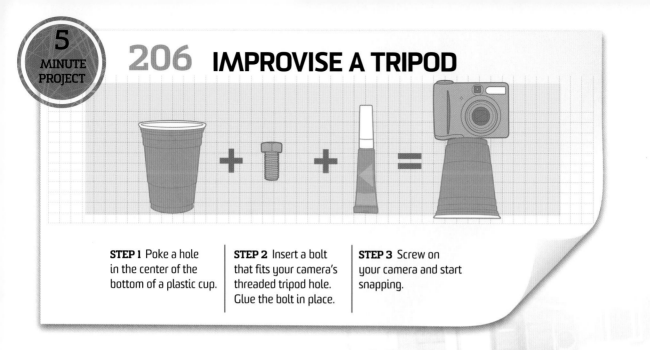

STEP 1 Poke a hole in the center of the bottom of a plastic cup.

STEP 2 Insert a bolt that fits your camera's threaded tripod hole. Glue the bolt in place.

STEP 3 Screw on your camera and start snapping.

207 MOUNT A CAMERA TO YOUR BIKE

Document your epic rides with a bike-bell mod.

MATERIALS

Bicycle bell
Camera
Bicycle
Screwdriver

STEP 1 Find a bike bell with a central screw that fits the tripod mount on the bottom of your camera. Most tripod mounts measure ¼ inch (6.35 mm).

STEP 2 Attach the bell to the handlebars.

STEP 3 Use a screwdriver to remove the bell's dome.

STEP 4 Screw the camera's tripod mount to the bell's central screw. Orient the camera whichever way you like, and start shooting your photographic travelogue.

Camera

Central screw

Bicycle bell

BUILD A TIME-LAPSE CAMERA STAND

Upgrade your kitchen timer for slick panoramic photos on the cheap.

MATERIALS

Kitchen timer
Drill
¼-inch (6.35-mm) 20 set screw
⅜-inch (9.5-mm) bolt
⅜-inch (9.5-mm) 20 bushing
Craft knife
Rubber mat
Glue
Tripod
Tripod mount
Camera
Computer with photo-editing software

STEP 1 Drill a ¹⁵/₆₄-inch (6-mm) hole into the center of a kitchen timer's dial. Insert a ¼-inch (6.35-mm) 20 set screw.

STEP 2 In the bottom of the timer, drill a hole ¹¹/₃₂ inches (8.75 mm) in diameter. Screw a ⅜-inch (9.5-mm) bolt into the hole to create threads for a ⅜-inch (9.5-mm) bushing (a threaded insert that will allow you to mount the timer to the tripod).

STEP 3 Measure and cut a piece of rubber mat, leaving a hole for the bushing, and glue it to the bottom of the timer.

STEP 4 Mount the timer on a tripod, attach the tripod mount and camera, and set the timer. Adjust the camera's settings to take pictures at regular intervals, and then transfer the shots to a computer and create a panoramic time-lapse montage with photo software.

Camera

Tripod mount

Kitchen timer

Tripod

209 RIG A PLASTIC-BOTTLE DIFFUSER

STEP 1 Cut out a small section of an empty frosted plastic water jug.

STEP 2 Cut a hole in the section large enough for the camera's lens to fit through.

STEP 3 Place the diffuser on the camera so it covers the flash. Snap away.

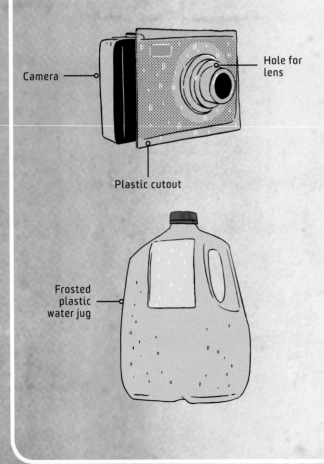

Camera

Hole for lens

Plastic cutout

Frosted plastic water jug

210 MAKE YOUR CAMERA WATERPROOF

STEP 1 Cut a piece of toilet-paper tube to match the depth of your camera lens and cover your lens with it.

STEP 2 Stretch an unlubricated condom open. Add a packet of desiccant gel—it will prevent moisture—and slide your camera inside with the tube in place.

STEP 3 Tie the condom slack into a knot and superglue the knot to make it watertight.

STEP 4 Stretch a second condom open and insert the wrapped camera, knot side in. Tie and glue the knot again. Dive in and document.

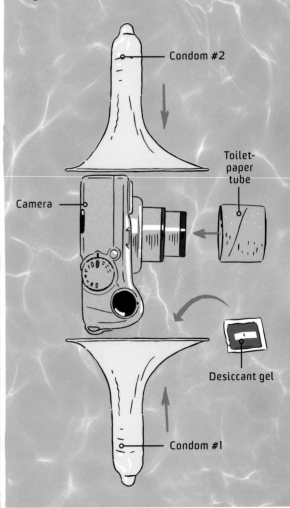

Condom #2

Toilet-paper tube

Camera

Desiccant gel

Condom #1

211 CREATE A PEEPHOLE FISHEYE LENS

STEP 1 Turn on your camera and extend the zoom as far as it will go.

STEP 2 Grab a standard peephole from a home-supply store and, making sure the peephole is facing the right way out, pop it over the camera lens.

STEP 3 Hold it in place or attach it to the lens with heavy-duty tape. (Look for tape that doesn't leave a residue, which could make your lens stick.)

212 ADAPT A MANUAL LENS TO YOUR DSLR

STEP 1 Procure a twist-on adapter ring and a compatible manual-focus lens from a vintage film camera. (These options are both way less expensive than the lenses you can buy for a DSLR, and you can even find old macro, fisheye, and ultrazoom lenses relatively inexpensively—just make sure they're compatible with your DSLR before purchasing.)

STEP 2 Insert the lens into the adapter. There is usually a dot or some kind of marking on both the lens and the adapter that makes it easy to see how the two fit together.

STEP 3 Twist the lens while holding the adapter in place, as if you were mounting the lens onto a camera body. The lens should make a click or locking sound when it's secured.

STEP 4 Mount the lens and adapter combination onto your camera like any other lens and get shooting.

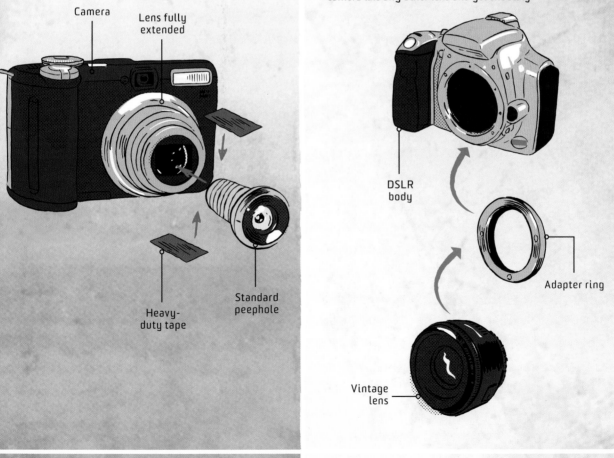

Camera

Lens fully extended

Heavy-duty tape

Standard peephole

DSLR body

Adapter ring

Vintage lens

213 Snap a Self-Portrait with a DIY Remote Shutter Release

Trigger your camera's shutter from afar with basic household parts.

MATERIALS

Rotary tool
Pill bottle with snap-on lid
Craft knife
Rubber tubing that fits snugly over the nozzle of your squeeze bottle
Shutter release cable
Plastic squeeze bottle

Short piece of plastic tubing that fits snugly into the rubber tubing
Balloon
Thread
Talcum powder
Cork that fits into the pill bottle

STEP 1 Use a rotary tool to drill a hole into the pill bottle's lid big enough to fit the rubber tubing.

STEP 2 Drill a hole in the bottom of the pill bottle for the trigger of your shutter release cable. Insert the trigger.

STEP 3 Use a craft knife to cut the rubber tubing long enough to cover the longest distance that you anticipate being from the camera. Insert the nozzle of your squeeze bottle into one end of the rubber tubing.

STEP 4 Thread the tubing's other end through the hole in the pill bottle's lid and onto the short plastic tubing.

STEP 5 Pull the balloon's opening around the piece of plastic tubing and tie it on securely with thread.

STEP 6 Dust the piece of cork with talcum powder and insert it into the pill bottle. Lower the balloon into the bottle so that it rests against the cork.

STEP 7 Test that everything is airtight, then hook the cable to your camera and get in front of the camera, holding the squeeze bottle. When you're ready, squeeze the bottle, and the balloon will inflate, pushing the cork against the cable's trigger. Say "cheese," anyone?

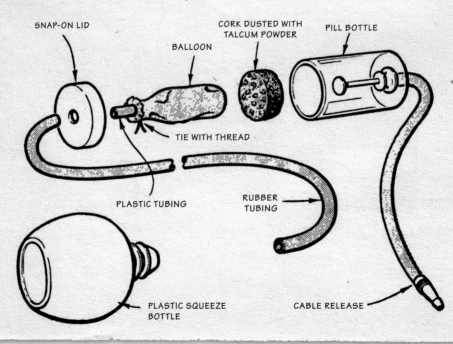

SNAP-ON LID

BALLOON

CORK DUSTED WITH TALCUM POWDER

PILL BOTTLE

TIE WITH THREAD

PLASTIC TUBING

RUBBER TUBING

PLASTIC SQUEEZE BOTTLE

CABLE RELEASE

214 SET UP A HIGH-SPEED AUDIO-TRIGGERED FLASH

Light up superquick action with a superquick audio-triggered flash.

COST	$$
TIME	⏲ ⏲ ⏲
EASY ● ● ● ● ○ HARD	

MATERIALS

Disposable flash camera

Two AA and two AAA alkaline batteries

Voltage meter

Sensitive-gate, 400-volt, 0.8-amp silicon-controlled rectifier (SCR)

Wire strippers

Soldering iron and solder

3.5-mm stereo cable

Cassette recorder

Electret microphone

Camera capable of "B" (bulb) or prolonged exposures (at least two seconds)

Tripod

STEP 1 Remove the exterior plastic, film advance system, and shutter assembly from the disposable flash camera. Make sure it has fresh batteries.

STEP 2 Locate the camera's flash terminals, located near where the shutter was. Use a voltage meter to determine which terminal is positive and which is negative.

STEP 3 Solder the cathode pin of the silicon-controlled rectifier to the negative flash terminal and the anode pin to the positive flash terminal.

STEP 4 Snip off one jack of the 3.5-mm stereo cable. Peel back its plastic to expose the red, white, and ground wires.

STEP 5 Solder the stereo cable's red and white wires to the silicon-controlled rectifier's gate pin and its ground wire to the negative flash terminal (with the cathode pin).

STEP 6 Plug an inexpensive electret microphone into the tape recorder's mic input. Plug the jack of the 3.5-mm stereo cable into the audio output.

STEP 7 Remove the tape recorder's door and look for the recorder's write-protection button, a small movable "finger" opposite the record head. Hold down this button and press the recorder's red record button to start charging the disposable camera's flash. When the amber ready light glows steadily, you can start using it.

STEP 8 Find a dark area, mount your camera onto a tripod, and set the shutter of the camera you'll be shooting with for a bulb exposure. (Cameras that can deliver timed 1- to 4-second exposures can also work.)

STEP 9 Kill the lights, hold the flash trigger near your subject, open the camera's shutter, and record a high-speed event that is accompanied by a noise—such as the pop of a water balloon or the smack of a slap. Take your pick and take some pics.

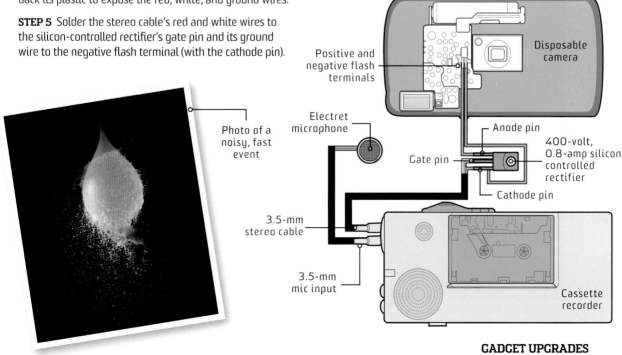

Photo of a noisy, fast event

Positive and negative flash terminals

Disposable camera

Electret microphone

Gate pin

Anode pin

400-volt, 0.8-amp silicon controlled rectifier

Cathode pin

3.5-mm stereo cable

3.5-mm mic input

Cassette recorder

GADGET UPGRADES

215 A CAMERA THAT SHOOTS HUGE PHOTOGRAPHS

This beast of a camera allows you to capture huge images on X-ray film. Problem is, you'll have to build it first.

Darren Samuelson had just taken his last photo of Manhattan when the police arrived. He and his father had been working from an empty dock across the Hudson River, and the authorities wanted to know what they were doing with a folding contraption that was more than 6 feet (1.8 m) long and 70 pounds (32 kg) pointed at the city. Samuelson pleaded that it was a camera, and that he was just a tourist. They believed him and he got his shot—a photo so detailed that the print could be blown up to half the length of a volleyball court and still remain sharp.

Samuelson specially built this camera for X-ray stock that measures 14 by 36 inches (35 cm by 90 cm) and is cheaper than large-format photo paper. He began by constructing the massive accordionlike bellows required to adjust the camera's focal length manually, spending two weeks on the floor folding, cutting, gluing, and inserting the ribs that would give it form. The camera and bellows unfold and slide out on rails, with a lens at one end and the film holder at the other. To focus, he slides either end in or out. The result is not point-and-shoot, Samuelson admits, and the build wasn't easy (the parts list runs to 186 rows on a spreadsheet). "But when I hold up a print and see the amazing detail," he says, "I think, 'Yeah, this was worth it.'"

MEGA PRINTS
Each print measures 3 feet (90 cm), and while shooting Samuelson drapes an immense black cloak over himself and the camera to block out light.

THINGS THAT GO

216 RIDE WITH A GREASE-FREE PANT LEG

STEP 1 Dig up an old toe strap from a pair of retired bike pedals. Apply a strip of adhesive reflective tape to the strap; it'll keep you safe during night rides.

STEP 2 Gather your chain-side pant leg, or roll it up to about mid-calf.

STEP 3 Wrap the toe strap around your calf, thread the buckle, and tighten. Adjust on the fly.

Toe strap
with
reflective
tape

Hiked-up
pant leg

Retired
bike pedal

217 REINFORCE YOUR TIRE WITH A SEAT BELT

STEP 1 Head to the junkyard or second-hand store and find an old seat belt.

STEP 2 Use scissors to cut off the buckle and latch plate.

STEP 3 Lay the belt inside your bicycle tire and cut it so that the ends don't overlap.

STEP 4 Insert your tire tube as you normally would and stretch the tire back onto the rim, making sure the tube still fits well inside the tire.

Seat belt

Tire

Tube

Discarded seat-
belt ends

218 STAY SAFE WITH A BEER-VIEW MIRROR

STEP 1 Obtain a piece of mirror that fits into your bottle cap. (Or use a glass cutter to score and punch out a small circle from a larger mirror.)

STEP 2 Using a drill bit that matches the diameter of a bicycle spoke, drill two holes in the rim of a bottle cap. The holes should be directly opposite each other.

STEP 3 Thread the spoke onto the cap. Once the spoke is through both sides of the cap, secure it by placing putty on the spoke's end.

STEP 4 Squeeze some glue into the back of the bottle cap and set the mirror down into it. Arrange the cap so the mirror will face you when it's installed on the helmet. Bend the cap and mirror on the spoke about 90 degrees, then wait 24 hours for the glue to dry completely.

STEP 5 Take a good look at your helmet to devise a proper mounting method. If your helmet has holes, you'll need to thread the spoke through one of them and then use needle-nose pliers to bend the spoke's end into a loop, then secure one end of the loop through the helmet's hole. Other helmet styles will call for other tactics—just make sure it's mounted in a way that won't poke you.

STEP 6 Hold the spoke in front of your helmet and determine how much length you'll need, given your mounting method and how far you'd like it to extend in front of you. Cut it to this length.

STEP 7 Secure it to your helmet and ride safe.

Spoke

Helmet

Mirror

Bottle cap

219 KEEP YOUR HANDLEBAR GRIPS TIGHT

STEP 1 If your handlebars start to slip around, remove the rubber grips. Wipe out the inside of the grips with a soft cloth.

STEP 2 Spray a few pumps of hair spray—the non-aerosol kind works best—inside the grips.

STEP 3 While the hair spray is wet, slide the grips into place on your handlebars.

STEP 4 Let the hair spray set overnight. Enjoy your no-budge grips.

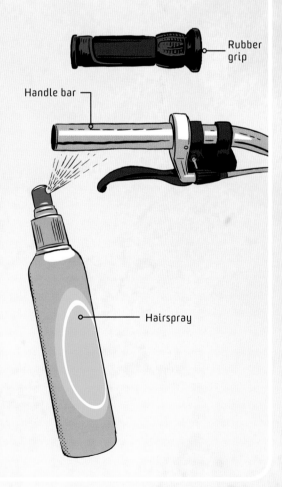

Rubber grip

Handle bar

Hairspray

220 BRING THE PARTY WITH A BIKE SPEAKER

Everyone knows that bike rides are best when they come with a soundtrack.

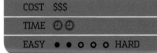

COST	$$$
TIME	◔ ◔
EASY ● ● ○ ○ ○ HARD	

MATERIALS

Bike with a rear rack
10-inch (25-cm) speaker with cable
Marker
Four bolts with washers and nuts to fit
2-by-2-inch (5-by-5-cm) wood board

Waterproof plastic container
Drill
Small screws
Foam
Tripath-based amp
Bike-light mount
Media player with clip holder
Superglue

STEP 1 Set the speaker on your bike rack and mark places for four holes on its underside for bolts.

STEP 2 Take the grille off the speaker and remove the woofer. Drill the holes you marked and put the bolts in so that they stick out from the speaker box's bottom.

STEP 3 Cut the 2-by-2-inch (5-by-5-cm) board to the size of your speaker's bottom. Make two holes in each board for the bolts in the speaker.

STEP 4 Put the woofer and the grille back into the speaker box, and use the washers and nuts to bolt the speaker to the board on the rack.

STEP 5 Screw the waterproof plastic container onto the speaker's top. Drill two holes in one side of the container and line its bottom with foam. Place the amp inside.

STEP 6 Connect the speaker to the amp's right channel with the speaker cable, threading it through one of the holes in the container's side.

STEP 7 Attach the bike-light mount to your handlebar, and glue on your media player's clip holder. Slide your media player in.

STEP 8 Thread your media player's cord through the second hole in the plastic container's side to connect it to the amp. Press play and put the top on.

STEP 9 Watch parties erupt as you ride by.

Waterproof plastic container with tripath-based amp inside

10-inch (25-cm) speaker

Board on rack

Media player

Cord to amp

221 STAY WARM ON CHILLY RIDES

STEP 1 Wad or fold newspaper to the length of your chest.

STEP 2 Insert the paper into your jacket and zip it up. Add more if you want extra warmth.

STEP 3 Ride on in the cold.

222 MAKE A UNICYCLE OUT OF A BIKE

Turns out unis aren't so tricky to make, but they're still just as tricky to ride.

MATERIALS

Old fixed-gear bicycle with a straight fork
Hacksaw
Metal file
Allen wrench
Steel pillow blocks

STEP 1 Remove the bicycle's front fork. Use a hacksaw, if necessary, to cut the frame where it's attached to the fork. File the edges of the cut pieces to smooth them.

STEP 2 Remove the handlebar and stem from the front fork using the Allen wrench.

STEP 3 Remove the rear wheel and crank. To do this, take the chain off the gears of the rear wheel and unfasten the bolts that hold it to the frame.

STEP 4 Attach the front fork to the wheel axle by clamping the steel pillow blocks on each side of the fork and attaching the blocks to the axle at the spacers, using the bottom lock nut. Reattach the crank and pedals.

STEP 5 Insert the seat post into the front fork and unicycle away. (Just spare us the clown suit.)

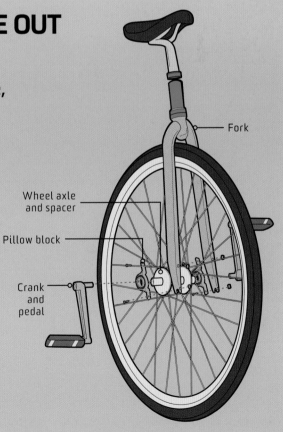

Fork

Wheel axle and spacer

Pillow block

Crank and pedal

THINGS THAT GO

223 NAVIGATE WITH AN OLD-FASHIONED GPS

Because the best bike adventures lack cell reception.

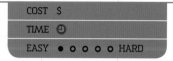

COST	$
TIME	◔
EASY ● ○ ○ ○ ○ HARD	

MATERIALS

Bicycle
Sturdy plastic mesh
Scissors
Large zip-top storage bag
Two Velcro strips 6 inches (15 cm) in length
Velcro strip 5 inches (12.5 cm) in length
Map

STEP 1 Cut the plastic mesh so that when you slide it inside the storage bag it lies flat.

STEP 2 Remove the mesh and make four slits in it just large enough for the Velcro strips to fit through. Two horizontal slits go in the upper corners; two vertical slits go in the center (where your bike's top tube is).

STEP 3 Slip the mesh inside the bag and adjust it so that it butts up against the zipper. Mark the location of the top slits on the back and front of the bag. Mark the location of the center strips on the back of the bag only.

STEP 4 Remove the mesh from the bag. Cut slits along the bag's markings.

STEP 5 Pass the Velcro strips through the slits in the bag. Wrap the 6-inch (15-cm) strips around the handlebars and the 5-inch (12.5-cm) strip around the top tube, and fasten them into loops. Insert the mesh back into the bag.

STEP 6 Open the bag and slide a printout of your route inside it.

STEP 7 Start riding, referring to your map when needed.

Velcro

Plastic mesh

Zip-top storage bag

224 MAKE YOUR BIKE'S TIRES SNOW PROOF

Brave the winter with DIY snow chains for your bike.

STEP 1 Make sure your bike has a coaster brake, a disc brake, or, if it's a fixed gear, no brake. (This particular trick won't work with rim brakes.)

STEP 2 Gather two zip ties for each spoke gap on both of your bicycle's tires.

STEP 3 Wrap a zip tie around the tire and rim, positioning the zip tie's head halfway between the outside of the tire and the rim. Fasten it shut.

STEP 4 Continue placing zip ties in the spoke gaps, alternating the side on which the head faces and leaving enough clearance between the zip ties and your fenders.

STEP 5 Trim the end of each zip tie just to the head. Ride off into the slush.

225 PROTECT YOUR BIKE SADDLE FROM THEFT

Deter bike saddle thieves with simple, persuasive inconvenience.

STEP 1 Making sure your seat post is at maximum height, measure a length of chain long enough to wrap through the saddle rails and seat stays.

STEP 2 Break the chain at your measured loop length and cut a used inner tube to the length of the chain.

STEP 3 Drop the chain through the inner tube.

STEP 4 Thread the chain between your saddle's seat rails and seat stays, then use a chain tool to rejoin the chain.

STEP 5 Never ride home without a saddle again.

Saddle rails

Inner tube

Chain

Seat stay

QUICK
HACKS

226 REUSE A BUSTED BIKE TUBE

A flat tire can really ruin your day. Get revenge
on it with these simple reuse ideas.

SUPER-SIZE RUBBER BANDS
Cut them into long strips and use them to secure all sorts of things. You can also make a really big rubber-band ball, or shoot them into the sky. (If you shoot them at people, you didn't get this idea here!)

GET A GRIP
Wrap a tube around the handle of common household tools (such as screwdrivers, brooms, rakes, and hammers) to improve your grip.

KEEP PAINT LOOKING SPIFFY
Protect the paint on vulnerable areas of your bicycle—such as where your lock rubs against the frame—by wrapping inner tubes around those areas.

EMERGENCY HEADLIGHT
If your bike light dies and you've got a flashlight handy, fish a spare inner tube out of your bag. Cut a piece that is 2 inches (5 cm) longer than your flashlight, then make a hole near each of the tube's ends. Run the tube under your handlebar so that it is perpendicular to the bar, and thread the flashlight through the holes with the light pointing forward. Turn it on and go.

BUNGEE CORDS IN A PINCH
Cut a sliver of inner tube and use it as a zip tie or bungee cord to lash whatever's loose.

227 SHRED ON A FAN-PROPELLED SKATEBOARD

Why cruise on a regular skateboard when you can blast by on this model?

Fast is cool, but few would disagree that faster is even better. This skateboard build has you adding the engine, propeller, and remote-control transmitter from a model airplane (which you can pick up as independent parts in a hobby shop, or salvage from a spare model plane near you) for a version that'd make even Marty McFly jealous.

COST	$$$
TIME	☺ ☺ ☺
EASY ● ● ● ○ ○ HARD	

STEP 1 Blow the template at right up to size so it's about 4½ feet (1.35 m) in length and trace it onto your piece of wood. Use a jigsaw to cut out the board, and sand the edges so they're splinter-free. Drill holes so you can mount the trucks and risers.

STEP 2 Cut out and sand the two pieces from the remaining wood that will serve as mounting planks for the fan, gas tank, and engine, as well as create a compartment for the electronics. Make the mounting planks tall enough so that they'll provide clearance for your fan model's cage, keeping it off the ground and the skateboard bottom.

STEP 3 Apply adhesive-backed grip tape in your desired colors to the board and mounting compartment pieces.

STEP 4 Screw the trucks and risers to the board using the predrilled holes.

MATERIALS

4½ feet (1.35 m) of 1-by-10-inch (2.5-by-25-cm) wood
Jigsaw
Sandpaper
Drill
Adhesive-backed skateboard grip tape
Skateboard trucks and risers with wheels
Screws and washers
Remote-control transmitter with bundled receiver and servo

Wire
Battery for transmitter
OS 1.60 FX model airplane engine
950-cc gas tank and gas
Hose clamp
Fan cage
Three-blade propeller
Standard glow starter with meter
12-volt starter motor

Fan cage

Model airplane engine

Glow plug

Gas tank

Skateboard covered in grip tape

Electronics compartment

Trucks and risers

Three-blade propeller

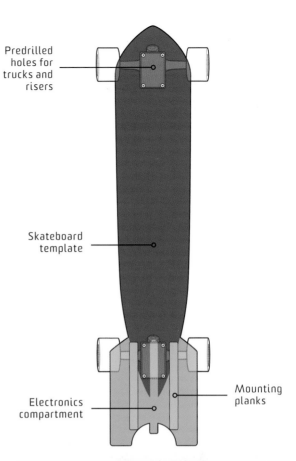

Predrilled holes for trucks and risers

Skateboard template

Mounting planks

Electronics compartment

STEP 5 Screw the two mounting planks securely into the back end of the board from the underside, after predrilling holes for them with a smaller bit. Cut another piece of scrap wood the width of the space between the mounting planks. Screw it in between the planks near their tops as a roof for the compartment that will house the electronics.

STEP 6 Wrap a short piece of wire around the servo's horn (the part where the arm screws on), and wrap the other end around the engine's throttle lever.

STEP 7 Plug the servo's connector into the receiver, then hook the battery to the receiver. Next mount the engine above the electronics compartment, screwing through the engine mount holes into the tops of the mounting planks. Secure the servo, receiver, and battery inside.

STEP 8 Screw a hose clamp to the outside of the mounting planks, then tighten the hose clamp around the gas tank to mount it. Connect the gas tank to the engine.

STEP 9 Unscrew the cage from a fan and insert the propeller. Slide the propeller onto the engine, tightening the propeller's bolt, then secure the cage onto the electronics compartment's roof with screws and washers.

STEP 10 Plug the glow starter into the engine's glow plug and use the starter motor to rotate the propeller. Once it's started up, set aside the starter motor, remove the glow plug, and give the remote to someone you trust. Zoom off.

YOU BUILT WHAT?!

A MOTORIZED SKATEBOARD

If you ever see a grown man whizzing by on a skateboard doing 20 miles per hour (32 km/h), that would be John Carnett, and in case you don't get a good look, his ride is a souped-up, motorized board he built from the ground up. He wanted to create a skateboard that would be superior to commercial models—a fast, hot-looking board that ran on all terrains. He cut an aluminum deck and bent the ends and side rails, then he outfitted it with axles and 8-inch (20-cm) knobby tires. Then there was the matter of installing a disc-braking system and a 500-watt electric motor. It's the sweetest ride on the road—or off it.

228 GIVE YOUR MOTORCYLE A FUTURISTIC VIBE

Ride straight out of the movie *TRON* with this illuminated motorcycle trick.

COST	$$$
TIME	☺ ☺ ☺
EASY	● ● ● ● ○ HARD

MATERIALS

Motorcycle
Flexible LED light strips
Heavy-duty tape
Wire strippers
Two clamp connectors

Soldering iron and solder
18-gauge black wire
18-gauge red wire
Zip ties
On/off switch

STEP 1 Locate your motorcycle's battery—it's probably under the seat.

STEP 2 Place the LED strips where you want them along your motorcycle's frame. If the strips themselves are not adhesive, secure them with tape, and run the wires through the frame body toward the battery.

STEP 3 Using the wire strippers, strip some of the insulation from the ends of all the LED strips' wires. Place the negative wires into a clamp connector and the positive wires into another clamp connector.

STEP 4 Solder the black 18-gauge wire to the clamp housing the black LED wires, and the red 18-gauge wire to the clamp housing the red wires.

STEP 5 Gather the wires and secure them with a zip tie.

STEP 6 Mount the on/off switch somewhere you can easily reach while you're riding. Strip the ends of the black and red 18-gauge wires. Connect the red 18-gauge wire to the on/off switch, soldering on another length of 18-gauge red wire to extend to the battery.

STEP 7 Connect the black 18-gauge wire to the battery's negative terminal and the red 18-gauge wire to the battery's positive terminal.

STEP 8 Start your motorcycle, flip the switch into the "on" position, and make sure all the LED strips light up—if they don't, check your connections.

STEP 9 Suit up and ride off into an alternate reality.

229 LIGHT UP YOUR MOTORCYCLE HELMET

Make your helmet extra safe—and extra cool, too—with conductive paint.

MATERIALS

Motorcycle helmet
Fine sandpaper
Paper towel
Pencil
Masking tape
Conductive paint
Paintbrush
Wire strippers
Electrical wire
Soldering iron and solder

9-volt battery
9-volt battery snap
On/off switch
Epoxy
Wooden sticks for mixing and applying epoxies
LEDs
Conductive epoxy
Clear spray enamel

STEP 1 Sand the surface of your helmet where your design will go and then wipe it with a damp paper towel.

STEP 2 Draw a circuit directly onto the helmet. Trace components (such as the LEDs, battery, and on/off switch) onto the helmet and mark positives and negatives.

STEP 3 Mask out the area around your circuit to contain the conductive paint.

STEP 4 Paint inside the tape, mapping your circuit. Make sure to stir the paint thoroughly and often, as the particles tend to settle. Apply multiple coats, if needed.

STEP 5 Let the paint dry for a few minutes and carefully remove the masking tape. Then let dry for 24 hours.

STEP 6 Snap the battery snap onto the 9-volt battery. Strip the ends of two pieces of wire and solder positive and negative leads to the snap's positive and negative ports. Then solder these leads to the positive and negative terminals of your on/off switch.

STEP 7 Use wooden sticks to mix and apply epoxy, then affix the on/off switch and battery to the helmet. Let dry.

STEP 8 Trim the leads of the LEDs. Use conductive epoxy to attach the LEDs where you want them, and then affix the switch wires.

STEP 9 Let dry for 24 hours, then seal over and around the conductive paint with epoxy to waterproof.

STEP 10 Tape off areas of your helmet you want to protect—like fabric parts or LED bulbs—and spray your helmet with clear spray enamel.

STEP 11 To turn the lights on, flip the on/off switch.

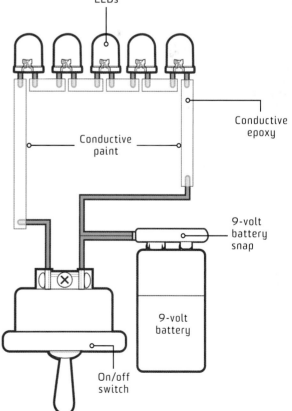

LEDs

Conductive epoxy

Conductive paint

9-volt battery snap

9-volt battery

On/off switch

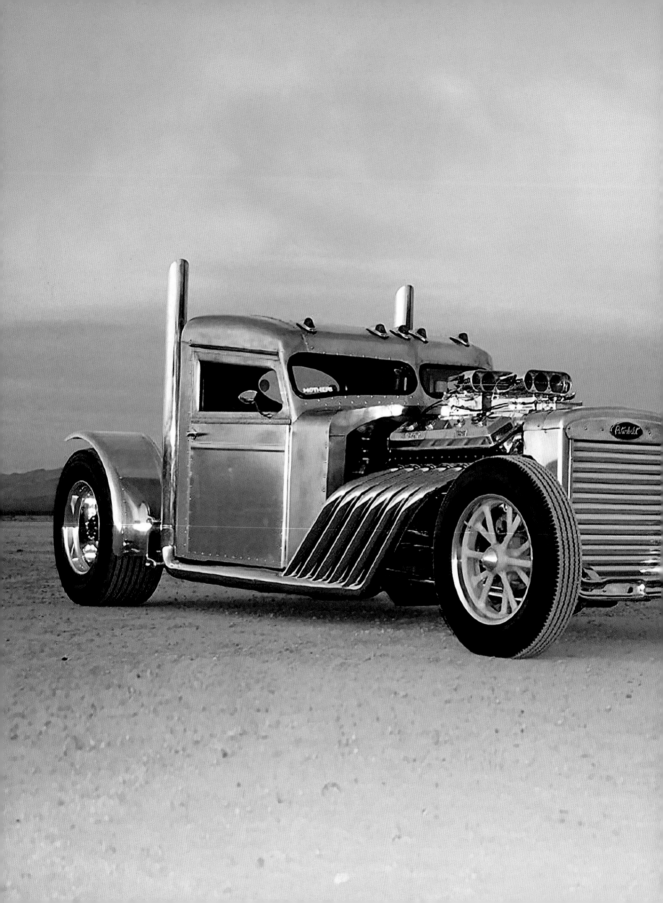

230 THE VROOMING HOT-ROD HAULER

An old logging truck is transformed into a sleek street racer.

Randy Grubb couldn't get it off his mind. For years he had been driving past an old logger's place near his home in rural Oregon, and one of the long-haul trucks in the man's yard kept catching his attention. In late 2008, Grubb finally stopped for a closer look, and the toothless, cigar-chomping trucker let him rev the engine. He was sold, but he had a big change in mind: He was going to transform it into a hot rod.

The 49-year-old Grubb had built a number of other vehicles out of forgotten engines in his backyard shop. But making a dragster out of this ancient truck—a 1965 Peterbilt Model 351 with a giant 12-cylinder, two-stroke diesel engine—was unlike any of his past jobs. The engine hadn't been used in a decade, so he found a diesel mechanic to help him tune it up, replaced the original 13-speed transmission with a four-speed automatic normally used in Greyhound buses, installed new fuel lines, and then polished every cubic inch. Next came the body. He shortened the truck's grille by 10.5 inches (26.25 cm), took the front and rear axles from another truck and narrowed them to hot-rod scale, and machined and welded all the connective hardware to complete the transformation.

Grubb refers to the car—dubbed Piss'd Off Pete because it's a Peterbilt with attitude—as an aluminum sculpture. In fact, the vehicle will most likely soon be in a private collection. But he hardly treats it like a museum piece. As soon as he was finished, he drag-raced it at more than 100 miles an hour (160 km/h).

OFF THE SCRAP HEAP
Piss'd Off Pete runs on a 12-cylinder engine Grubb calls "the biggest, baddest diesel ever made." Just how much did making it cost him? $100,000.

231 MOUNT A RAD HOOD ORNAMENT

STEP 1 Use epoxy to glue a plastic figurine of your choosing to a circular magnet with a center bore.

STEP 2 If your car has a hood ornament, remove it. Thread a screw through the magnet of your new one and turn to secure the screw to the ornament.

STEP 3 Screw it onto your car's hood in the old ornament's hole, or just use the magnet to hold it in place.

232 HANG A DIY AIR FRESHENER

STEP 1 Cut out a T-shirt image you like and trace it onto a sheet of fabric softener and a piece of fabric.

STEP 2 Staple the dryer sheet in between the two pieces of fabric.

STEP 3 Punch a hole in the top and insert a rubber band; knot the band to secure it.

STEP 4 Hang it up in your car to cover up stink.

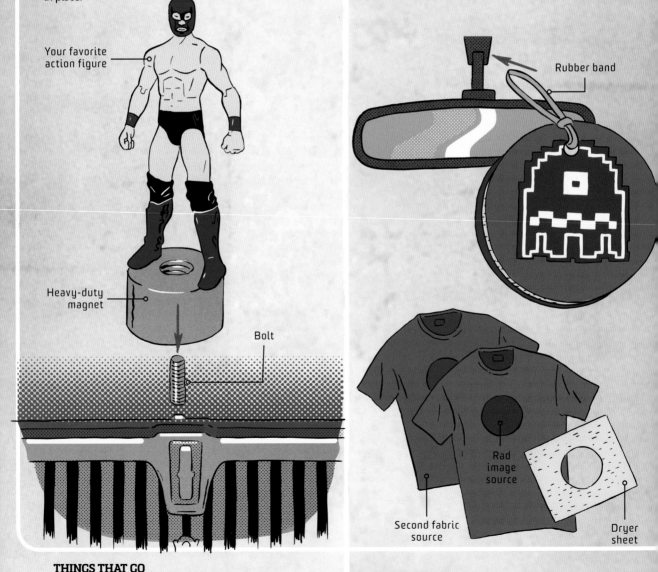

Your favorite action figure

Heavy-duty magnet

Bolt

Rubber band

Rad image source

Second fabric source

Dryer sheet

233 BLACK OUT YOUR TAILLIGHTS

STEP 1 Remove your taillight lenses by unscrewing the bolts holding them onto the car.

STEP 2 Clean them, and then cover the lights entirely with strips of masking tape, pressing the strips into the grooves with a pen.

STEP 3 Draw your design onto the masking tape.

STEP 4 Cut out your design by tracing your drawing with a razor blade or a craft knife. Remove the excess tape.

STEP 5 Put tape around the light's edges.

STEP 6 Lightly sand the unmasked surfaces.

STEP 7 Spray the taillight with black paint in quick passes. Do two to three coats, allowing them to dry in between.

STEP 8 Apply a coat of clear spraypaint. Gently remove the tape.

STEP 9 Reinstall your badder-than-before taillights and hit the streets (after investigating how your local law enforcement will feel about them).

234 INSTALL AIR HORNS IN YOUR CAR

STEP 1 Open up your hood and detach the battery's negative terminal with a wrench.

STEP 2 Locate the factory-issued horn at the front of the engine and disconnect the power harness from it, starting with the ground wire. (The power harness is the bundle of wires that keeps the horn juiced, and it will power your new horn and air compressor.)

STEP 3 Remove the old horn from the mount. Using the brackets that came with your air horn kit, mount your new horns in the same place as the factory-issued horn. Aim the new horns slightly downward.

STEP 4 Find a clear spot under the hood and along the firewall (the sheet metal that separates the engine from the passenger section). Mount the air compressor here using the mounting bolts that came with the kit.

STEP 5 Connect the wiring harness's hot wire and the air compressor's hot wire to a relay.

STEP 6 Ground the relay's ground wire to a bolt, then connect the relay's hot wire to the car battery.

STEP 7 Run a tube from the compressor to the horns.

STEP 8 Reconnect the negative terminal to complete the circuit. Let those bad boys blast.

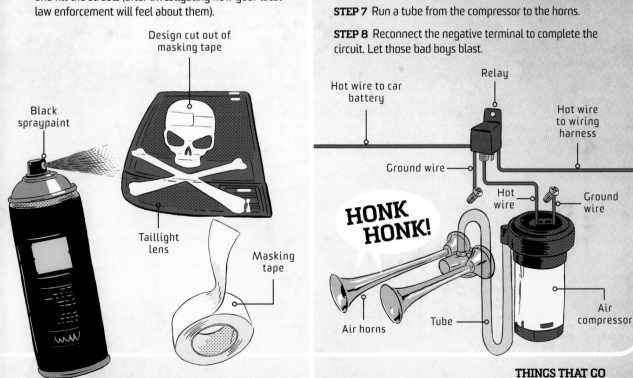

Black spraypaint

Design cut out of masking tape

Taillight lens

Masking tape

Hot wire to car battery

Relay

Hot wire to wiring harness

Ground wire

Hot wire

Ground wire

HONK HONK!

Air horns

Tube

Air compressor

235 FEND OFF FENDER BENDERS WITH A SONIC DISTANCE SENSOR

Back up with confidence thanks to a device that beeps when you're about to crash.

COST $$

TIME 🕐🕐

EASY ● ● ● ○ ○ HARD

MATERIALS

Ping ultrasonic distance sensor

Electrical wire

Arduino Uno

Buzzer

Epoxy

STEP 1 Wire the Ping sensor to your Arduino according to the circuitry diagram.

STEP 2 To hook up the buzzer, wire its positive end to the Arduino's pin 8, and the negative end to a ground pin.

STEP 3 Load up the Arduino code for the Ping sensor, which you can find at www.popsci.com/thebigbookofhacks.

STEP 4 Mount the sensor on the back of your car with epoxy, running the wires through the trunk to the inside of the car.

STEP 5 Mount the buzzer with epoxy somewhere inside the car where you'll be able to hear it.

STEP 6 When the sensor comes within 1 foot (30 cm) of an obstacle, the buzzer will sound to warn you. You may now parallel park without fear.

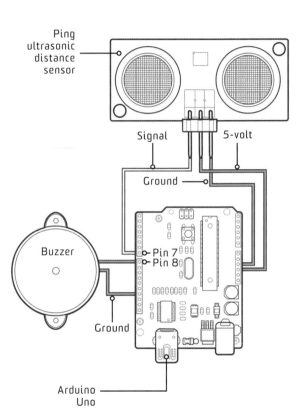

Ping ultrasonic distance sensor

Signal 5-volt

Ground

Buzzer

Pin 7
Pin 8

Ground

Arduino Uno

236 HACK AN EMERGENCY USB CHARGER

On the lam without your car charger? Splice some wires and be on your way.

MATERIALS

USB cable for your device
Knife

Any 5-volt car cigarette lighter
adapter
Tape

STEP 1 Cut the USB end off the cable for your device and strip the insulation. You'll use the black and red wires to connect to the adapter. Twist together the other two wires.

STEP 2 Cut off the end of the cigarette lighter adapter that does not plug into the cigarette lighter. Use the knife to strip the insulation to reveal the black and red wires.

STEP 3 Twist the two red wires together and the two black wires together. Wrap tape around the joints to insulate them.

STEP 4 Plug it in and charge up your phone in the car.

5 MINUTE PROJECT

237 SHIFT WITH A CUSTOM GEAR KNOB

STEP 1 Pry off your old shift knob. Measure the size of the knob's mount.

STEP 2 Choose an object to use as a new shift knob (resin, wood, and plastic work well).

STEP 3 Drill a hole in the object's bottom to fit the knob mount.

STEP 4 Glue your new knob onto your shifter using epoxy. Upshift in style.

238 BUILD A BED IN YOUR VAN

Get on the road again with a mod that makes your van at least as comfy as that Best Western.

COST	$$
TIME	☺ ☺ ☺
EASY ● ● ● ○ ○ HARD	

MATERIALS

Sweet van

Tape measure

Paper and pencil

Storage bins, if desired

Two sheets of 1¼-inch (3-cm) plywood

2x4s

Wood screws

Screwdriver

Jigsaw

Mattress

STEP 1 Measure the space you have available in the back of your van, accounting for any obstructions, such as wheel wells. You may want to remove the last row of seats to provide more space.

STEP 2 Make a plan for a bed frame based on your van's measurements, and include a flat bottom, two risers that lift the bed off the van floor, and a flat top. If you want to use the space under the bed for storage, figure storage bins into your plan.

STEP 3 Construct your risers. Lay out a long 2x4 and attach four shorter 2x4s perpendicular to it, spaced evenly along it. Reinforce the riser by doubling up your 2x4s as necessary. Repeat to build a second riser. (Use screws instead of nails if you want to be able to deconstruct and remove the bed easily.)

STEP 4 Use a jigsaw to customize the bottom of the bed, cutting out holes for any brackets or wheel wells that would keep the bottom from sitting flat in your van.

STEP 5 Attach the two risers to the sheet of plywood that will serve as the bed's bottom, then slide the bottom into your van. You may need to tilt it to get it inside.

STEP 6 Attach evenly spaced crosspieces to the risers.

STEP 7 Use a jigsaw to trim the top of the bed to avoid obstructions as needed, then screw it to the crosspieces.

STEP 8 Add a mattress or other padding and slide your storage bins underneath the bed.

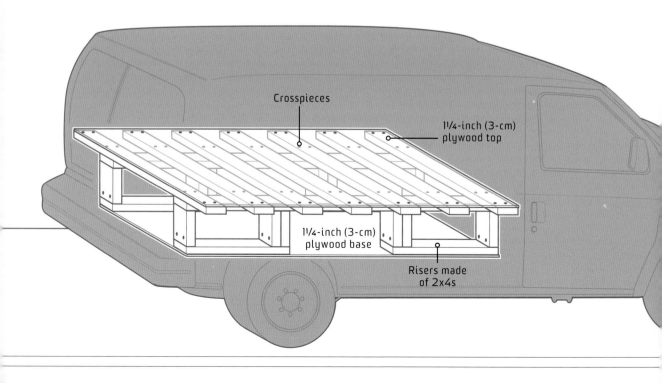

Crosspieces

1¼-inch (3-cm) plywood top

1¼-inch (3-cm) plywood base

Risers made of 2x4s

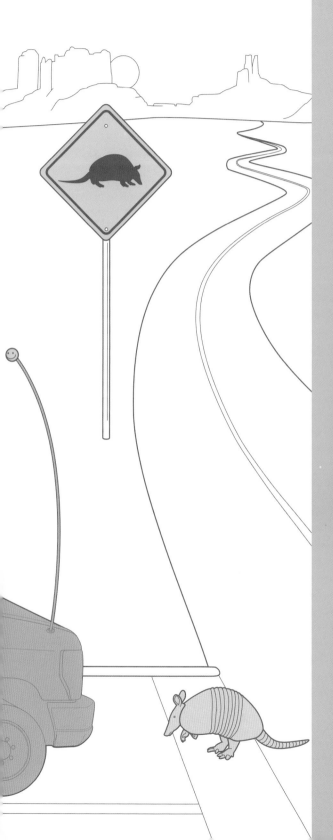

239 RIG A CAMPING SHOWER

MATERIALS

Hose
12-volt output pump
Two PVC elbows
Small-diameter PVC pipe

Showerhead
12-volt car lighter
Bucket of water

STEP 1 Attach a small piece of hose to the outlet on a 12-volt output pump.

STEP 2 Add a PVC elbow fitting to the hose, and connect a length of small-diameter PVC pipe. Run the pipe to another elbow, then screw a showerhead to the second elbow's end.

STEP 3 Wire the pump to a 12-volt car lighter plug, and drop the pump in a bucket of water.

STEP 4 Hang up your shower to a tree near you, securing it however you see fit. Enjoy showering outdoors.

PVC pipe

Elbow

Elbow

Showerhead

Bungee cord

Hose

12-volt pump's wire

Bucket containing water and pump

240 KIT OUT A SOLAR-CHARGING MESSENGER BAG

Mod a basic bag and charge your gadgets with the sun's rays.

COST	$$
TIME	☺ ☺ ☺
EASY ● ● ● ○ ○ HARD	

MATERIALS

Messenger bag
Scissors
Grommeting kit
Clear vinyl sheeting
Superglue
Photovoltaic panel
78M05 voltage regulator
Project box
0.47F 50-volt electrolytic capacitor

0.1F 50-volt tantalum capacitor
Electrical wire
Soldering iron and solder
USB cable with female connector
Digital multimeter
A device to charge that connects to the USB cable

STEP 1 Use the grommeting kit to punch holes in your bag. (These holes are for the wires connecting the photovoltaic panel to the voltage regulator and your device.) Reinforce the holes with grommets.

STEP 2 Use clear vinyl sheeting to create a pocket for the photovoltaic panel. Glue it in place over the grommets so it's on the bag's outside.

STEP 3 Mount the voltage regulator inside your project box, then follow the circuitry diagram to hook up the capacitors and voltage regulator. Solder these connections.

STEP 4 Snip off the male connector from the USB cable. Open the cable end and separate the four wires: red, black, green, and white. Connect the red wire to the output lead of the 78M05 voltage regulator and the black wire to the voltage regulator's ground lead.

STEP 5 With the photovoltaic panel in the clear pocket, connect its positive terminal to the input lead of the voltage regulator. Connect its negative terminal to the voltage regulator's ground lead, threading the wires through the holes in the bag.

STEP 6 Place the photovoltaic panel in direct sunlight and test the voltage readings with a digital multimeter at four points: the photovoltaic panel terminals, the voltage regulator input, the voltage regulator output, and the USB pin 1 + 4. The readings at the first two points should both be approximately 7 to 8 volts. The readings at the last two points should be exactly 5.15 volts.

STEP 7 If everything checks out, hook up a suitable device and charge out there.

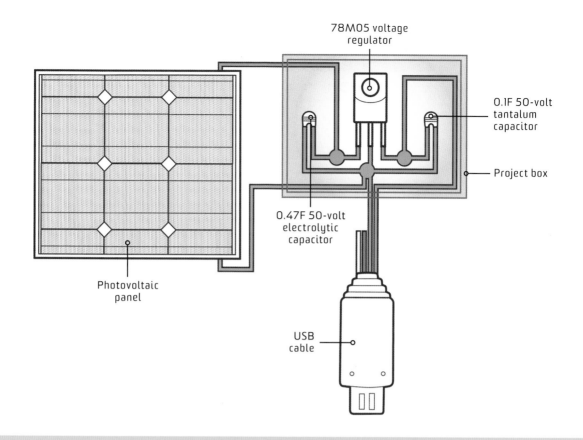

78M05 voltage
regulator

0.1F 50-volt
tantalum
capacitor

Project box

0.47F 50-volt
electrolytic
capacitor

Photovoltaic
panel

USB
cable

241 STAY COOL ON THE GO
WITH AD HOC A/C

**If you're camping, you've already got a
cooler. Hook up a fan to feel the breeze.**

MATERIALS

Styrofoam cooler

Saw

Ice

Portable fan

STEP 1 Cut a hole in the lid of the cooler; it should be as
large as the fan's face.

STEP 2 Cut holes in the side of the cooler. They should
face in the general direction in which you'd like the cool
air to blow.

STEP 3 Add ice to the cooler and replace the lid.

STEP 4 Place the fan facedown over the hole in the lid,
and turn it on.

STEP 5 Pull up a chair and swelter no more.

242 REFILL A TINY TOOTHPASTE TUBE

STEP 1 Detach the tops of two toothpaste tubes and place them together with their closed ends touching.

STEP 2 Use a ring of Sugru to attach the closed ends. Wait 24 hours for it to dry.

STEP 3 Drill a hole through the center of the attached tops. Brush out any shards of plastic.

STEP 4 Attach a full large tube of toothpaste to one side, and an empty travel-size tube to the other. Squeeze to refill.

243 ASSEMBLE A COLLAPSIBLE TRAVEL HANGER

Because wrinkled clothes are for suckers, but so are hanging bags.

MATERIALS

Wire hanger
Wire cutters
3 feet (90 cm) of ½-inch (1.25-cm) PVC
4 feet (1.2 m) of rope
Pliers

STEP 1 Measure the length of each side of a wire hanger. Cut three sections of PVC pipe, sized to match those measurements.

STEP 2 Cut the hook off the wire hanger, slicing about 1 inch (2.5 cm) below the twisted base of the hook on either side. Use pliers to bend the two ends up at the base.

STEP 3 Line up the PVC sections so they match the layout of the original hanger, then thread the rope through all three sections, leaving enough slack so that the hanger will be able to collapse—about 6 inches (15 cm). Tie a knot in the rope.

STEP 4 Thread the base of the hook through the rope at the top of the hanger, using pliers to close the upturned ends around the rope.

STEP 5 To collapse the completed hanger, just fold it up— if it doesn't fold, use a longer piece of rope.

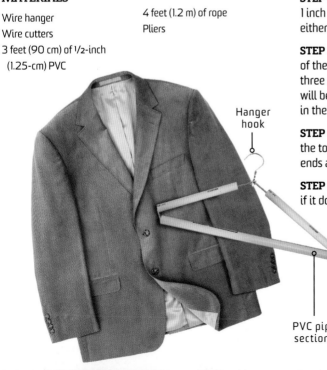

Hanger hook

Rope threaded through the PVC

PVC pipe sections

244 GIVE YOUR SUITCASE THE GIFT OF WHEELS

Forget lugging that luggage—upgrade it and let it roll itself to the terminal.

MATERIALS

Metal plate
Four casters
Suitcase
Marker

Drill
Grommet kit
Nuts and bolts
Rubber washers

STEP 1 Choose a metal plate that fits the side of the suitcase you're modifying. Decide where you'd like the casters to go, then line up the tops of the casters on your metal plate and mark their positions. Also mark a few sets of holes along each edge of the plate—you'll use these to secure the plate to your bag.

STEP 2 Drill your marks, using a drill bit that matches the size of your bolts.

STEP 3 Place the drilled metal plate in its final position on your suitcase. Use a pen to mark the position of each hole.

STEP 4 Using a grommet kit, punch a hole through your suitcase at each point you marked. Place a grommet on either side of each hole, then hammer the two pieces together using the equipment in your kit. Repeat until you've protected each hole with a grommet.

STEP 5 Line up the plate again, and use nuts and bolts to connect the plate to the bag. Then connect the casters—the bolts for these should run through the plate and into the bag. To add extra weatherproofing, use rubber washers on the inside of all bolts.

245 PACK YOUR RAZOR SAFELY

No more reaching into your toiletries bag and coming out with a bloody fingertip.

MATERIALS

Binder clip
Razor

Rubber band

STEP 1 Fold back the binder clip's arms and open it.

STEP 2 Insert the head of your razor and close the clip, folding down the arms. Use a rubber band to secure the binder clip in place over the razor.

STEP 3 Pack your razor without fear of cutting yourself when you unpack.

TAKE AERIAL PHOTOS WITH A WEATHER BALLOON

Keep your drone envy in check with a rig that snaps shots from the sky.

COST $
TIME ⏱
EASY ● ○ ○ ○ ○ HARD

MATERIALS

Digital camera
3,500 feet (1,070 m) of heavy-duty nylon string
Gaffers tape
Large plastic bottle
Box cutter
Weather balloon
Helium
Rubber band

STEP 1 Choose a camera with a large SD card (at least 4 GB) and a continuous setting.

STEP 2 Make a 3-foot (90-cm) loop of string, wrap it around your camera, and knot it securely against the camera body, with the excess creating another loop.

STEP 3 Secure the string around your camera with gaffers tape. When you dangle it by the loop, your camera should be supported on either side of the lens. (Don't skimp on tape and buy the cheap stuff, or you'll pay for it later.)

STEP 4 Cut a large plastic bottle in half. Put the camera inside the top half of the bottle, lens facing down, with the loop of string sticking out through the neck of the bottle.

STEP 5 Cut out two 8-by-2½-inch (20-by-6.25-cm) plastic strips from the plastic bottle's bottom half. Tape them to the top half of the bottle. (They'll help stabilize the camera during flight.)

STEP 6 Inflate the weather balloon with helium, close it up, and tie the string to the balloon's opening. (If you don't have an especially large balloon, you can make your own by taping two Mylar sleeping bags together and inflating them, then taping them together.)

STEP 7 Attach the camera in its protective cover just below the balloon using the loop of string that's secured to the camera. Tie the 3,500-foot (1,070-m) string to the balloon as well. The weather balloon should lift the camera easily.

STEP 8 Set your camera to continuous mode and use a rubber band to hold down the camera's trigger. Allow the balloon to rise quickly, letting out the string carefully to avoid tangles.

STEP 9 Head in the direction of the area you'd like to document from above. Avoid trees and other structures that could tangle your string. When you're done, just pull the balloon back in by its string.

STEP 10 Use digital photo-stitching software to create huge, detailed maps of your 'hood.

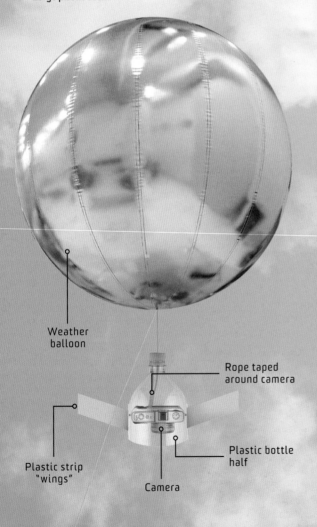

Weather balloon

Rope taped around camera

Plastic strip "wings"

Camera

Plastic bottle half

String

247 MAKE A MINI HOVERCRAFT

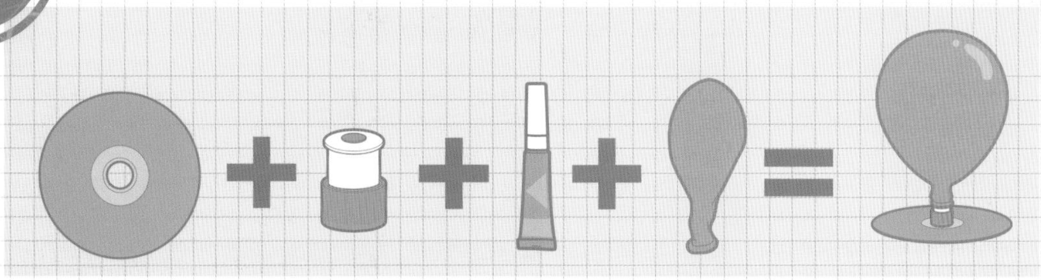

STEP 1 Remove the push-up cap from any sports-drink bottle.

STEP 2 Glue the bottle cap to the top of a CD. Make sure the valve can still open and shut.

STEP 3 Glue a balloon to the cap. Blow it up from underneath, and watch it soar above the floor.

248 LAUNCH A MINI ROCKET

Combine simple household items to make a rocket propulsion system.

MATERIALS

Paper
Pencil
Scissors
Glue

Alka-Seltzer tablets
Water
Empty film canister

STEP 1 Design your rocket, drawing it on paper. A simple cylinder, nose cone, and a pair of fins will suffice. It should stand around 6 inches (15 cm) tall and be approximately 1½ inches (3.75 cm) in diameter.

STEP 2 Cut out your rocket components (cylinder, nose cone, and fins) and glue them together.

STEP 3 Open the film canister and drop one-half of an Alka-Seltzer tablet into it.

STEP 4 Fill the canister half full of water and snap the canister cap into place. Slide the rocket over the cap, place the assembly cap-down, and get back. Watch the rocket blast off.

THINGS THAT GO

249 Build a Better Canoe Paddle

Because tech geeks can be wilderness geeks, too.

MATERIALS

¾-by-20-by-8-inch
 (1.9-by-50-by-20-cm)
 piece of wood board
Keyhole saw
Wood glue
Two rectangular wooden strips,
 5 feet (1.5 m) long
 and ¾ by 1¼ inch
 (1.9 by 3 cm) thick

Rubber bands
Block plane
Sandpaper
Wood finish
Steel wool

STEP 1 Make the paddle blades by cutting the wood board diagonally lengthwise, then remove a triangle with a 1-inch (2.5-cm) base from a corner of each board as shown below. Reserve these for later use.

STEP 2 Use wood glue to connect the two wood strips together, forming the shaft. Hold the strips together with rubber bands and let them dry.

STEP 3 Glue the two paddle halves to the shaft as shown, aligning them carefully. Glue the two triangles in place as the handle grips. Again, hold these parts in place with rubber bands while the glue dries.

STEP 4 Once all the glue is dry, remove the rubber bands. Use the keyhole saw to trim around the blade, contouring its shape as desired.

STEP 5 Use the block plane to contour the center of each blade half for a slightly concave paddle blade, and to shape the shaft and handle.

STEP 6 To round the shaft, hold the grip end in one hand. Slowly rotate the paddle so that the block plane shapes it uniformly on all sides.

STEP 7 Sand the paddle to smooth it and apply wood finish. Let this coat dry before smoothing with steel wool and applying additional coats.

STEP 8 After that last coat of varnish has dried, hit the river or lake and paddle off into the sunset.

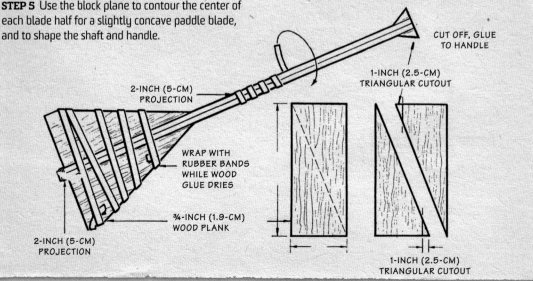

CUT OFF, GLUE
TO HANDLE

1-INCH (2.5-CM)
TRIANGULAR CUTOUT

2-INCH (5-CM)
PROJECTION

WRAP WITH
RUBBER BANDS
WHILE WOOD
GLUE DRIES

¾-INCH (1.9-CM)
WOOD PLANK

2-INCH (5-CM)
PROJECTION

1-INCH (2.5-CM)
TRIANGULAR CUTOUT

250 UPGRADE YOUR KAYAK INTO A SAILBOAT

Pull that old kayak out of the garage and set it sailing.

COST	$$
TIME	⊕ ⊕
EASY ● ● ● ● ○ HARD	

MATERIALS

Aluminum sheeting
1-inch (2.5-cm) PVC pipe
Epoxy
1¼-inch (3-cm) PVC pipe
Drill
Polyethylene kayak
1¼-inch (3-cm) polyethylene irrigation pipe
Plastic welder

Scrap polyethylene plastic
Nylon rope
Boat tarp
Grommeting kit
PVC elbow
Two three-way connectors
Dock ties

STEP 1 Cut the aluminum sheeting to create a rudder and centerboard. The centerboard should be a 1-by-1-foot (30-by-30-cm) square, and the rudder should be about 1 foot (30 cm) in length and 6 inches (15 cm) in height.

STEP 2 Attach the centerboard to a length of 1-inch (2.5-cm) PVC pipe using epoxy.

STEP 3 Make a hole in the kayak's floor immediately in front of the seat. The hole should be large enough for the 1-inch (2.5-cm) pipe. Insert the centerboard pipe into this hole from the bottom, then use a plastic welder and scrap polyethylene to secure the pipe to the kayak's floor.

STEP 4 For the rudder mount, use a section of 1¼-inch (3-cm) polyethylene pipe that's cut to approximately the same height as the tail end of your kayak. Weld the rudder mount onto the kayak's back.

STEP 5 Cut a piece of 1-inch (2.5-cm) PVC pipe so it's a little longer than the rudder mount. Epoxy the aluminum rudder to this pipe and slide it through the rudder mount.

STEP 6 Cap off the rudder pipe with a PVC elbow, then attach a 1-inch (2.5-cm) pipe to the rudder pipe. Drill a hole in the end of this pipe.

STEP 7 Cut two short pieces of polyethylene pipe to use as rudder control handles and make holes in them. Thread a long piece of rope through the handles and through the hole in the pipe attached to the rudder.

STEP 8 For the sail, cut three long pieces of 1-inch (2.5-cm) PVC pipe to the size of your boat tarp and attach them together in a U shape with three-way connectors. Use the grommeting kit to make grommets down the tarp's edges. Attach the sail to the pipes by stringing rope through the grommets and around the pipe frame. Leave a piece of pipe extending that will fit into the mast base.

STEP 9 For the mast base, weld a piece of 1¼-inch (3-cm) PVC pipe to the floor of the kayak with scrap polyethylene. To secure the mast farther up, weld both ends of a half-ring shape that fits the 1¼-inch (3-cm) pipe to the inside front of the kayak. Fit the mast into the base.

STEP 10 Attach lengths of rope to the sail and secure the ropes to the kayak with dock ties. Sail away.

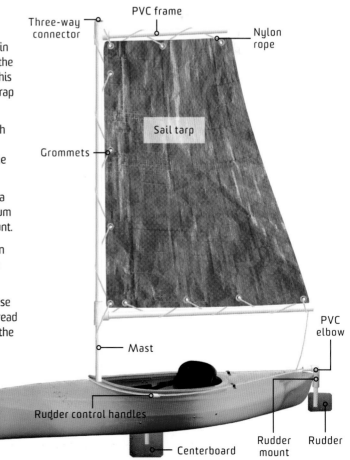

Three-way connector
PVC frame
Nylon rope
Sail tarp
Grommets
Mast
PVC elbow
Rudder control handles
Centerboard
Rudder mount
Rudder

YOU
BUILT
WHAT?!

251 THE INCREDIBLE AMPHIBIOUS TANK

Half boat, half car, all adventure.

Avid hunter Stan Hewitt wanted to tackle the prime duck habitat of the Alaskan tundra, an area hard to access using regular vehicles. He knew he needed a tank to do it—one with speed and maneuverability that would be able to handle the water currents there.

Hewitt designed a 21-foot (6.4-m) craft with two wide, tanklike rubber treads that can pivot 180 degrees when afloat. When on the ground, the treads spread the vehicle's weight over a large surface area, improving traction and exerting minimal pressure on the ground. Hewitt installed a simple hydraulic pump to lift and lower these treads vertically in and out of the water. In sea mode, the Chevy TrailBlazer engine drives an outboard propeller. In land mode, the treads drop so the engine can muscle the craft up onto shore. His creation is the first-ever amphibious vehicle with a fully retractable drive assembly—one that needs just 18 seconds to go from sea cruiser to land rover.

The craft can reach speeds of up to 30 miles per hour (48 km/h) and effortlessly trek through mud flats, bogs, rivers, ice, snow, and lakes—and do it with a 1,500-pound (680-kg) load. There's room for a crew of five and all the gear they need for search and rescue, patrol, geological surveying, and other fieldwork. Ironically, though, Hewitt hasn't gotten around to taking it duck hunting yet.

SEA MONSTER
Hewitt increased the cab's ability to resist water by adding foam sandwiched between layers of aluminum to its panels.

THINGS THAT GO

252 HACK AN OVERSIZE AIR HOCKEY PUCK

STEP 1 Cut a hole in the top of a smoke-detector case. Make sure the hole is large enough to mount the propeller and motor from a remote-controlled plane or helicopter.

STEP 2 To protect the entire outer surface of the smoke detector, cover it completely (except for the bottom rim) with a coat of Plasti Dip.

STEP 3 Connect six AAA batteries in series using aluminum-foil duct tape. Glue the cells onto a round piece of plastic with ventilation holes, making sure that the weight is evenly distributed.

STEP 4 Wire the motor, an on/off switch, and the battery together, and attach the cap to the smaller end of the smoke detector with hot glue.

STEP 5 Place the larger end on the floor. The air should be sucked up through the detector vents.

STEP 6 Enjoy air hockey beyond the confines of the tabletop version.

253 SCORE WITH PING-PONG PADDLE GLOVES

STEP 1 Using a handsaw, cut the handles off two Ping-Pong paddles.

STEP 2 Cut two pieces of plywood into wedges. The widest part should measure 3 inches (7.5 cm) in width and the narrowest should measure 1 inch (2.5 cm) in width. Both should be 4 inches (10 cm) long.

STEP 3 Drill a hole in each of the two plywood pieces, one that's large enough for your thumb, and one that's large enough for your fingertips to protrude.

STEP 4 Sandwich the wood pieces between the paddles so that the glove fits your dominant hand and the thumb and finger holes align. Secure with wood glue.

STEP 5 Dominate at the table.

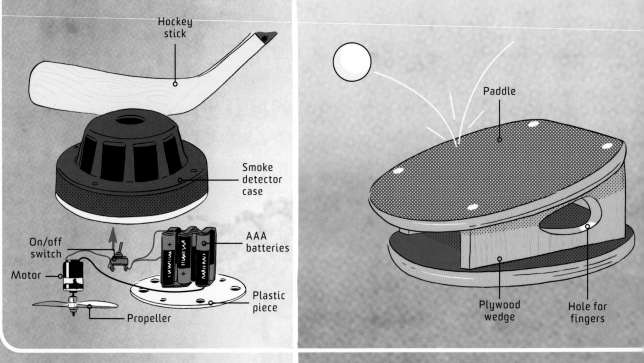

Hockey stick

Smoke detector case

AAA batteries

On/off switch

Motor

Propeller

Plastic piece

Paddle

Plywood wedge

Hole for fingers

254 ASSEMBLE A PVC-PIPE SOCCER GOAL

STEP 1 Use a handsaw to cut twelve lengths of 1½-inch (3.75-cm) PVC pipe so that you have four 2-foot (60-cm) sections, four 6-foot (1.8-m) sections, two 8-foot (2.4-m) sections, and two 10-foot (3-m) sections.

STEP 2 Put the goal together without glue first, using six 1½-inch (3.75-cm) rounded PVC elbows and four 1½-inch (3.75-cm) T-style PVC connectors. Make sure that all the pieces fit together correctly.

STEP 3 To glue, pull apart one joint at a time and spread PVC glue on the inside of the connector and the outside of the pipe. Reconnect the joint. (If you want to keep your soccer goal portable, leave a few joints unglued.)

STEP 4 Once you've glued all the joints, leave the structure to set.

STEP 5 To make the net, wrap netting around the goal and cut it to size, leaving a bit of extra netting around the edges. Attach the net using zip ties wrapped around the frame every 6 inches (15 cm).

STEP 6 Find a goalie to stand in front of your soccer goal, and get kicking.

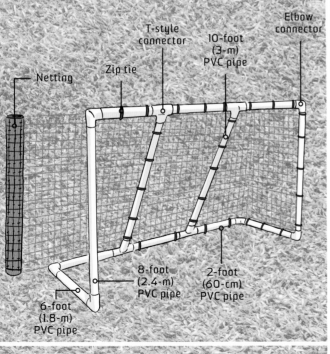

255 TRANSFORM A BIKE INTO A B-BALL HOOP

STEP 1 Detach the entire front section of the bicycle frame, from the handlebars down to the fork.

STEP 2 Adjust the handlebars to a horizontal angle, then mount the detached section of the frame to a large piece of wood using three U-clamps: one directly under the handlebars, two at the fork's top.

STEP 3 To use an old bicycle wheel for the hoop, remove the tire and clip off the spokes with wire cutters, leaving the hoop empty in the middle.

STEP 4 Set the hoop in the center of the handlebars, then use hose clamps to attach it. Make sure that the hoop rests parallel to the ground when the backboard is vertical.

STEP 5 Attach a net using zip ties or wire.

STEP 6 Shoot some hoops.

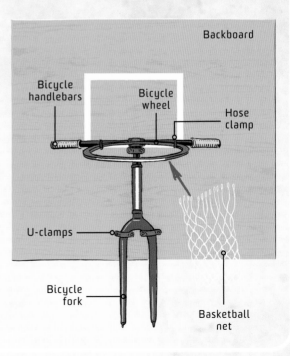

QUICK HACKS

256 **SERVE UP A TENNIS BALL**

This is one piece of sporting equipment that's useful both on and off the court.

STEALTHY SHOOTER
Poke a hole in a tennis ball and fill it with water for an instant squirt gun.

SUPER GRIP
Slice a tennis ball in half and use one half as a grip to twist off pesky stuck lids on jars.

HAMMER TIME
Protect surfaces while you hammer nails by cutting an X into the ball and sliding the head of the hammer inside it.

LIGHTBULB MOMENT
Got a broken lightbulb that you need to remove? With the light's switch and breaker turned off, clear the shards away from the bulb, press the tennis ball against the socket, and unscrew with the ball protecting your hand.

DOOR STOPPER
If you've ever had a doorknob smash through a wall when someone flung the door open, you know it can really hurt your chances of getting your apartment security deposit back. Cut a hole in a tennis ball and put it over the doorknob—it'll help keep your drywall intact.

257 Turn Your Backyard into a Badminton Court

Badminton—it's the gentleman's tennis. Set up your own court and show that birdie who's boss.

MATERIALS

Shovel
Landscaper's rake
2x4 boards
Topsoil

Sand
Chalk line marker
Court divider net
Posts for the net

STEP 1 Identify a spot on your land where there's room to build the court. Mark off a 20-by-44-foot (6-by-13.2-m) rectangle, allowing for a little extra room around the edges.

STEP 2 Use a landscaper's rake to level off this area, and also to create a slight slope. The whole court should slope 4 inches (10 cm) toward one end and 1 inch (2.5 cm) toward one side for drainage.

STEP 3 Use a shovel to excavate the area to a depth of 3 inches (7.5 cm), and then set in 2x4 boards along the edges as borders.

STEP 4 Mix together the topsoil and sand, and fill in the area with the mixture. Use the rake to smooth it out.

STEP 5 Mark the boundaries of the court with a chalk line marker according to the diagram.

STEP 6 Drive posts into the ground on either side of the court's center line. Tie the net to the posts so that it hangs at a height of 5 feet (1.5 m) in the center of the court.

STEP 7 If desired, set up lights around the court to enable nighttime play.

STEP 8 Grab a racket and start practicing your backhand.

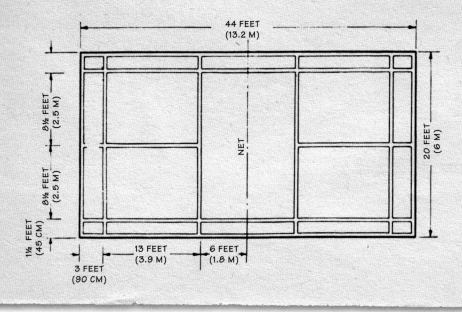

44 FEET (13.2 M)

8½ FEET (2.5 M)

8½ FEET (2.5 M)

1½ FEET (45 CM)

NET

20 FEET (6 M)

3 FEET (90 CM)

13 FEET (3.9 M)

6 FEET (1.8 M)

258 MAKE A MINI-GOLF COURSE

Practice your swing on a Pebble Beach course you designed yourself.

MATERIALS

3/4-inch (1.9-cm) medium-density fiberboard
Deck balusters
Craft knife
Wood glue
Drill with 4-inch (10-cm) hole saw
Green felt
Dropcloth
Spray adhesive
PVC pipe fitting
Composite wood balusters
Artificial turf

STEP 1 Sketch out a diagram of the course, marking any obstacles you want to add. The materials you'll need will depend on this design, so be sure to measure everything out before beginning your build.

STEP 2 Cut a sheet of medium-density fiberboard to size according to your diagram. You may need several sheets to create a long or irregularly shaped course.

STEP 3 Line up deck balusters along each edge of the sheet, cutting them to size as necessary. Use wood glue to hold the balusters in place, then allow the structure to dry.

STEP 4 Once the balusters are set, use a drill fitted with a 4-inch (10-cm) hole saw to cut a hole in the fiberboard sheet, placed according to your diagram. This will be the course's hole.

STEP 5 Cut green felt so it will cover the fiberboard sheet and wrap over the balusters.

STEP 6 Set the fiberboard sheet down on a dropcloth, balusters down, and spray the top with adhesive. Spray the felt with the adhesive, too, and let both pieces dry.

STEP 7 Place the fiberboard sheet top-down on the center of the felt, and spray more adhesive on the balusters and around the hole. After this has dried, wrap the excess felt over the balusters, trimming as needed.

STEP 8 Slice the felt inside the hole into sections, and fold it back so that the hole is clear.

STEP 9 Flip the sheet over, cut a PVC pipe fitting to just fill the space between the top of the hole and the floor, and insert it into the hole as a liner.

STEP 10 Line the edges of the course with lengths of composite wood baluster.

STEP 11 Build obstacles and use artificial turf for rough.

STEP 12 Hit the links.

BATTER UP

Frank Barnes, a 30-year-old industrial artist, dreamed up this 265-pound (120-kg) quasi-human-shaped robot made from a jumble of salvaged auto parts, steel piping, and pneumatic hoses for the sole purpose of belting every fastball thrown its way. The Headless Batsman won't make the majors, but Barnes suggests another career option: "Put some wheels on it, drive it around—I figure I can use it for security."

259 INSTALL AN AT-HOME ROCK WALL

We can't all have Mount Everest in our backyards. But you can still get your climb on with this rock wall.

COST	$$
TIME	🕐 🕐 🕐
EASY ● ● ● ● ○ HARD	

MATERIALS

Tape measure
Stud finder
Pencil
3/4-inch (1.9-cm) plywood
Saw
2x4s
Screws

2-inch (5-cm) drywall screws
3/8-inch (9.5-mm) T-nuts
Drill
Hammer
Nails
Handholds

STEP 1 Scout for a good wall. It absolutely must be load-bearing to support the weight of your wall (and you on it!). Come up with a design that will fit the space.

STEP 2 Use a stud finder to locate the studs in your wall, and then mark them with a pencil. (You'll be mounting your climbing wall alongside your original wall, and you'll want the studs of both walls to align.) Be sure to mark the top of where you'd like your wall to end as well.

STEP 3 Cut your 3/4-inch (1.9-cm) plywood to size based on your design.

STEP 4 Measure the height of your plywood, then subtract the widths of the 2x4 plates you'll be mounting on top and on bottom. Cut at least four studs to this height, then measure the width of your plywood and cut your top and bottom plate to this width.

STEP 5 Screw the four studs into place on your bottom plate so that they match the placement of the studs in your existing wall. Then screw on the top plate.

STEP 6 Before attaching your plywood to the existing wall, place T-nuts in the back of the plywood in a design of your choosing. This is where your handholds will go.

STEP 7 Line up your plywood wall with the existing wall. Predrill holes along the studs every 8 inches (20 cm) vertically and use long screws to attach the plywood.

STEP 8 Once your wall is securely mounted, screw handholds into the T-nut holes. (You can leave some T-nut holes empty and reposition or add additional handholds later to change up your course.)

STEP 9 Release your inner Spider-Man.

3/4-inch (1.9-cm) plywood sheeting

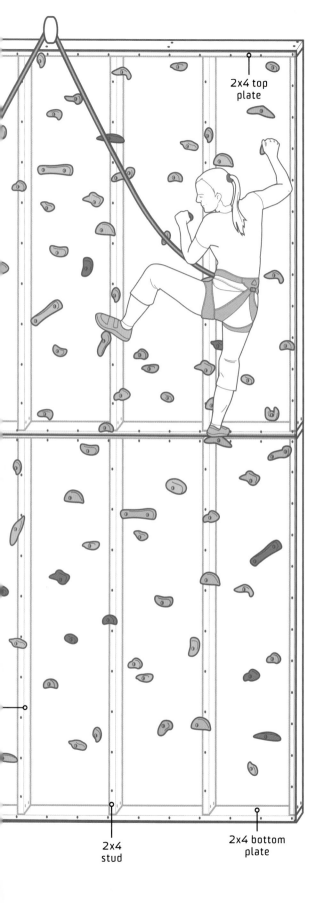

2x4 top plate

2x4 stud

2x4 bottom plate

260 HANG PVC FITNESS RINGS

Quit the gym but still get a workout with this simple build.

MATERIALS

Twine
1-inch (2.5-cm) PVC pipe
Sand
Duct tape
Baking sheet

Aluminum foil
Oven mitts
Paint cans
Heavy-duty nylon rope
Lashing straps

STEP 1 Soak two 3-feet (90-cm) lengths of twine in water, then thread them each through 2-foot (60-cm) lengths of PVC pipe, letting 6 inches (15 cm) dangle from each end.

STEP 2 Fully cover one end of each pipe with duct tape, leaving the twine sticking out. Fill each pipe with sand, then cover the other ends with tape.

STEP 3 Set your oven to 200°F (93°C). Place the pipes on a foil-covered baking sheet and heat them for 8 to 10 minutes.

STEP 4 Using oven mitts, remove the pipes from the oven and wrap them around old paint cans to mold them into a circular shape. Tie the ends of the twine together to hold the pipe in this shape as it cools.

STEP 5 Once the pipes have cooled, remove the duct-tape caps, sand, and twine. Loop a length of heavy-duty nylon rope twice through each pipe, then tie the rope off with a square knot. Thread any excess rope back through the pipe.

STEP 6 Use lashing straps to hang the rings from a sturdy structure with the knot at the top of each ring.

STEP 7 Start practicing your inverted cross.

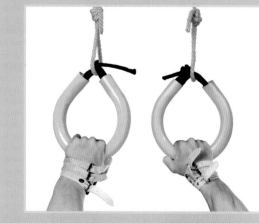

THINGS THAT GO

261 A TILTING PING-PONG TABLE THAT THROWS OFF OPPONENTS

A group of young designers reinvent ping-pong. Welcome to "swing pong."

Internships are often mindless, coffee-fetching black holes of boredom. But not at Syyn Labs, a Los Angeles collective that creates unusual interactive art and science projects for commercials and music videos. Last summer, student interns Hoon Oh, Robb Godshaw, and Jisu Choi took it upon themselves to reinvent the sport of table tennis. Their project could pass for an extra in *Transformers:* It's part ping-pong table, part machine, and so difficult to play that it reduces pros to the level of rank amateurs.

Oh came up with the idea of doing a ping-pong project because the game is a staple of so many cultures around the globe, and is normally relatively easy to play. They wanted to make the game more social than competitive, so they eliminated the potential for humiliating one-sided contests by building a table that tilts on demand and makes it tough for even highly skilled players.

They started by scrounging for parts in the Syyn Labs warehouse. A rectangular piece of Plexiglas that had once been used in an illuminated dance floor became the tabletop. To drive the tilting surface, Godshaw suggested using pneumatic pistons left over from a commercial for a Google science fair. Choi worked on the drive system and other aspects of the design, while Oh wrote software to control the pistons and switch the table from level to off-kilter. The group found that getting the angles correct was tricky. "We wanted to make it tilt at a dramatic angle but not hit anybody in the jaw," Godshaw says.

They were right about leveling gameplay—when table-tennis pro Adam Bobrow visited Syyn Labs, he won his match by only a single point. In fact, the game is such strange, absurd fun, Godshaw says, that competition is an afterthought: "Most games never make it to nine."

262 ORGANIZE CORDS ON THE GO

STEP 1 Cut a sheet of foam into a dog-bone shape, then cut a slit into each end.

STEP 2 Tuck your media player's cord into the slit to secure it and wrap the excess cord around the bone's center.

STEP 3 Pump jams while you jog without having to jump rope over cords.

263 RUN IN NO-SLIP SHOES

Experience the joy of added traction in the most rugged terrain.

MATERIALS

Running shoes
Thirty sheet-metal screws
½ to ⅜ inch (1.25 to 9.5 mm), depending on thickness of shoe soles)

Drill
Clamps

STEP 1 Decide how to distribute the screws on the sole of each shoe. Use about 15 screws per shoe, scattered evenly between the front and back of the sole. Mark where you want to place each one, avoiding any pockets of air or gel in the sole.

STEP 2 Use a drill to insert the screws at your marks. You may need to exert extra pressure on the drill for tough rubber—try clamping the shoe if necessary. Tighten the screws only until the heads touch the rubber.

STEP 3 Test them out (outside, unless you don't mind leaving gouges in your floor). If the screws make you feel off balance, try removing or adding some to compensate.

264 THE MOTORIZED EASY CHAIR

Getting to class just got a little faster.

Chris McIntosh's first recliner was not your standard La-Z-Boy: It was electric-powered and capable of going 15 miles per hour (24 km/h). After he finished making it, he pulled a doughnut on his high school's front lawn, circled the gym during a pep rally, and ruled the street near his home in Orinda, California.

McIntosh spent his youth building ad hoc vehicles (he once made a mini hovercraft out of a leaf blower), so when the chair's paltry electric motor burned out, he decided it was time for a monster makeover. "I wanted to go fast," he says.

To upgrade the recliner, he removed the electric motor he had installed, the motor's controller, a pair of batteries, and other parts. He bought a 9-horsepower, four-stroke dirt-bike engine, which fit perfectly in the space beneath the seat, and welded on a fixed rear axle so that the engine could power both rear wheels instead of just one. Bike engines need to be kick-started, but the recliner's lever snapped when he tried to use it. He welded on a motorcycle kick-start lever instead.

Then there was the danger of the vehicle catching on fire. The dirt-bike engine's exhaust pipe got so hot that it sometimes glowed red and threatened to set the upholstery (and McIntosh) ablaze. To avert disaster, he rerouted the pipe, mounting it farther from the underside of the chair, and covered it with fireproof wrap. His parents were pleased.

Still, the first test drive was frightening: McIntosh immediately popped an accidental 45-degree wheelie. He added 30 pounds (13.6 kg) of weights near his feet to keep the front down, along with a roll bar and harness for safety. The chair has no suspension at all. "The ride gets a bit bumpy," McIntosh says. "But then again, there's plenty of padding."

He says he has now mastered climbing hills and turning corners, although he's planning to add a rearview mirror to reduce the large blind spot behind the backrest. The newly completed gas-powered version now goes 40 miles per hour (64 km/h) and, just as important, he says, "It sounds like a Harley."

STREET ILLEGAL
McIntosh figured the chair wouldn't be street legal, so he designed it to fit in the back of his hatchback. To load it, he slides off the backrest, leans a ramp against the back of his car, and pushes the heavy frame up and in. He typically uses it in parking lots, but he does occasionally take it around local streets and even took it to USC's homecoming parade.

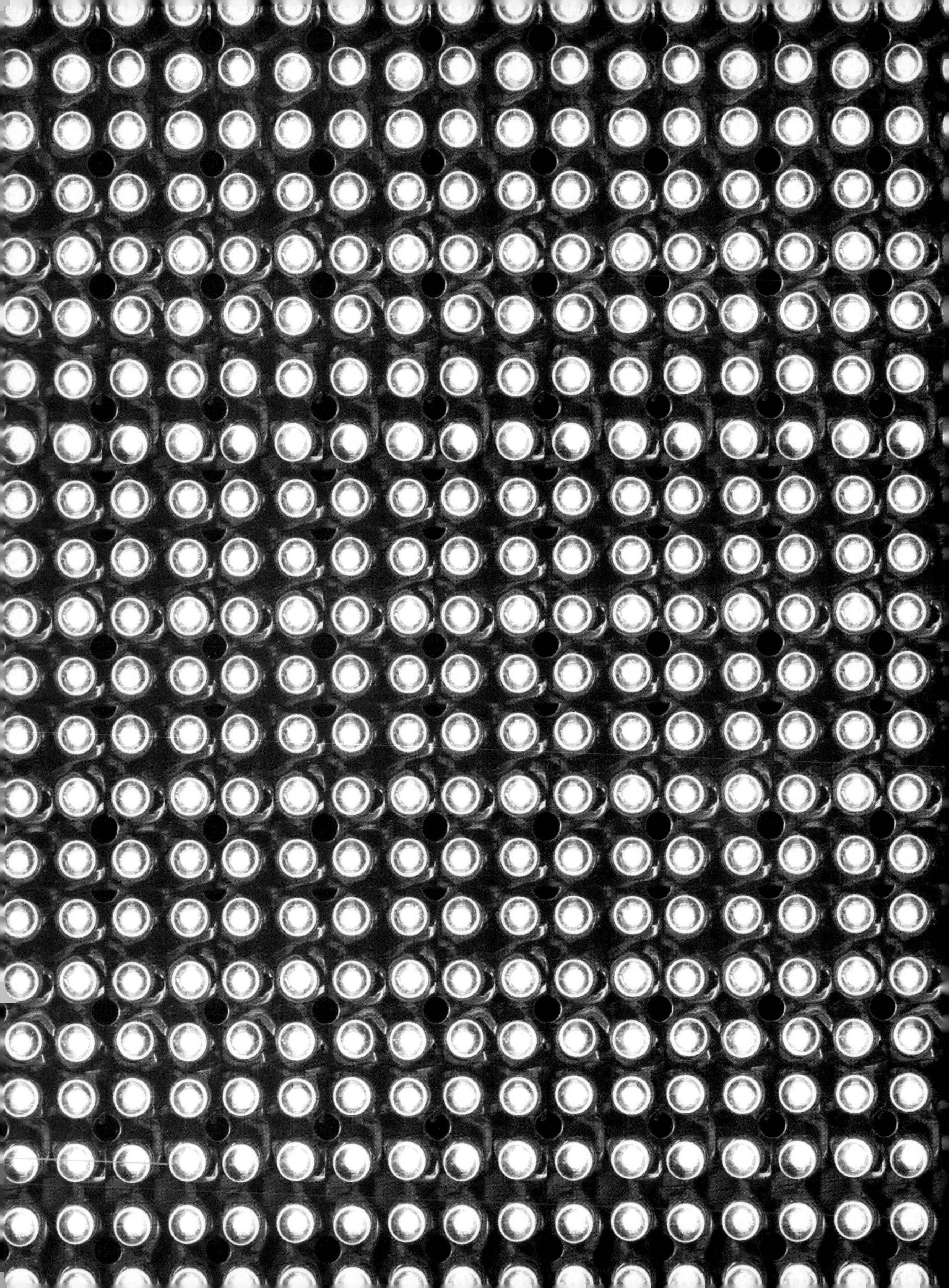

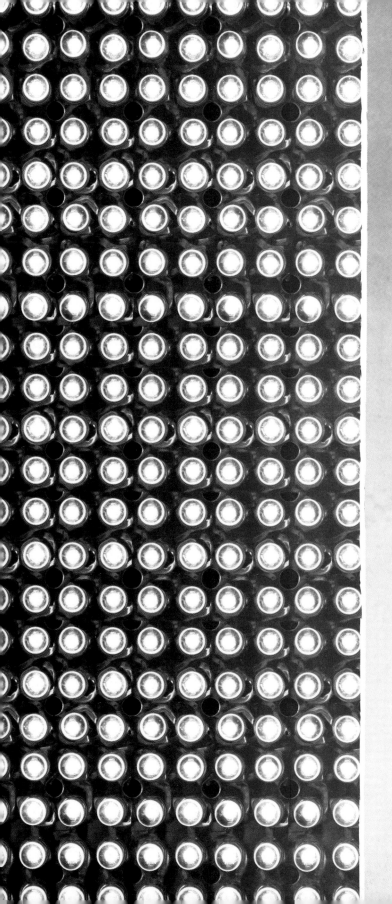

RESOURCES

GLOSSARY

ALLIGATOR CLIP Spring-loaded clip that can be used to connect a component to a wire in a temporary circuit.

ALUMINUM FLASHING Thin sheet of aluminum; often used in weatherproofing to prevent water from flowing through a joint.

AMPLIFIER Component that augments the power of a signal. In circuits, an amplifier is usually used to increase the voltage or current.

ANTENNA Wire, thin metal pole, or other device that can transmit or receive electromagnetic waves, such as TV or radio waves.

ARDUINO Common, open-source microcontroller. There are various types of Arduino microcontrollers, but all can be programmed using the same programming language.

BLACK LIGHT Type of lamp that gives off ultraviolet light. Many substances emit fluorescence that can be seen under a black light, but not in normal lighting conditions.

BREADBOARD Base used to set up temporary circuits and test them out before soldering components together.

BREAKOUT BOARD Electrical component that allows you easier access to tightly spaced pins on a microchip or densely bundled wires. The device connects the hard-to-reach pins or wires to an easier-to-access interface.

BUSHING Connector used to join pipes of different diameters; one end has a smaller opening, the other end a larger one. A bushing can also be called a *reducing coupling*.

CAPACITOR Electrical component that stores energy within a circuit. Unlike a battery, a capacitor does not produce energy, it simply contains or filters the energy already flowing through the circuit.

CIRCUIT Closed loop through which electrical current flows. A circuit is often used to power an electrical device.

CIRCUIT BOARD Thin, insulated board on which electrical components are mounted and connected together. A printed circuit board has thin conductive strips printed on the board, allowing connections to be made between components largely without the use of wires.

CLAMP Device used to hold an object tightly in place. Clamps can vary widely in size and construction, and can be intended for temporary or permanent use.

COAXIAL CABLE Cable with a central conductive wire, surrounded by an insulating layer, which in turn is surrounded by a conductive tube. A coaxial cable is often used to transmit radio or cable television signals.

COIN BATTERY Also called a button cell, a coin battery is a small, flat, disc-shaped battery that is often used to power portable electronic devices.

CONDUCTIVITY Capacity to transmit an electrical current; it can also refer to the measure of a substance's ability to transmit electrical current.

CONTACT Point where an electrical component is connected to a wire or circuit board.

COUPLER Short section of piping used to join two pipes together.

CRAFT KNIFE Small, fixed-blade knife used to make precise cuts.

DESOLDERING Removing solder to detach components from a circuit or circuit board. Desoldering can be used to fix a fault in a circuit, or to replace a component.

DIODE Electronic component with one terminal that has high resistance, and another terminal with low resistance. A diode is used to allow current to flow in one direction but not another.

DRILL Tool used to cut holes in a variety of materials. A drill is usually powered by electricity, and comes with an array of interchangeable bits in different sizes.

ELECTRICAL TAPE Type of tape covered in an insulating material, often used to cover and connect electrical wires.

ELECTRICAL WIRE Insulated strand of conductive material used to carry electricity.

ELECTRODE Conductor used to transmit current to a non-metallic material. Electrodes are used in arc welding to fuse objects together.

EPOXY Adhesive made from a type of resin that becomes rigid when heated or cured.

EXHAUST FAN Fan used to ventilate a workspace; it is particularly important to use an exhaust fan when working with materials that emit toxic fumes.

FIBER OPTIC CABLE Cable made up of thin fibers that transmit light from one end of the fiber to the other. A fiber optic cable can carry signals and provide illumination.

FLASH DRIVE Small data-storage device that can be connected to a computer, often via a USB port.

FRESNEL LENS Thin lens made of a number of smaller lens segments. A Fresnel lens magnifies a light source, and is often used in projectors and spotlights.

GROUND WIRE Wire in a circuit that provides a return path for current, often leading to the earth. A ground wire can prevent the buildup of dangerous static electricity in a circuit.

HACKSAW Fine-toothed saw held in a frame. A hacksaw can be used to cut metal or other hard materials.

HEAT-SHRINK TUBING Tubing that contracts when heated; often used

to insulate wires or to create a protective seal.

HEAT SINK Device that channels heat away from an electronic system, keeping it cool enough to operate properly.

HOLE SAW Cylindrical saw blade, used to cut holes of uniform size. A hole saw is usually used in a drill, in place of the drill bit, to create a large hole.

HOLOGRAPHY Technique that allows for the capture of a lifelike 3D image. The resulting hologram looks different when viewed from different angles, much as a real-world scene would.

INSULATION Material, such as the nonconductive coating around an electrical wire, that prevents current or heat from flowing.

INTEGRATED CIRCUIT Also called a *microchip*, this small, thin device is a complete circuit etched or imprinted on a semiconductive surface. An integrated circuit allows for complex circuitry to be condensed into an extremely small space, and is vital to the operation of many modern electronic devices, notably computers.

JIGSAW Tool (usually a power tool) with a long, thin saw blade. A jigsaw is useful in cutting curves and irregular shapes.

JOINT The point at which two objects are connected together. In woodworking, creating a join may involve cutting a notch or angle into the pieces of wood to be joined; in metalworking, the process often involves soldering or welding.

LASER Device that emits a tightly focused beam of light. Lasers vary widely in intensity, and can be as weak as a laser pointer, or strong enough to cut through extremely hard and thick materials.

LCD MONITOR Display that uses liquid crystals to bend and shape light to create an image. In an LCD monitor, the liquid crystal material is sandwiched between two electrodes and filtered through a layer of polarizing film.

LEAD A wire extending from an electronic component that is used to connect that component to another electronic part.

LED Diode that gives off light. They are usually more energy-efficient than incandescent light sources, and can be much smaller.

LITHIUM-ION BATTERY Type of rechargeable battery often used in consumer electronics. A lithium-ion battery commonly carries a large amount of energy for its size, and loses charge relatively slowly when not in use.

MICROCONTROLLER Tiny dedicated computer, contained on a single chip that can be embedded within a larger device.

MULTIMETER Device that measures electrical current, resistance, and voltage. A multimeter is very helpful for monitoring and identifying problems in circuits.

O-RING Circular seal used in joining cylinders together. An O-ring is usually seated inside a joint to prevent leaks.

OHM Unit of measurement of electrical resistance.

OPTICAL MOUSE Computer mouse that uses an LED to sense motion, as opposed to the rolling ball used by a mechanical mouse.

PARTICLEBOARD Composite wood-based material manufactured from small chips or shavings of wood joined together by resin.

PEG-BOARD Plank or sheet of wood pre-drilled with a grid of evenly spaced small holes, A Peg-Board is useful for mounting hooks and tools on a wall.

PHOTOCELL Device that produces a flow of current when exposed to light. A photocell can detect the presence (or absence) of light or other radiation.

PLEXIGLAS Hard, transparent plastic; looks like glass but is more lightweight and durable.

POLARIZING FILM Sheet of material, often used in LCD monitors, that allows only light polarized in a specific direction to pass through.

PORT Point of interface between one device and another. On computers, common ports include Ethernet ports and USB ports.

POTENTIOMETER Three-terminal electrical component that acts as a variable resistor. These adjust the flow of current through a circuit, and are often used in dimmer switches or volume controls.

PROGRAMMING LANGUAGE Language used to convey instructions to a computer or other machine. Many distinct programming languages are used for different purposes and types of hardware.

PROJECT BOX Box designed to contain the components of a circuit; useful for mounting and protecting the elements of a device.

PVC PIPE Type of durable, lightweight plastic pipe often used to carry liquids in plumbing.

PVC PIPE CEMENT Adhesive designed to connect pieces of PVC material together.

REBAR Ridged bar of steel, often used in construction to reinforce concrete or masonry.

RECIPROCATING SAW Power tool that cuts with the back-and-forth motion of a saw blade.

REED SWITCH Switch composed of metal reeds enclosed in a tiny glass container. The reeds react to the presence of a magnetic field by either opening or closing the switch.

RESISTOR Two-terminal electrical component that resists the flow of an electric current. A resistor is used in a circuit to control the direction and strength of the current flowing through it.

ROTARY TOOL Power tool with a wide variety of interchangeable bits that can be used for different purposes. A rotary tool can cut, polish, carve, or grind, and is particularly good for detail work.

SAFETY GOGGLES Glasses that shield the eye area from heat, chemicals, and debris.

SCHEMATIC Two-dimensional map of an electrical circuit. A schematic uses a set of symbols to stand for the components of a circuit, and shows the connections between components.

SKETCH When working with Arduino microcontrollers, a sketch is a program that can be loaded into an Arduino.

SLAG Scrap metal that results from the welding process.

SOLDERING Connecting two metal objects together by melting solder (a type of metal) with a soldering iron to create a strong joint between the objects.

SUGRU Type of silicone-based putty that can be molded for about 30 minutes after it is removed from its packaging. Sugru cures to a solid but somewhat flexible state after 24 hours.

SWITCH Component that can stop the flow of current in a circuit, or allow it to continue. These include push-button switches, rocker switches, toggle switches, and many other devices.

TABLE SAW Machine that cuts wood or other materials with a rapidly spinning serrated metal disc. A circular saw is usually powered by electricity, and often mounted within a safety guard.

T-CONNECTOR Short section of pipe with three openings; used to connect lengths of pipe into a T shape.

TERMINAL End point of a conductor in a circuit; also a point at which connections can be made to a larger network.

TOUCHSCREEN An electronic display screen that users interact with by touching with their fingers; the screen detects touch within the display area.

TRANSFORMER Device that transfers current from one circuit to another. A transformer can also be used to alter the voltage of an alternating current.

TRANSISTOR Semiconducting electrical component with at least three leads; can control or amplify the flow of electricity in a circuit.

USB Universal Serial Bus; an extremely common type of connector for computer and other electronic components.

VISE Type of clamp, often affixed to a table, that uses a screw to hold an object tightly in place.

VOLT Unit of measurement for electrical potential.

WELDING Process of joining pieces of metal together by melting them slightly and introducing a filler material at the joint.

WIRE CUTTER Pliers with sharp diagonal edges used to cut lengths of wire.

WIRE STRIPPER Device composed of a set of scissor-like blades with a central notch; used to strip the insulation from the outside of electrical wires.

ZIP TIES Self-closing fastener. When the end of a zip tie is inserted into the slot at its head and tightened, it creates a loop that can't easily be loosened.

INDEX

THANKS TO OUR MAKERS

Lots of inventive people contributed their ideas and how-to tutorials to the pages of this book. Look them up to find out more details about their projects, as well as any new cool stuff they're up to.

GEEK TOYS

014: John B. Carnett (carnettphoto.com) **015:** Elizabeth Hurchalla and Kent Hayward **019:** Kip Kay (kipkay.com) **021:** Jamie Price (jamiepricecreative.com) **023:** Scott McIndoe **024:** Kyle Pollock **025:** Windell H. Oskay (evilmadscientist.com) **026:** Alessandro Lambardi **027 (potato gun):** Spudtech (spudtech. com) **027 (pumpkin gun):** Gary Arold and John Gill **029:** R. Lee Kennedy, Associate Professor, Department of Drama, University of Virginia **030:** Michel Mota da Cruz **031:** Bob Munz **033:** Mike Andersen, Grant Elliot, Schyler Senft-Grup, and Scott Torborg (scotttorborg. com) **034 (Rubens' tube):** Nik Vaughn **034 (fireball gun):** Vin Marshall (te-motorworks. com) **035:** Courtesy of campfiredude.com **039:** Courtesy of waterzooka.com **041:** Inspired by a tutorial by Instructables username hunrichs; furthered by Emelie Griffin **042:** Kimanh le Roux (scissorspaperwok.com) **043:** Emelie Griffin **044:** Anthony Le (masterle247.wix.com) **047 (jetpack):** Raymond Li (jetlev-flyer.com) **050:** Harout Markarian **051:** Daniel Wolf (cookrookery.com) **052:** Jason Wilson **053:** Robert Waters **054:** Eddie Zarick **055 (LEGO pinball):** Gerrit Bronsveld and Martijn Boogarts **056:** Joshua Zimmerman (browndoggadgets.com) **058:** A.C. Jeong **059:** Michael Nagle **061:** Andrew Lim (cofounder of Recombu.com) **062:** Aram Bartholl (deaddrops.com) **065:** Bard Lund Johansen **066:** Lindsay Lawlor (electricgiraffe.com) **067:** Inspired by Kang Chang, Kyle Milns, and Mike Fleming; further developed by Ian Cannon **068:** Courtesy of illphabetik.com **073:** Tim Lillis **074:** Michael Greensmith (steampunkwayoflife. blogspot.com.au) **078:** Maayan Migdal (created at the Bezalel Academy of Art and Design, under professors Ytai Ben-Tsvi, Shachar Geiger, and Itay Galim) **080 (theremin):** Dave Prochnow **080 (lasers):** Stephen Hobley (stephenhobley.com)

HOME IMPROVEMENTS

081: Jeni Rodger (jenirodger.com) **082:** Brian Jewett **085:** Ben Katz (build-its.blogspot. com) **086:** Kip Kay (kipkay.com) **093:** Dave Prochnow **094 (wearable LED TV):** David Forbes **099 (graffiti laser):** Chris Poole **100:** Eric Dyer and Maggie Hoffman (radiohole. com) **102:** David Prochnow **105:** Daniel Julian **106:** Jared Bouck (inventgeek.com) **111:** Damon Hearne **118:** Dave Prochnow **120:** Perry Watkins (perrywinklecustoms.co.uk) **123:** Juan Francisco Paredes **124:** Patrick Lalonde **125:** Dan Poff (tophatlabs.wordpress.com) **129:** Ben Diaz **131:** Dave Prochnow **134:** Scott McIndoe **140:** Melanie Rapp Mimikry **141:** John B. Carnett (carnettphoto. com) **142:** Merijn van Wouden **143:** Dean Segovis (hackaweek.com) **144:** Ed Lenz (windstuffnow. com) **145:** Dave Prochnow **148 (lawnmower):** Korey Atterberry (atterberry.net) **148 (golf cart):** Bill Rulien (beavercreekgolfcarts.com) **149:** Dave Prochnow **151:** Kai Grundt

GADGET UPGRADES

152: William Finucane (adapted with permission from his original guide in the Mad Science World on wonderhowto.com) **157:** Wallace Kineyko **161:** Dave Prochnow **162:** Dylan Hart (householdhacker.com) **167:** Jennifer Lee (jen7714. wordpress.com) **169:** Adapted from *More Show Me How* **170:** Windell H. Oskay (evilmadscientist. com) **172:** Instructables username unclesam **173:** Ian Cannon **175:** Phil Herlihy (braindeadlock.net) **176:** Jeffrey Davies **178:** Dave Fortin (failsworld. com) **180:** Toma Dimov (outfab.com) **181:** Bard Lund Johansen **185:** Ian Cannon **186:** Jani "Japala" Pönkkö (editor of metku.net) **188:** Ingo Schommer (chillu.com) **190:** Pamela Stephens (pbjstories. com) **195 (portable X-ray machine):** Adam Munich **196:** Bionerd23 (youtube.com/user/ bionerd23) **197 (plasma globe):** Burak Incepinar (tacashi.tripod.com) **197 (DIY SEM):** Ben Krasnow (youtube.com/user/bkraz333) **199:** Kip Kay (kipkay.com) **201:** Markus Kayser (markuskayer. com) **204:** Chris Barnardo **208:** Larry Towe (getawaymoments.com) **214:** Dave Prochnow **215:** Darren Samuelson (darrensamuelson.com)

THINGS THAT GO

227 (fan-propelled skateboard): Ryan Bavetta
227 (motorized skateboard): John B. Carnett
(carnettphoto.com) 229: Ian Cannon 230: Randy
Grubb 235: William Finucane (adapted with
permission from his original guide in the Mad Science
World on wonderhowto.com) 238: Allison Button
(modmischief.blogspot.com) 240: Dave Prochnow
242: Adam Stetten 244: Alan Chatham (unojoy.com)
246: Public Laboratory for Open Technology and
Science (publiclaboratory.org) 248: Dave Prochnow
251: Stan Hewitt 252: Ari Horowitz 255: Claude
Siset (synergyparamotors.com) 258 (batting machine):
Frank Barnes (robocross.de) 259: Conor Buckley 261:
Hoon Oh (hoon-oh.com), Robb Godshaw (robb.cc), and
Jisu Choi (jisuchoi.com) 264: Chris McIntosh

IMAGE CREDITS

All images courtesy of Shutterstock Images
unless otherwise noted.

Courtesy of the *Popular Science* Archives: 49, 57, 79, 83,
104, 119, 147, 160, 213, 249, 257.
Chris Barnardo: 204 Ryan Bavetta: 227 (photograph
of skateboard) Luis Bruno: 100, 102, 131, 149 Conor
Buckley: 15, 22, 24–26, 27 (potato gun illustration),
28–32, 34 (Rubens' tube illustration), 39–43, 45, 47
(roller coaster illustration), 48, 55 (Nintendo belt
illustration), 56, 58–65, 67–69, 75–76, 78, 81, 84–86,
88–93, 94 (gaming chair), 99, 101, 103, 107–109, 111–116,
118, 121–126, 132–133, 135, 142–144, 146, 148 (lawnmower
photograph), 150, 152, 159, 162–167, 172–177, 180, 183–186,
193–194, 196, 198–200, 202–203, 206–208, 214, 221–
225, 228–229, 235–242, 247–248, 250, 259, 262 John
B. Carnett: Back cover (firegun photograph), 14, 21, 27
(pumpkin gun photograph), 33, 34 (firegun photograph),
141, 145, 148 (golf cart photograph), 151, 161, 215, 227
(motorized skateboard photograph), 251, 258 (baseball
photograph) Luke Copping: 195 (portable
X-ray machine photograph) Scott Erwert: Front
cover, 87, 106, 158, 178–179, 181, 195, 197 (plasma globe
photograph), 220, 243–246, 258 (mini-golf course
photograph), 260, 263 Hayden Foell: 153 Getty
Images: 80 (Léon Theremin photograph) Michael
Greensmith: 74 JP Greenwood: 66 Jeannette Grubb:
230 Stephen Hobley: 80 (laser harp photograph)
D.G. Hubbard: 47 (Jetflyer photograph) Dan Julian: 105
Brian Jewett: 82 Theron Kirkman: 99 (graffiti laser
photograph) Timothy Lillis: 192 Scott McIndoe: 23,
134 Stephen Meckler: 94 (LED TV vest photograph)
Jeff Newton: 261 Cody Pickens: 197 (electron
scanning microscope photograph), 264 Amos Field
Reid: 201 Tyler Stableford: 44 Nik Vaughn: 34
(Rubens' tube photograph) Carl Wiens: Back cover
(mint-tin guitar illustration, steamer illustration,
aquarium illustration, air freshener illustration), 16–19,
35–38, 50–53, 70–73, 95–98, 127–130, 137–140, 154–157,
168–171, 188–191, 209–212, 216–219, 231–234, 252–255
Jonathon Worth: 120 Eddie Zarick: 54

weldon**owen**

President, CEO Terry Newell

VP, Sales Amy Kaneko

VP, Publisher Roger Shaw

Senior Editor Lucie Parker

Project Editors Emelie Griffin, Jess Hemerly

Creative Director Kelly Booth

Designer Michel Gadwa

Image Coordinator Conor Buckley

Production Director Chris Hemesath

Production Manager Michelle Duggan

415 Jackson Street, Suite 200
San Francisco, CA 94111
Telephone: 415 291 0100
Fax: 415 291 8841
www.weldonowen.com

Popular Science and Weldon Owen are divisions of

BONNIER

POPULAR SCIENCE

ACKNOWLEDGMENTS

Weldon Owen would like to thank Katie Cagenee, Andrew Jordon, Katharine Moore, Gail Nelson-Bonebrake, Jenna Rosenthal, Katie Schlossberg, and Marisa Solis for their editorial expertise and design assistance.

We'd also like to thank our technical editors, Michael Rigsby and Tim Lillis, and our in-house builder and circuity diagram consultant, Ian Cannon.

Popular Science would like to thank Matt Cokeley, Todd Detwiler, Kristine LaManna, Stephanie O'Hara, Thom Payne, and Katie Peek for their support over the years.

We would also like to thank Gregory Mone for penning the You Built What?! entries included in this book.

And a big thanks to Mark Jannot and Mike Haney—the How 2.0 column's first editor—for getting it all started.